THE

911

HANDBOOK

THE 911

HANDBOOK

BIBLICAL SOLUTIONS TO EVERYDAY PROBLEMS

KENT CROCKETT

HENDRICKSON PUBLISHERS

The 911 Handbook: Biblical Solutions to Everyday Problems
Copyright © 1997, 2003 by Kent Crockett
Published by Hendrickson Publishers, Inc.
P.O. Box 3473
Peabody, Massachusetts 01961-3473

Printed in the United States of America

First printing, softcover edition—July 2003

ISBN 1-56563-903-0

Except where otherwise indicated, all Scripture quotations are taken from The New
American Standard Bible, © 1960, 1962, 1963, 1968, 1971, 1972, 1973, 1975, 1977 by
The Lockman Foundation. Used by permission.

Verses marked (TLB) are taken from The Living Bible © 1971 owned by assignment by
Illinois Regional Bank N.A. (as trustee), used by permission of Tyndale House Publishers,
Inc., Wheaton, Illinois, 60189. All rights reserved.

Cover design by Paetzold Design, Batavia, Ill.
Interior design by Pinpoint Marketing, Kirkland, Wash.
Edited by Judy Bodmer, Agnes Lawless, and Scott Pinzon

The Library of Congress has cataloged the hardcover edition as follows:

Crockett, Kent, 1952–
    911 Handbook: Biblical solutions to everyday problems / Kent Crockett.
    p. cm.
    Includes bibliographical references (p. 223)
    ISBN 1-56563-295-8 (cloth)
    1. Christian life–Biblical teaching. I. Title.
BS880.C47C76   1997
242–dc21   97-23128
                                                                        CIP

Dedication

To my mother, Dot Crockett.

If it weren't for you, Mom,
this book would not have been written.

ACKNOWLEDGMENTS

I give thanks to:

My Lord Jesus Christ, who saved me from eternal punishment and transferred me into his kingdom of light. Any wisdom gained from this book came from the Father above, not from the human instrument he chose to communicate through.

Cindy, the most wonderful wife, greatest mother, and best unpaid editor in the universe.

Hannah and Scott, my two special gifts from God, for making fatherhood a blessing rather than a burden.

His servants, Alesa Meschberger, Ronda Jameson, Jo Ann Jameson, Debbie Foster, Debbie Cenatiempo, and many others for your prayers and critiques of my manuscript.

Peter Lord, Doug White, Paul Baskin, Pete Shultis, and David Lino for your wealth of pastoral wisdom.

Billie Wilson and the Florida Christian Writers Conference for your wonderful ministry and encouragement to Christian writers.

The members of Cornerstone Church, truly a treasure from God and my second family, a congregation any pastor would love to shepherd, for your incredible love and support.

My editor, Judy Bodmer, for putting me on the writer's rack and stretching me to new dimensions.

Dan Penwell, my acquisitions editor, for your faith in me and your words of encouragement. Thanks for being available every time I needed you.

Everyone at Hendrickson Publishers for multiplying this work for the brothers and sisters in the family of God.

CONTENTS

Introduction   1

1. **When You Need God to Provide**   3
   Does God Consider the Odds?

2. **When Your Faith Is Weak**   11
   Without a Doubt

3. **When You Are Discontented**   20
   May I Change Seats, Please?

4. **When You Are Tempted**   28
   Adam and Eve's Instruction Manual

5. **When You Can't Forgive Someone**   39
   Who Is in Your Dungeon?

6. **When You Can't Forgive Yourself**   48
   Canceling Guilt Trips

7. **When You Are Disappointed**   58
   God's Recipe for Leftovers

8. **When You Need to Make a Change**   65
   Breaking Out of Comfort Zones

9. **When You Are Depressed**   75
   The Elijah Complex

10. **When You Feel Like Quitting**   85
    Preventing Burnout

11. **When You Are Criticized**   95
    Coping with Criticism

12. **When You Are Tired of Waiting**   107
Giving Birth to Ishmael

13. **When You Are Afraid**   117
No Fear!

14. **When You Need to Make a Decision**   125
The Deciding Factor

15. **When You Feel Like Complaining**   143
The Empty-Net Syndrome

16. **When You Are Middle-Aged**   149
Calming Mid-life Crisis

17. **When Your Life Is Missing Something**   157
Lepers Anonymous

18. **When You Carry Heavy Burdens**   166
Check Your Baggage Here

19. **When Opinions Differ**   175
Is Right Ever Wrong?

20. **When You Are Angry**   184
The Danger of Anger

21. **When Bad Things Happen**   194
The Rest of the Story

22. **When You Have Drifted from God**   203
Heartbreak Highway

23. **When You Are Afraid of Dying**   212
Scared to Death of Death

24. **When You're Not Sure You're Saved**   218
Heaven's Entrance Exam

Source Notes and Study Guide   225

SEVERAL YEARS AGO, I purchased a family medical handbook for my library. I realized if someone in my family had a medical emergency, I could dial 911 and consult my reference guide to tell me what to do. Then it occurred to me that most people don't have a handbook for their spiritual problems. They know the answers are in the Bible somewhere, but they don't know where to find them.

The 911 Handbook is designed to help you find solutions to the problems you face every day. If you are being tempted, you can dial 911 by reading "When You Are Tempted: Adam & Eve's Instruction Manual." If you are experiencing a time of depression, you can get immediate help by turning to "When You Are Depressed: The Elijah Complex" and following the instructions.

This handbook is not written to be a laborious book of instructions but is designed to be encouraging and uplifting to help you walk in victory rather than defeat amid life's difficulties. Each biblically based chapter will have humor, stories, insights, and solutions to problems that you can apply in your daily Christian walk. Although you may be inclined to begin your reading with the chapter of your most urgent need, I would encourage you to start with chapter 1 and read through the book.

Our society is quick to blame syndromes and disorders for its problems, rather than sin. In chapter 3, I humorously create a new disorder, Contentment-Deficit Disorder, to show how easy it is to run from problems rather than deal with them. Although there can be no denying that disorders affect some people, we should never assume a syndrome is the problem until we have first examined the sin factor. It is possible that sin is causing the "sindrome"!

If a doctor misdiagnoses a medical problem, his treatment will be ineffective. The same holds true for psychological and spiritual problems. Until we correctly diagnose the roots of the problems, we will only treat the symptoms. Treating misdiagnosed problems is as ineffective as a gardener trying to kill weeds by mowing over them with a lawnmower. At first, it looks like the problems have been solved. But then the weeds spring right back up because the root has not been dealt with. The roots of most of our problems can be traced back to sinful attitudes toward God and people.

The Bible is your gardening manual to instruct you how to diagnose your problems and uproot the weeds so your life becomes fruitful. Within the pages of your Bible are the answers to your problems, and we are about to take a journey to help you find them. It is my prayer that this book will help open your eyes to the truths presented in God's Word so you can apply them to your life.

Kent Crockett

CHAPTER 1

When You Need God to Provide
Does God Consider the Odds?

And when they had come to Capernaum, those who collected the
two-drachma tax came to Peter, and said, "Does your teacher not
pay the two-drachma tax?" He said, "Yes." And when he came into
the house, Jesus spoke to him first, saying, "What do you think,
Simon? From whom do the kings of the earth collect customs or
poll-tax, from their sons or from strangers?" And upon his saying,
"From strangers," Jesus said to him, "Consequently the sons are
exempt. But, lest we give them offense, go to the sea, and throw
in a hook, and take the first fish that comes up; and when you
open its mouth, you will find a stater. Take that and give it to them
for you and Me."

(Matthew 17:24–27)

I WENT TO McDONALD'S the other day. Their latest promotion
was the Monopoly game where I had a chance to win one
million dollars. The winning piece was "Boardwalk." When
I read the fine print on the official rules, I learned my chance of
winning was one in 518,071,190. I figured there was only one winning piece printed for the entire country. Not good odds.

Even though I am not a gambler, I pulled the sticker off my
french fries' container to see if I was about to become a millionaire.

Nope. Not even an "instant winner" of a small drink. I got
"Atlantic Avenue" for the fifth time. Wasn't God's will, I guessed.

Maybe your odds don't look too good. You are losing hope. The
candle is about to burn out. You are thirty-five years old and still not
married. In your mind, the odds of finding Boardwalk are better
than finding the right mate.

Perhaps you are climbing a financial mountain of debt that appears to be insurmountable. Or maybe you are in a situation that is so hopeless, the solution will require nothing short of a miracle. If God doesn't intervene soon, disaster will occur. Your predicament seems so impossible, it is hard for you to imagine how God could possibly meet your need.

But God doesn't have to consider the odds when it comes to his providing for you. With God involved, the chances of something happening really don't matter. This passage gives us an amazing example of how he can do miracles and provide no matter how impossible the situation may look. Four facts are established in this passage:

Fact # 1	**God knows our needs before we ask him.**

Peter received an unexpected bill. One day he was standing outside the house when the tax collectors arrived. They wanted to know if Jesus was going to pay the tax to support the temple, which was a commandment found in Exodus 30:13. When Peter went into the house to inform him, Jesus spoke about the tax before Peter could say anything. Even though Jesus wasn't outside to hear the conversation, he wanted Peter to know he had supernatural knowledge of this need even before he asked.

Sometimes we think that the purpose of prayer is to inform God of our needs. We believe he is ignorant of what is going on in our lives, and if we don't tell him, he will never know. We assume he is too busy counting hairs on people's heads to be concerned about real needs.

But in Matthew 6:8, Jesus said the Father knows what we need before we ask. The purpose of prayer is not to inform God concerning things that are happening in our lives. We pray because God says our prayers make a difference in bringing things to pass on earth. Some things will not happen unless we pray.

Shortly after Dallas Theological Seminary was founded in 1924 in Dallas, Texas, it almost had to shut down. The creditors were going to foreclose at noon on a certain day. President Lewis Chafer met with his faculty in the office, praying fervently that God would provide. One of the men, Dr. Harry Ironside, prayed, "Lord, we know that you own the cattle on a thousand hills. Please sell some of them and send us the money."

In the meantime, a Texas businessman stepped into the seminary's business office and said, "I just sold two carloads of cattle in Fort Worth, and I feel compelled to give the money to the seminary. I don't care if you need it or not, but here's the check."

The surprised secretary took the check and timidly knocked on the door of the prayer meeting. Dr. Chafer took it out of her hand and discovered it was for the exact amount of the debt. He then turned to Dr. Ironside and said, "Harry, God sold the cattle!"[1]

What are the odds of that happening? Without God, one in a billion. But with God, the odds change to one in one. He knew the needs of Dallas Theological Seminary before the faculty asked, and prearranged for the businessman to sell his cattle and bring in the money.

He also is aware of our needs and prepares ahead of time the solution to our problems. And we probably are not going to figure out how he will do it. Isaiah 55:8–9 says, "'For My thoughts are not your thoughts, neither are your ways My ways,' declares the Lord. 'For as the heavens are higher than the earth, so are My ways higher than your ways, and My thoughts than your thoughts.'" God has a much higher IQ than we have!

My little dog Bandit has an IQ of about one, maybe two. On a good day he can play dead. Sometimes he will tilt his head and look at me as if he were trying to figure out what I am thinking. But he will never be able to understand my thoughts because people thoughts are so much higher than dog thoughts.

If I read Bandit every book I have in my office library trying to educate him, it would be a waste of time. And if I opened the hood of my car and tried to explain to him how to repair it, he would comprehend nothing. He isn't capable of understanding these things because dogs are not as intelligent as people. It would be useless to explain things to him that were beyond his ability to grasp.

In the same way that human thoughts are higher than dog thoughts, God's thoughts are higher than our thoughts. We can't comprehend how he supernaturally moves people and events when the situation looks impossible. How does God cause a businessman to sell his cattle for the exact amount needed at Dallas Seminary, then lead him (without his knowledge of the school's problem) to donate the money just before the bank was about to foreclose? How does he guide two people who don't know each other and don't know they are being led to meet at a certain place and eventually get married? We are not capable of understanding how God does these things any more than Bandit understands how to read a book or how to repair a car. But just because we don't understand how God will meet our needs doesn't mean he doesn't know how he will do it. He is able to do far beyond all that we are able to ask or even think (Eph. 3:20).

| *Fact # 2* | **God controls events that we can't control.** |

After Jesus revealed to Peter that he already knew his need, he told him to go to the sea and throw in a hook. When he caught the first fish, he would find a coin inside its mouth with which he could pay the tax.

Now out of all the ways he could have chosen to meet this need, why did he choose this way? Aren't there easier ways to get money? Of course there are. He did it for a reason. God did it to demonstrate to Peter (and to us) that he controls events we can't control.

Peter was probably thinking, "Wait a minute, Jesus. I know how to fish better than you do. Remember, I had a fishing business, and the best way to catch fish is to use a net, not a hook." And Peter was right. It is much easier to use a net to catch fish. But Jesus told him to use a hook for a reason. He didn't want Peter to catch a whole net full of fish. He only wanted him to catch one fish, the right fish. Out of all the fish in the sea, only one had a coin in its mouth.

If you are single, how are you going to find the right person to marry? There are over five billion people in the world. But you need to remember, you don't need to marry five billion people. All you need is one. The right one. If God can lead a fish to a man, then he can lead a woman to a man. Thousands and thousands of fish swam in the Sea of Galilee, but Peter didn't need to catch them all. He only needed to catch the one with the coin inside its mouth.

Peter had no control over the fish he would catch. All he could do was hold the fishing pole and trust what Jesus had said. And God made sure that the right fish would bite on Peter's hook. Imagine being that fish under water trying to locate that tiny hook out of the entire sea. What are the odds of the right fish finding that little hook? Without God, one in a billion. With God, one in one.

Jimmy Smith, a student at Houston Baptist University, was interested in becoming a missionary. Two missionaries had invited him to visit their work in Guatemala. Money was tight, so he and his wife knew the trip would be impossible unless God intervened.

Several weeks later, Smith went fishing with a deacon in his church named Gene Alexander. They talked about an upcoming fishing tournament with a $20,000 prize for catching a particular fish. The deacon knew of Smith's desire to visit Guatemala and said, "I'll give you $5,000 for the trip if I catch the winning fish." Upon learning of the prize fish, Mrs. Smith logged it in her prayer journal and prayed for God to provide.

On the day of the tournament, Gene Alexander cast out his line and reeled in his first catch of the day. When he took the fish off the hook, he was surprised to discover it was marked as the $20,000 prize fish! Not only did Jimmy Smith and his wife make the trip to Guatemala, they later returned to the country to serve as foreign missionaries.[2]

Officials speculated the odds of landing that fish were one in 6.8 billion. But that's without figuring God into the equation. With him, the odds are one in one.

Fact # 3	**God's timing is perfect.**

Just as we misapprehend God's thoughts and misunderstand his sovereignty, we may miscalculate his timing. Because we are so impatient, we usually think God is either late or he has forgotten about us. But God's timing is always perfect.

Peter went to the sea and threw out the line. It was no accident that the right fish was at the right place at the right time. God had set up a divine appointment for the fish to meet Peter when he arrived at the correct spot on the sea.

God specializes in making divine appointments. It was no accident that:

- When Saul was looking for lost donkeys, he met Samuel at the appointed time set by God (1 Sam. 9:3,15–17, 24).

- The arrow shot by a soldier at random had the correct direction and timing to strike wicked King Ahab in a tiny joint in his armor, which fulfilled a prophecy (2 Chron. 18:16, 33).

- Mary and Joseph had traveled to Bethlehem for the census at the same time she gave birth to Jesus, fulfilling the prophecy of Micah 5:2 (Luke 2:1–6).

- At the exact moment when Peter denied Jesus for the third time, the rooster in the courtyard crowed twice, fulfilling the prophecy of Jesus (Matt. 26:74–75).

- The whale was at the appointed spot in the ocean at the right time to catch Jonah when the men threw him overboard (Jonah 1:15–17).

- The ram was caught in the thicket at the exact moment when Abraham was about to offer up Isaac (Gen. 22:10–13).

You see, not only is God in control, he also has perfect timing. He knows the exact moment when he needs to come through.

Franklin Graham, son of evangelist Billy Graham, was a newly licensed pilot flying from Vero Beach, Florida, to Longview, Texas. He met bad weather over Mobile, Alabama. Air-traffic controllers told him to fly north toward Jackson, Mississippi, to avoid the coming storm.

As he rose above the clouds, the instrument-panel lights flickered. A minute later the radio and instruments went dead; then all the lights went out. Franklin realized his situation was desperate, so he asked God to intervene.

He dropped below the clouds, hoping to see the ground. When he spotted the distant lights of Jackson, he headed for the airport's rotating beacon. He circled the control tower, and since he didn't have any electrical power, lowered the landing gear manually.

At that moment, all the runway's emergency landing lights came on, and he landed. As soon as he was on the ground, the lights went off. That's odd, he thought, at least they could have waited until I taxied to the ramp.

After he got out of the plane, a man from the tower asked, "Who gave you permission to land?" No one in the tower had seen the small plane circling overhead.

Why would the lights be turned on if they hadn't seen him? They investigated and discovered the runway lights had been turned on by an air-traffic controller who was explaining to his visiting pastor what he would do in case a plane ever attempted to land without radio communications![3] At the exact moment when Franklin needed the lights, the controller turned them on without knowing the plane was there.

What are the odds of that happening? Without God, one in a billion. With God, one in one.

Fact # 4	**God supplies needs to those who obey him.**

Jesus told Peter to throw the hook into the sea. That's not too difficult. But if he had not obeyed, he would never have caught the fish. It is essential that we fulfill our part in what God asks us to do.

Peter was responsible for only two things. The first thing he had to do was find the right sea. He could have gone to the Dead Sea, but there aren't any fish living in it. It was pretty obvious that wasn't the sea Jesus wanted him to fish in. Some people aren't catching anything because they are fishing out of God's will in the Dead Sea.

The other thing he had to do was throw in a hook. God didn't make the fish jump into the boat. Peter had to throw out a line. Many times when God wants to provide, he asks us to do something, such as throwing out lines.

Peter could have thrown out a net, trying to increase his chances of catching the fish with the coin in its mouth. But if he had done so, he would have been disobedient. Jesus specifically instructed him to throw out a hook. We must obey God, even if it makes better sense to do it in a different way than what he says.

So Peter did it. He threw out his line into the sea and waited for a nibble. After a few seconds, he noticed his cork begin to bob, then disappear beneath the surface of the water. He pulled back on his pole, lifting the fish out of the water and into the boat. When he opened the mouth of the fish, he discovered a coin inside. It was a stater, the exact amount needed to pay the tax for both Jesus and Peter. The only way it could have been more miraculous would be if he had taken the coin out of the fish's mouth and the fish had said, "Ta-da!" The right fish was at the right place at the right time with the right amount. God's divine appointments never disappoint.

But there's one more question we need to answer. How did the coin get in the fish's mouth? Did God create the money in its mouth? I don't think so. If Jesus was going to create money, he could have turned a couple of flat stones into coins in front of Peter. Besides, it would have made Jesus a counterfeiter if he had created the coins because it wouldn't have been the official currency of the government.

No, someone in a boat on the Sea of Galilee either threw a coin in the water or accidentally dropped a coin overboard. As it drifted toward the bottom, the fish caught it in its mouth and without swallowing it, kept it there until Peter threw in his hook and caught him.

What are the odds of that happening? Without God, one in ten billion. With God, one in one!

Fishing for Provision

- Are you fishing in the Dead Sea? If so, change your fishing location.

- What lines does God want you to throw out? (This would include praying, knocking on doors, sending out resumes, etc.)

- After throwing out the lines, are you patiently holding the fishing pole as you wait for the "fish" to bite?

- Are you trusting God to put the "fish" on the hook?

CHAPTER 2

When Your Faith Is Weak
Without a Doubt

Now when John in prison heard of the works of Christ, he sent word by his disciples, and said to Him, "Are You the Expected One, or shall we look for someone else?" And Jesus answered and said to them, "Go and report to John what you hear and see: the blind receive sight and the lame walk, the lepers are cleansed and the deaf hear, and the dead are raised up, and the poor have the gospel preached to them. And blessed is he who keeps from stumbling over Me."

(Matthew 11:2–6)

MANY WOULD SAY JOHN the Baptist was at his lowest point in his ministry. At one time, depending upon your viewpoint, he was the most famous or infamous person in Israel. His preaching had swayed multitudes.

But now things were different. Most of his disciples were following Jesus. His popularity had dwindled. John himself had said, "He must increase, but I must decrease." But decrease this far? He had no idea he would decrease to the bottom of a dark dungeon.

It's enough to make a guy start wondering. Maybe even doubt. Doubts about himself. Doubts about his ministry. Even some doubts about Jesus. John asked himself, "Is he really the Messiah? Or did I make a mistake?" So he decided to send word through his disciples to Jesus to get his questions answered.

Dear Jesus,

I am writing to inform you that I have been thrown into prison by Herod. I have had a lot of time to think since I have been here. I have been thinking about all of the things I have preached about you, even before you began your ministry.

Remember how I told everyone that your winnowing fork was in your hand and you would thoroughly clean your threshing floor? Remember how I said you would burn up the chaff with unquenchable fire? To me that meant that you would take care of all injustice and would correct all wrongs with your righteousness.

To be quite honest with you, Jesus, I never thought I would have to write a note like this. Things haven't quite worked out like I thought they would. I was sure you would have straightened things up around here by now. Rumors have it that Herodias wants my head. If you are wondering when to get out your winnowing fork to start cleaning up, now would be a pretty good time. That is, if you are the one we are expecting.

Respectfully yours,
John the Baptist

P.S. If we are to look for someone else, please let us know.

A few days later, the mailman delivered a letter to John's jail cell. He anxiously opened it, hoping to receive news that Jesus was arranging for his quick release from prison. Instead, John read this reply:

Dear John the Baptist,

The blind receive sight, the lame walk, the lepers are cleansed, the deaf hear, the dead are raised, the poor have the gospel preached to them.

Agape,
Jesus

P.S. Blessed is he who keeps from stumbling over me.

We expect doubters to become believers. But not for believers to become doubters. That's a little bit hard to swallow. Especially when you're talking about John the Baptist. We might expect Thomas to doubt. The guy was one big question mark. But John the Baptist? This man was an exclamation point! His whole ministry was filled with courage and confidence, being the first one to boldly proclaim that Jesus was the Lamb of God who takes away the sin of the world.

Remember the time when he called the Pharisees and Sadducees a brood of vipers? Boy, were they mad at him that day. He didn't so much as blink in response to them. John didn't have a doubt in his mind he was right. And you should have seen him when he told King Herod it was unlawful to have his brother's wife. He had the king sweating bullets. Not an inkling of a doubt there, either.

If you take a good look at a resumé of John's life, it reads like a *Who's Who of Non-doubters.*

Resumé of John the Baptist

Name: John (the Baptist)
Birth: Miraculous. My mother was advanced in years and was barren. An angel appeared to my father Zacharias and told him my mother would give birth and that my name would be called "John."

Prophet Qualifications
- Filled with the Holy Spirit in my mother's womb.
- Forerunner before Messiah in the spirit and power of Elijah.
- Fulfilled prophecies in the Old Testament (Isa. 40:3, Mal. 4:5–6).

Ministry Experience
- Baptized Jesus in the Jordan River.
- Saw the heavens open and the Spirit descend upon Jesus as a dove.
- Heard a voice from heaven telling me about Jesus, "This is My beloved Son, in whom I am well-pleased."
- Preached to the multitudes. Started with no disciples, but grew a following of thousands.

Other Comments
Willing to live on meager salary. Cheap to clothe and feed. My garments are made of camel's hair. My diet consists primarily of locusts and wild honey.

How can a prophet like that possibly experience doubt? Many of us wrongly assume all the great men of the Bible never had any doubts, but we find that was not the case.

David, a man after God's own heart, experienced doubts. He wrote, "How long, O Lord? Wilt Thou forget me forever? How long wilt Thou hide Thy face from me?" (Ps. 13:1). The great prophet Elijah also doubted. After he had conquered the prophets of Baal and Asherah, he fled from Jezebel because he thought God wouldn't protect him (1 Kings 19:3). Jonah put his doubt into action when he ran from God and hid in the bottom of a ship going to Tarshish (Jon. 1:3, 5). How about Jeremiah? Yep, even Jerry dabbled in doubt. He thought God had deceived him (Jer. 20:7). And of course, we all know Thomas doubted that Jesus rose from the dead. But how many of us remember that all the disciples refused to believe he rose from the dead (Mark 16:11, 14)?

What is doubt, anyway? Doubt is not unbelief, but it is not faith, either. It wavers between faith and unbelief, unable to make up its mind what it wants to be. It is like the hitchhiker who was thumbing a ride with his hand in one direction—and thumbing a ride with his other hand in the other direction. He wasn't sure which way he wanted to go.

James 1:8 tells us that doubt is being double-minded, which makes a person unstable in all his ways.

> But let him ask in faith without any doubting, for the one who doubts is like the surf of the sea driven and tossed by the wind. For let not that man expect that he will receive anything from the Lord, being a double-minded man, unstable in all his ways. (James 1:6–8)

A double-minded man has certain characteristics. The one who doubts is:

Up and Down Emotionally. He is tossed by the wind like the surf of the sea. If you have ever been on the sea in a boat, the waves will take you up, then down. Up, then down. Whenever we doubt, we are controlled and manipulated by our ups and downs. One minute we are up emotionally, and the next minute we are down emotionally. We can't take this very long without becoming seasick.

Tossed To and Fro Doctrinally. James 1:6 says he is driven by the wind. He is being directed by outside forces rather than being guided from the inside by faith. Ephesians 4:14 talks about being tossed to and fro by every wind of doctrine. The one who doubts does not have a firm grasp on what he should believe doctrinally.

Answering Yes and No Mentally. He is a double-minded man. He says yes at first, then a little while later changes the answer to no.

Scientists once studied a snake that was double-minded. It was born with two heads. Each head had a mind of its own and would try to control the body. One moment it would crawl one way, then the other mind would take over, and the snake would crawl in a completely different direction. It truly was double-minded.

That's the picture of the one who doubts. As confused as a termite inside a yo-yo, he doesn't know which way is up and which way is down. He is lacking direction, looking back on past decisions and wondering if he's made a mistake.

We have all experienced doubts. Doubt means we don't know what to do next. We are not sure what we believe. We are having second thoughts about the decisions we have made in the past, which makes us even more uncertain about the decisions we need to make for the future.

That's why John doubted. He had paved the highway for the Messiah to journey on, but now he was locked up in prison while Jesus traveled down the road without him. Jesus didn't seem to appreciate all the work John had done for him. The least a Messiah could do would be to visit him in prison, which was what Jesus told his disciples to do (Matt. 25:36).

What John had said about Jesus being a Great Deliverer seemed to be nothing more than a Great Disappointment. Jesus appeared to be unconcerned that John was in prison and about to lose his head. In John's mind, everything he had preached about justice and righteousness was now in question.

How to Deal with Doubts

Doubts occur when what we expect to happen *isn't* happening, or what shouldn't be happening *is* happening. Circumstances are in direct conflict with what we believe. This causes us to be confused and waver between the two, wondering which is right.

How then, can we deal with doubts? Is there any way we can increase our faith and decrease our doubts? Yes, there is.

First

Question your doubts, not your faith.

Instead of questioning your faith, question your doubts. That is what John did. Rather than letting his doubts continue to plague him, he investigated them. He knew truth would stand up for itself because it could pass the test of scrutiny.

So John packed up his doubts and sent them to Jesus. The answer Jesus sent back revealed John needed to make some adjustments in his belief system. He had been preaching about Jesus, quoting from Isaiah concerning the Messiah's *second* coming. When Jesus sent word back, he quoted verses from Isaiah concerning his *first* coming. John was confused because he had the right person but the wrong timing.

John wasn't wrong in what he believed about Jesus, but he needed to make adjustments in his theology. Doubts can be a stepping stone, rather than a stumbling block, if we will allow them to expose weak points in our belief system so we can correct them.

We are all growing in our understanding of God. Apollos, who was mighty in the Scriptures, was teaching accurately the things concerning Jesus. But Priscilla and Aquilla took him aside and explained the way of God to him more accurately (Acts 18:24–26). Faith will always grow and doubts will diminish whenever we adjust our belief system to line up more accurately with God's Word.

Second

Concentrate on what you know, not on what you don't know.

Doubts will arise when we think about things we don't know the answers to. Jesus responded to John's questions by trying to get him to recall the things he knew to be true.

"John, I have made the blind to see. I have healed people who have been paralyzed and have cleansed lepers. I have made deaf people hear, and I have even raised people from the dead. I have also preached the gospel to the poor, not just the wealthy. Now, John, you know I did these miracles. Who else can do these things, except the Messiah? If you will concentrate on these facts, your doubts will leave."

After Jesus healed a man's blindness, the Pharisees were questioning the former blind man as to whether or not Jesus was a sinner. He answered, "Whether He is a sinner, I do not know; one thing I do know, that, whereas I was blind, now I see" (John 9:25). He concentrated on what he knew to be true, not on what he didn't know.

You also know many things that are true. "Finally, brethren, whatever is true…let your mind dwell on these things" (Phil. 4:8). You may recall when God answered a prayer, spoke to you clearly, or did something miraculous in your life. He might have touched you in a special way, and you knew it was God who did it. Concentrating on those facts rather than concentrating on your doubts will help you grow in faith.

	Trust in the Lord with your heart, not your head.
Third	Trust in the Lord with all your heart, and do not lean on your own understanding. (Prov. 3:5)

When we doubt, we have a hard time making decisions. We are unable to make up our minds because we have so many questions. God wants to help us in the decision-making process, but it requires that we trust him. That sounds easy, but the difficulty arises when he instructs us in ways that contradict our minds. That's why he tells us to trust him with our entire heart and to not depend on logic in making decisions. Trust comes from believing that our Father knows what is best for us. He will lead us through speaking to our hearts, even when our minds may tell us differently.

Inside every airplane are instruments that are critical to flying the aircraft. The instruments will give a true reading of how the aircraft is flying, even if a pilot's mind tells him differently. On a clear, sunny day, a pilot may not need some of these instruments, but at night or in poor visibility, these instruments become vital to his survival. Many planes have crashed because the pilot became disoriented and failed to trust his instruments.

While attending Texas A&M, Jeff Patton and I became friends as members of the Corps of Cadets. He is now Lt. Col. Jeff Patton and flew as an F-15 fighter pilot in Desert Storm. On the first night of the war, his mission was to escort a large formation of fighters in bombing a chemical-weapons plant in northern Iraq. The date for Desert Storm was chosen because the absence of moonlight and the high clouds helped prevent the enemy defenses from detecting the attacking Allied fighters. Flying in total darkness, the pilots became completely dependent upon their instruments.

Shortly after crossing into Iraq, Lt. Col. Patton's jet was "locked on" to by an Iraqi surface-to-air missile radar. He violently maneuvered his aircraft to break the radar's lock on him. He successfully broke the lock, but it created a new problem. Those radical movements in the dark threw off the balance in his inner ear (which is what happens when a person gets dizzy), causing him to become disoriented.

His mind was telling him his plane was in a climbing right turn, but when he checked his instruments, they indicated he was in a 60-degree dive towards the ground! He was sure he was in a climb instead of a dive, and his mind was screaming at him to lower the nose of his F-15 to halt the climb. While his mind commanded him to correct the plane in one direction, his instruments instructed him to do just the opposite. Because he was flying in total darkness, he had to decide quickly whether to trust his mind or his instruments. His life depended on making the correct choice.

Even though it took everything within to overcome what his mind was telling him, he decided to trust his instruments. He rolled his wings level and pulled his F-15 upward, which drew seven times the force of gravity, pulling the aircraft out of its dive. It only took a few moments to realize he had made the right decision. If he had lowered the nose of his jet like his mind had been telling him, he would have crashed the plane. Trusting his instruments saved his life.

Immediately, he looked at his altimeter, which told him the elevation of his aircraft. He had narrowly escaped colliding with the mountains of Iraq by just two thousand feet. Although he had made the correct decision by trusting his instruments, he realized if he had delayed just three more seconds, his plane *still* would have crashed into the mountains. Even right decisions can be wrong ones if they are made too late.

God will guide the "instruments" inside our hearts through his Spirit, even though our minds may tell us to do just the opposite. We cannot continue to vacillate between God's instructions and our own logic, trying to decide which to believe. There comes a time when we, like Lt. Col. Patton, must decide whom we are going to trust.

When we put our trust in the Lord rather than our own understanding, doubts will disappear. But don't take too much time trying to decide. The consequences of indecision can be disastrous.

Doubting Your Doubts

- What doubts do you need to investigate?

- List some facts you know to be true about God.

- Make a decision to concentrate on facts rather than doubts.

CHAPTER 3

When You Are Discontented
May I Change Seats, Please?

Not that I speak from want; for I have learned to be content in whatever circumstances I am. I know how to get along with humble means, and I also know how to live in prosperity; in any and every circumstance I have learned the secret of being filled and going hungry, both of having abundance and suffering need.

(Philippians 4:11–12)

AN ABNORMAL SPIRITUAL CONDITION is reaching epidemic portions throughout our country. Unfortunately, counselors have not been able to successfully treat this disorder. The abnormality I am describing is what I call "Contentment-Deficit Disorder."

Symptoms of Contentment-Deficit Disorder

- Lack of commitment to other people

- Compulsion to move to another city or state

- Strong desire to quit your job

- Urgency to leave your spouse

- Desire to drop out of school

- Restlessness compelling you to run from your present circumstances

- Attitude that anything is better than what you have right now

Fortunately, God has a cure for Contentment-Deficit Disorder.

Dr. Jack Hyles told of an experience he once had on a flight from San Francisco to Chicago. He was seated in 4A and, as he usually did, spoke to the person next to him. He said, "Good morning. How are you today?" The man did not reply. Dr. Hyles thought the man might be hard of hearing, so he spoke louder, "Good morning, how are you today?" Once again, the man didn't acknowledge him.

Dr. Hyles started making hand motions like sign language, thinking he might be deaf. The man glanced over at him and then quickly looked away. Dr. Hyles said he knew right then he was seated next to a crab, that is, a very difficult person.

He continued to try to strike up a conversation, "It's a nice day." Again, no response. He asked, "Where are you going?" He knew that was a dumb question because everyone on the plane was going to Chicago. The man didn't respond.

The flight attendant came by and took the man's order for breakfast. The man spoke to her, but wouldn't speak to Dr. Hyles. So Dr. Hyles asked, "Do you have some problems?" The man still ignored him. Dr. Hyles thought, "This old crab is ruining my trip. I have to sit beside this person for four hours. He is not going to ruin my trip."

So he called the stewardess and asked, "Ma'am, may I change seats, please?"

She said, "I'm sorry, the plane is full. You must stay in your assigned seat."

He looked at the man and said, "If you think you're going to ruin my trip, you're mistaken." The man never looked up.[1]

All of us are boarded on a plane heading toward a destination. In order to enjoy the trip, you need to understand a couple of things. First, God has assigned you a seat in life. Second, you are probably going to be seated next to a crab.

That crab may be a difficult person you work with. That crab may be your spouse. It may be a relative or a next-door neighbor, or it may even be some difficult circumstances you are going through. And that crab is ruining your trip.

So you cry out to God and pray, "May I change seats, please? Can I move away from this situation?"

He answers, "No, this is your assigned seat in life. Buckle your seat belt and enjoy the trip!"

How do we enjoy the trip through life when we are seated next to a crab?

| First | **Accept the fact that God has given you an assigned seat.** |

There are a lot of seats that we would never choose on our own, but God has assigned them to us. Paul wrote Philippians from a Roman prison. The prisons in Biblical times were different from today's. Paul didn't have cable TV, nor a recreation room in which to lift weights. He didn't have air-conditioning or heating or three balanced meals a day. No, he was bound by chains, without the entertainment features prisoners have today.

If Paul could have had a choice, he would not have chosen to go to prison for preaching the gospel. He would have preferred to be preaching on the streets or on a missionary journey. But his assigned seat at that time was not on the streets or on a ship. It was in a Roman prison.

So what did Paul do? He learned to accept his assigned seat. He learned to be content in whatever circumstances he was in.

Have you learned to be content in your situation? Have you accepted the seat God has assigned you? Until you do, you will always be asking him to let you change seats.

I once knew a man who had been married for ten years to his wife, and they had three children. The family moved forty times in those ten years of marriage. That's four times a year, once every three months. Why did he move his family so much? It was because he had Contentment-Deficit Disorder. He moved from job to job, from state to state, always looking for that perfect place where he would be happy. But there was one place he forgot to look. He forgot to look inside his own heart. God had assigned him a seat in life, but he didn't want to sit in it.

| Second | **Learn to coexist with the crab.** |

Paul said he had learned how to get along with humble means and prosperity. He had learned the secret of being filled and going hungry, of having abundance and suffering need.

I'm sure Paul was seated next to some crabs in prison. Thieves and murderers were there. Probably some perverts, too. No doubt some people hated him because of his preaching to them about Jesus. Others had obnoxious personalities that rubbed him the wrong way. They probably stunk, since they had no deodorant or fabric softener to make their clothes smell fresh. No mints for their bad breath, either. These were the crabs Paul learned to coexist with. He wasn't going to let them ruin his trip.

The grizzly bear is the meanest animal in the forest. It can end the life of any other creature with one swipe of its paw. There is one animal the grizzly bear will not attack. He has even allowed this animal to eat with him, although it is his adversary.

The animal I am talking about is the skunk. The grizzly bear does not like the skunk, but he has decided it is better to coexist with him than to create a stink. Sometimes it is better to learn how to get along with the crab in your life than fight him and make your situation even worse.

If you are working with a crab or working for one, it is better to coexist with the difficult person than to quit your job. Many people become irritated by the crab they work with and, in a moment of frustration, quit their jobs. But they are hurting themselves more than they are hurting the crab. It is better to coexist than quit.

God has a purpose for the crab in your life. That's why he assigned you a seat next to him. He is using that crab to teach you some things. One of those things is how to love crabs! It's easy to love the lovely, but Jesus wants us to love our enemies.

> "And if you love those who love you, what credit is that to you? For even sinners love those who love them" (Luke 6:32).

A man was working a crossword puzzle and asked, "What is a four letter word for a strong emotional reaction toward a difficult person?"

Someone standing nearby said, "The answer is hate."

A lady interrupted and said, "No, the answer is love!"

Everyone is working that same crossword puzzle, but the way you answer is up to you.

| *Third* | **Realize that changing seats does not solve your problem.** |

People believe a lot of myths about seat changing. Let's examine some of them.

Myth #1: "If I could be with someone else, then I would be happy."

Some people think if they could get away from the crab and be with someone else, then all of their problems would be over. But that's not true, because discontentment is an internal problem, not an external one. Yet, many people have never figured this out. They are consumed with changing seats, because it's easier to change seats than deal with the crab.

Single people want to change seats and get married, while married people want to change seats and be single again. Like flies on a screen door, the flies on the inside are wanting to get out, and the flies on the outside are wanting to get in.

The grass always looks greener on the other side of the fence. That's because it's artificial turf. It is only an illusion. People with Contentment-Deficit Disorder (CDD) spend their entire lifetimes chasing illusions which are always just beyond their reach.

A man in the desert was craving something to drink and saw a lemonade stand on the next sand dune. He ran to it, but when he arrived, the lemonade stand disappeared and reappeared on the next sand dune. When he ran to the next and grabbed for the lemonade, it disappeared and reappeared again on the next dune. He continued to chase it from dune to dune until he died of thirst. He was chasing a mirage. It was nothing more than an illusion in his mind.

We must make a distinction between reality and illusion. Those with CDD believe that illusion is reality and will exchange whatever they have for what they perceive to be better.

A dog was crossing over a bridge with a bone in his mouth. He looked over the edge and saw his reflection in the water. Not realizing that he was looking at a mirror image, he coveted the bone in the other dog's mouth. When he opened his mouth to grab for the other dog's bone, he lost the bone he was carrying. He gave up the reality of what he possessed for a reflection.

Many discontented people have exchanged their spouses for what they imagined would be exciting new lives with someone else. The following letter was written to Ann Landers:

Dear Ann:

Sometimes you feel lonely and unloved in a marriage—even after 23 years. You feel as if there's got to be more to life, so you set out to find someone who can make you blissfully happy. You believe you have found that someone and decide he is exactly what you want. So you pack up and say good-bye to your 23-year marriage and all the friends you made when you were part of the couple.

You live the glorious life for a few years, and then, a light bulb goes on in your empty head. You realize that you have exactly the life you had before—the only difference is that you've lost your friends, your children's respect, and the best friend you loved and shared everything with for 23 years. And you miss him. You cannot undo what has been done, so you settle for a lonely and loveless life with emptiness in your heart.

Ann, please print my letter so others won't give up something that is truly precious—and let them know that they won't know how precious it is until they have thrown it away.

Heavyhearted in Philly[2]

Myth #2: "If I could just go somewhere else, then I would be happy."

My mother grew up dreaming of living in a house on the beach. She said it would be wonderful to sit on the shore, watching the sun set over the water. After she married my father, they moved to a little cottage on the beach, fulfilling her lifelong dream. But she discovered things were not as she thought they would be.

The humidity was terrible, causing her to always feel sticky. After a walk on the beach, they tracked in sand and deposited it all over the house. Sand found its way into the bed, onto the couch, and into the sandwiches they ate. After a while, she didn't even notice the sunsets. Many times the surroundings that are so exciting when we first see them are not noticed after a few months of viewing them every day.

At one time Mother had dreamed about moving to the beach, but when they moved away, she was glad. Some places are a great place to visit, but a different story once you live there.

Of course, that doesn't mean God never wants us to move. It simply means that the grass is never quite as green once we get to the other side. Problems that we can't see from a distance are on the other side of the fence. When we change seats, we exchange one set of problems for another.

Myth #3: "If I could just get something else, then I would be happy."

Contentment is not having everything we want, but wanting everything we have. God has supplied us with all things to enjoy (1 Tim. 6:17), but our hearts must be right before we can enjoy them. If we are not happy with the things we already have, we will never be happy with the new things we receive.

A little boy named Billy was spoiled by his permissive parents. Whenever he didn't get what he wanted, he threw a temper tantrum, and his parents immediately catered to his wishes. They believed if they gave him everything he wanted, he would never be unhappy.

One day Billy's mother heard him crying in the living room. She rushed in and said, "What's the matter? What can Mommy get for you?"

Billy pointed to a clock hanging on the wall and screamed, "I want that clock and I want it now!"

His mother hesitated giving it to him because it was expensive, and she knew he would probably break it. But she had never refused him anything.

"Well, are you going to give it to me?" Billy demanded.

His mother went over to the wall, reluctantly took it down, and handed it to him.

Then Billy started crying again.

His mother asked, "What's the matter now? What do you want?"

Between sobs Billy said, "I want—(sniff)—I want . . . I want something that I can't have!"

Because Billy wasn't happy with what he already had, he wasn't happy with what he received. God wants us to receive his blessings, but if our hearts are not in a position to enjoy them, we will simply toss them aside and whine for something else. That's why discontented people don't need to change their seats; they need to change their hearts.

	Don't allow the crab to ruin your trip.
Fourth	

Too many people are so concerned about the crab in their lives, they have forgotten how to enjoy the trip. God wants us to enjoy our trip through life, but in order to do this, we cannot allow the crab to ruin it. We must make up our minds right now, "Crabby person, you are not going to ruin my trip! Difficult situation, you're not going to force me to change seats! Lord, I'm going to be content in my situation and rejoice in it, no matter how difficult the crab may be."

Don't get the idea that contentment means God will never lead you to a new place. More than likely he will lead you to make a number of changes during your lifetime. He just doesn't want discontentment to drive you into a situation that is out of his will.

If God does allow you to change seats, just remember: another crab will always want to sit next to you. It's part of the cure for Contentment-Deficit Disorder.

Learning to be Content

- Think about different ways you can coexist with your crab.

- Rather than running from your difficult situation, think about how you can change your heart.

- If God leads you to make a change, read chapter 8, "When You Need to Make a Change."

CHAPTER 4

When You Are Tempted
Adam and Eve's Instruction Manual

Now the serpent was more crafty than any beast of the field which the Lord God had made. And he said to the woman, "Indeed, has God said , 'You shall not eat from any tree of the garden'?" And the woman said to the serpent, "From the fruit of the trees of the garden we may eat; but from the tree which is in the middle of the garden, God has said, 'You shall not eat from it or touch it, lest you die.'" And the serpent said to the woman, "You surely shall not die!". . .When the woman saw that the tree was good for food, and that it was a delight to the eyes, and that the tree was desirable to make one wise, she took from its fruit and ate; and she gave also to her husband with her, and he ate.

(Genesis 3:1–4, 6)

I F ADAM AND EVE had written a book, they might have entitled it, *Adam and Eve's Instruction Manual For Reducing Temptations.* They could give us a step-by-step document explaining how they were tempted and how others can avoid it.

Temptation hasn't changed much since the first one. The tactics are the same. The principles involved are identical. The only thing that has changed is the bait. Our forbidden fruit may not be hanging on a tree, but it is still off limits. Here are some lessons Adam and Eve can teach us from what they learned in the garden.

| *Lesson # 1* | We can reduce temptations by avoiding the places of temptation. |

Have you ever wondered why God put the forbidden tree in the middle of the garden? That was no accident. He could have put it anywhere, but God chose that spot because he wanted Adam and Eve to know exactly where it was *so they could avoid it.* It is always easier to avoid temptation than to overcome it. If they could avoid that place, they wouldn't be tempted. They knew where the forbidden tree was, so they could stay away from it and enjoy the rest of the garden.

A man broke his arm and went to see the doctor. He walked in clutching his arm in great pain. "Doc, you gotta help me," he moaned. "I broke my arm in two places. What should I do?"

The doctor said, "There's only one thing you can do. Stay out of those places!"

We get into trouble many times because we hang around the wrong places. Staying away from certain areas can keep us from getting into trouble.

Temptations usually begin with a thought to go to a certain place. The temptation began for Adam and Eve when they decided to take a trip to the middle of the garden. The tree of life was also in the middle of the garden, but that's not why they went there. They went to look at the wrong tree. When they chose to inspect forbidden fruit rather than legitimate fruit, they had entered into temptation.

Temptation always covers an area that can be entered into. Once we have crossed that invisible line, we have entered into temptation. Every boxing ring has rope around the area where the boxers fight. If we stay outside the ring, we will be safe. But once we enter into the ring, temptation begins to fight with us.

I once counseled a man who had a drinking problem. After he left his job every day, he stopped at the bar on his way home. When I asked him where the bar was located, he told me it was on the direct route between his job and his house. I explained to him that when he drove past the bar, he had entered into temptation. So I rerouted him home from work on different streets where he wouldn't have the option of stopping at the bar. He later told me this was an important factor in helping him overcome his temptation to drink.

Jesus taught us to pray, "Lead us not into temptation" (Luke 11:4). This doesn't mean that God leads us into temptation, and we must beg him to stop doing it. It means God can lead us in such a way that we will avoid the areas of temptation. That's why Jesus said, "Keep watching and praying, that you may not *enter into* temptation" (Matthew 26:41, italics mine). This is a pre-temptation instruction. Watching and praying can keep us from entering into the areas where we will be tempted.

Lesson # 2	We open ourselves to temptation when we decide to provide for the flesh.

Romans 13:14 tells us to make no provision for the flesh. We make provision for the flesh when we attempt to provide for our desires in the wrong way. Each person is "tempted when he is carried away and enticed by his own lust" (James 1:14). This means the desires of our flesh can carry us to the wrong places and tempt us.

Provision means "to think ahead." If a person wants to be tempted, he will think ahead and make plans to be in a place where he can provide for the flesh. It's hard to be victorious over temptation when you also want to be overcome by it.

One day little Richard was told by his mother to come straight home after school and not stop at the baseball field. After school, Richard decided to carry his ball glove with him just in case he was tempted. By thinking ahead and making plans to disobey, he made provision for the flesh.

My favorite ice-cream flavor is vanilla bean. When I am tempted by this delicacy, my taste buds become stronger than my mind, will, and emotions. If a carton of vanilla bean had been hanging on the tree in the garden, I would have been first in line with my spoon. Forget that it doesn't have one ounce of nutrition; my flesh loves this stuff. If I see an ice cream commercial on television, my taste buds dance. My salivary glands burst with excitement. I get the "jitters" for ice cream.

This is followed by a conversation inside my head: "Kent, you don't drink, do drugs, smoke, or chew. You're in pretty good health, and you deserve a break. You've been working hard lately. Reward yourself with a little ice cream."

Within moments I have the car keys in hand and tell Cindy, "Honey, I'm going to run to the grocery store for a few things; I'll be back in a little bit."

I don't fool her for one second. She knows that once I have decided to go to the store, I will provide for my ice-cream craving. Adam and Eve did the same thing when they decided to go to the middle of the garden. They made provision for the flesh by planning to look at the forbidden tree.

Lesson # 3	**When we move into the place of temptation, Satan will be waiting there to tempt us.**

When Adam and Eve arrived at the middle of the garden, guess who just happened to be waiting at the tree? Satan! How did he know to wait for them at that spot? Because he knew that was the place where they could be tempted. Satan can tempt us easier in some places than others. He likes to hang around the places of temptation.

Not only are we to make *no provision* for the flesh, but we are also to make *no place* for the devil (Ephesians 4:27). When I make a place in my mind for Satan to fill, I have made a place for the devil. He first gets me to think about eating vanilla bean. And if he can get me to think about eating ice cream while I am standing in the frozen-foods section of the store, I'm in double trouble.

Once I crack open the door of my mind, Satan sticks his foot in the door. If he can get a foothold, then he can make a stronghold. Satan knows that once I make a place in my mind to provide for the flesh, he can pour in thoughts of temptation.

So now we see a couple of things are involved in temptation. We struggle with the flesh on the inside and Satan on the outside. When we make provision for the flesh and a place for the devil, we become vulnerable to yielding to the temptation.

Lesson # 4	**After we have entered into temptation, we become blinded to the consequences.**

Outside of the area of temptation, we can easily see the consequences of what can happen to us if we yield. But after we have entered into temptation, we become blinded to them. Temptations don't usually look like temptations, especially when we have been observing them for a while. When Eve entered into temptation, she failed to recognize it as such.

This tree doesn't look too harmful, she thought. It has a lot of good points. It's good for food, it delights me to look at it, and I've been told it will increase my wisdom. I don't see any consequences if I eat from it.

It is no secret vanilla-bean ice cream is a delight to the taste buds and has the ability to make one fat. After I decide to go to the grocery store, I only remember the "delight to the taste buds" part. The "ability to make one fat" only applies to other people, not me.

Sometimes the "nutritional facts" label listing the calories and grams of fat can deter me from buying a food item. But once I have decided to buy vanilla bean, the nutrition label becomes irrelevant. "Let's see, 320 calories per cup, 18 grams of fat." This last warning doesn't even phase me. I divert my eyes from the nutrition label to the ingredients. I tell myself, "The milk products listed in the ingredients will be good for me. This isn't that bad."

After I have entered into temptation, I ignore all warning signs because I am blind to the consequences. The truth is, the result of delighting my tastes buds is fat added to my stomach. But Satan is quick to confirm what I already convinced myself: "You shall surely not get fat!" If we could only see the consequences of our actions before we did them, it would deter us from doing many things.

The manager of a historical mansion in Florida was having a problem with tourists touching the bedspreads and curtains in one of the furnished master bedrooms. The "Do Not Touch" sign seemed to encourage the visitors to touch them anyway. He decided to change the sign to "Wash Hands Immediately After Touching."

You can guess what happened. It immediately ended the touching. People thought the curtains and bedspreads might be treated with a harmful preserving chemical.[1] They stopped touching because they imagined harmful consequences if they yielded to the temptation.

The alcoholic never dreamed he would end up in the gutter when he took his first drink. But he could remember saying, "One drink never hurt anyone."

The man who cheated on his wife never dreamed he would lose his wife and children because of yielding for one fleeting moment. But he could remember thinking, "Who will ever know?"

The fish who took the bait never dreamed a hook was inside and he would end up in the frying pan. But he couldn't see the man standing on the shore with a fishing pole at the other end of the line.

Eve never dreamed she would lose her innocence, bring down the entire human race, and be banished from the Garden of Eden as a result of taking one bite from a piece of fruit. It never occurred to her that Satan had been lying. His power lies in his ability to deceive people into believing they can get away with yielding to temptation without suffering any consequences.

Lesson # 5	**The pull of the temptation increases the closer we get to the forbidden fruit.**

Many people want to play with temptation as long as they can, thinking they can walk away from it at any time. But it's not that easy, because the closer we get to the temptation, the more pull it has. Adam and Eve had walked to the middle of the garden, and now they were standing under the tree looking at the fruit. The closer they got to the tree, the more likely they would eat the forbidden fruit. It is hard to pick fruit if you are a hundred yards away, but it is easy if you are at an arm's length.

Willpower grows weaker as we get nearer to the temptation. Just like Superman weakens as he gets near the Kryptonite, we weaken when we get near the temptation. Martin Luther once said, "Don't sit near the fire if your head is made of butter." The closer we get to the fire, the hotter the fire feels to us. Even though the fire remains at the same temperature, the heat affects us according to how close we are to it.

In the cartoon *Cathy,* she struggled with her diet so she decided to make provision for the flesh by taking a drive.

Frame 1: I will take a drive but won't go near the grocery store.

Frame 2: I will drive by the grocery store but will not go in.

Frame 3: I will go in the grocery store but will not walk down the aisle where the candy is on sale.

Frame 4: I will look at the candy but will not pick it up.

Frame 5: I will pick it up but not buy it.

Frame 6: I will buy it but not open it.

Frame 7: Open it but not smell it.

Frame 8: Smell it but not taste it.

Frame 9: Taste it but not eat it.

Frame 10: Munch, munch, munch![2]

I can identify with that cartoon. Once I've entered into temptation, vanilla-bean ice cream has the power to get me off the couch and into my car, drive me down the road, carry me into the store, and walk me down the aisle to the frozen-foods department. Once I'm there, temptation's power is much greater than when I was in my home.

My temptation began with my thought to go to the store. That's also the easiest place to stop the pull of temptation. Cutting off the temptation by killing the thought at the beginning is the key to breaking free from temptation's pull.

Lesson # 6	**We must run away from the temptation rather than try to resist it.**

Adam and Eve had gone to the wrong place and were considering eating the forbidden fruit, but they still had not sinned. Most people in this situation would attempt to resist the temptation by trying not to do it. The Bible, however, never instructs us to "try not to do it."

When we try not to do something, we are like the country boy who was lying under a farmer's apple tree looking up at the apples.

The farmer saw him from a distance and said, "Hey you! What are you trying to do, son—steal my apples?"

The boy yelled back, "No sir, I'm trying not to!"

Most of us are trying not to. The harder we try not to, the more we fail. When we try not to, we are attempting to resist the temptation with the power of the flesh. This is absolutely the wrong thing to do because the flesh actually wants to yield. The very thing that got us into the temptation is now trying to get us out of it!

Trying to resist temptation in the flesh is like trying to...

...fight a lion with a leg of lamb.

...push a magnet away with an iron pipe.

...scare off a thundercloud with a lightning rod.

...put out a fire with a piece of dried kindling wood.

The flesh is the wrong weapon to use in fighting temptation. The spirit is willing, but the flesh is weak (Matt. 26:41). The flesh makes an attempt to resist, but its resistance isn't strong enough to overcome temptation's pull. Mark Twain once said, "I can resist everything but temptation." So can you! That's why you need to find a different battle plan than "trying not to do it."

It may surprise you to find that the Bible never tells us to resist temptation. God tells us to resist the tempter (Satan), but to flee or run from the temptation. We are to flee immorality (1 Cor. 6:18). We must flee idolatry (1 Cor. 10:14). Are we to resist youthful lusts? No. We are to flee from them (2 Tim. 2:22). That's quite the opposite of standing there, trying to resist. If we try to resist, we will lose.

Of course, don't say yes to temptation. But don't say no to it, either. Any time you get into a conversation with temptation, it will talk you into doing it. Rather than "Just Say No" in your attempt to resist, "Just Run Away" from it.

A couple of boys tried to walk through a corral when a bull saw them and charged. One of the boys said, "Let's stop and pray."

The other boy said, "No, let's run and pray!"

They didn't need to resist the bull inside of the corral. They needed to run out of the area where they were vulnerable.

That's what we need to do when we are being tempted. We need to flee *out of the area of temptation*. We must exit the area we have entered into. The only way I can break the pull of vanilla bean once I am in the frozen-foods department is to get out of the store as quickly as possible. Temptation's power can only be broken by running outside the area of temptation. God promises that when we are tempted, he will make a way of escape for us (1 Cor. 10:13).

Joseph found the way of escape when he was being seduced by Potiphar's wife. He didn't stand there, trying to push her away. He fled from her presence (Gen. 39:12). Adam and Eve didn't need to stand by the tree trying to figure out the best way to resist; they needed to run away from the middle of the garden.

| Lesson # 7 | Forbidden fruit is never as sweet as you have been told it will be. |

Eve picked the fruit from the tree and thought, I touched it and nothing happened. I thought I was supposed to die. Actually, God never said she would die if she touched it. He had given the command to not eat from the tree to Adam before Eve was created (Gen. 2:17–18). Adam passed the instructions to Eve, and something got crossed in the communication. He probably told her, "Woman, (her name wasn't Eve until Genesis 3:20), God said don't eat from the tree or we will die. Just to be on the safe side, don't even touch it, okay?"

But Eve did touch it. She decided to pick the wrong fruit, which was the last step before sinning. She was like the little boy who opened the cookie jar in the kitchen. His mother was in the next room and heard the lid rattle. She called out, "Johnny, is your hand in the cookie jar?"

He yelled back, "Yes, Mommy, but I'm not eating any!"

That's where Eve was. Her hand was in the cookie jar.

Satan whispered in Eve's ear, "Come on, Eve. If you eat the fruit, it will make you wise. I'm not asking you to eat the whole tree. I'm not even asking you to eat the whole piece of fruit. I'm just asking you to take one little bite, and if you don't like it—hey, the whole deal is off."

Eve thought, Well, I guess one little nibble never hurt anyone. She bit into the fruit, then gave it to Adam. After he ate, their eyes were opened, and they were ashamed of what they had done. We are always ashamed after we have yielded to temptation. Hindsight is always 20/20.

It was the first and the last bite of the fruit they ever enjoyed. Forbidden fruit leaves a bitter aftertaste of misery and bondage. Satan always presents his very best up front, but then afterward it quickly goes downhill. Each bite gets progressively less satisfying until we get to the point where we must have the forbidden fruit even though we don't enjoy it anymore. Satan's goal is to get us addicted to forbidden fruit, where we crave having it even though it doesn't satisfy.

| *Lesson # 8* | **When we are full of God's fruit, we won't be hungry for forbidden fruit.** |

God had given Adam and Eve all the trees of the garden to eat from except one. If they had been eating from the fruit God had provided, they would not have been hungry for the forbidden fruit.

When God created Adam, he gave him a hunger drive, a need to eat. Then he provided fruit trees, which were legitimate to eat from, to satisfy his hunger drive. Temptation is trying to fulfill a legitimate God-given drive in an illegitimate way. When Adam and Eve became hungry for forbidden fruit, they were attempting to satisfy their drive in an illegitimate way. It's never a good idea to inspect forbidden fruit, especially on an empty stomach. Fulfilling their hunger drive with the right fruit would have kept them from being hungry for the wrong fruit.

What if you went to your Aunt Margie's for Thanksgiving, and she had just baked your favorite dessert, homemade apple pie. You are about to indulge yourself when Aunt Margie interrupts and says, "You can't eat that now! Dinner is ready. You can have it for dessert."

She serves you turkey and dressing with all the trimmings and you are "eating freely," that is, stuffing yourself. You continue to eat until you are full. Then Aunt Margie comes out with a large piece of apple pie and places it in front of you. You tell her, "There's no way I can eat that now. I'm full!"

Thirty minutes ago you were craving the pie. Now it's repulsive to think about. What happened? Your hunger drive has been fulfilled, so the temptation is no longer there.

The same thing that works for hunger drives also applies to fellowship, sex, acceptance, and worship drives. If we don't fulfill them in the right ways, we will look for the wrong ways to meet these needs. Temptations begin when we quit eating fruit from the trees God has provided, which creates a hunger that needs to be fulfilled. If we fulfill our desires and drives by eating God's fruit, we won't be hungry for forbidden fruit. However, the reverse is also true. If we have been stuffing ourselves with forbidden fruit, we won't be hungry for God's fruit.

The Key to Victory over Temptation

Galatians 5:16 says if we will walk in the Spirit, we will not fulfill the desires of the flesh. God isn't interested in putting our flesh in a straight jacket, trying to restrain our evil impulses. We must have something to displace the desires of the flesh. The only thing that will displace the desires of the flesh is a genuine work of the Holy Spirit inside our hearts.

Years ago I knew a man who was heavily involved with drugs. When he had nowhere else to turn, he surrendered his life to Jesus Christ. Immediately, he knew his sins were forgiven and God had given him a new life.

Not long after his conversion, one of his former acquaintances offered him drugs. When he looked at the drugs in the other man's hand, what he had craved before he became a Christian was now disgusting to him. "I had about as much desire for those drugs," he said, "as if he had offered me manure!" God changed the desire in his heart.

When we yield to the Spirit's control, he puts his desires within us to want what he wants (Gal. 5:17). We begin to desire the things of the Spirit rather than the things of the flesh, then he fulfills our desires in his way.

Perhaps you have been continually defeated in your battle with temptation. You don't have to be defeated. God has promised that sin shall not be master over you (Rom. 6:14). Through the power of the Holy Spirit, you can walk in victory.

Reducing Your Temptations

- What places of temptation will you avoid?

- Identify the boundaries where you enter into temptation. Example: A store where pornography is sold. Make a commitment by God's grace to not cross the boundary line.

- Fulfill your desires with the fruit God has provided rather than with forbidden fruit.

- Ask someone whom you trust to hold you accountable for the weak areas in your life. Have the person ask you at least once a week how you are doing in those areas.

CHAPTER 5

When You Can't Forgive Someone
Who Is in Your Dungeon?

"For this reason the kingdom of heaven may be compared to a certain king who wished to settle accounts with his slaves. And when he had begun to settle them, there was brought to him one who owed him ten thousand talents. But since he did not have the means to repay, his lord commanded him to be sold, along with his wife and children and all that he had, and repayment to be made. The slave therefore falling down, prostrated himself before him saying, 'Have patience with me, and I will repay you everything.' And the lord of that slave felt compassion and released him and forgave him the debt. But that slave went out and found one of his fellow slaves who owed him a hundred denarii; and he seized him and began to choke him, saying, 'Pay back what you owe.' So his fellow slave fell down and began to entreat him, saying, 'Have patience with me and I will repay you.' He was unwilling however, but went and threw him in prison until he should pay back what was owed."

(Matthew 18:23–30)

DURING THE REVOLUTIONARY WAR, a pastor named John P. Miller learned one of his greatest enemies was to be hanged for his crimes. At once, Miller set out on foot sixty miles to visit Gen. George Washington and intercede for the man's life.

The general, when he heard the request, stated he was sorry, but he could not pardon Miller's friend.

Miller said, "He's not my friend. That man is my worst enemy."

Washington replied, "Well, that puts matters in a whole new light." Seeing the preacher's forgiveness for his enemy, Gen. Washington signed the pardon.

Then Miller quickly carried it another fifteen miles to the execution site, arriving just as the condemned man was trudging toward the scaffold. Miller's enemy was set free that day—by the pastor whom he hated the most.[1]

Now I know you are probably asking yourself, "Did the enemy become his friend?" I don't know. But when he made that kind of effort to set his enemy free, John P. Miller proved he was the real free man.

In Matthew 18, we find a man who was quite the opposite of John P. Miller. Rather than setting his enemy free, he threw him into prison. We are all in the process of either locking people up in prison or setting them free.

The slave in this parable owed a debt of ten thousand talents. A talent was not a coin as many people think. It was a measuring weight of about eighty to ninety-four pounds. A talent could be a sack of ninety-four pounds of gold and silver coins. You can imagine how much that would be worth. Well, just think about ten thousand of those sacks of coins. That was how much this slave owed the king.

In today's currency, that would be about fifty million dollars. Someone calculated that at slave's pay, it would take about forty-five hundred lifetimes to repay the debt. Since the slave could not pay it off, the king decided to sell his slave, along with his wife and children and all that they had. Each family member would be taken to a different location, probably owned by different masters, and they would never see each other again.

So the slave became desperate and did something ridiculous. He made one last ditch effort to keep this from happening. He threw himself on the floor before the king and wept uncontrollably. He could hardly get the words out of his mouth but in brokenness before the king, he said, "Have patience with me, and I will repay you everything."

What a ridiculous request! It would take him forty-five hundred lifetimes to repay that debt. No king would be so foolish as to think he could actually do it. But when he looked at the brokenness and humility of the slave, something happened to the heart of the king. Instead of feeling anger toward the slave, he felt sorrow. The king's pity quickly turned into compassion because the slave had touched the king's heart.

You have probably felt compassion for someone before. He or she touches your heart and you are moved to help that person. This king was so moved, he released the slave of the entire fifty million dollar debt. His pity for the other man outweighed the talents.

This is what God has done for you when you come to know him. You have a debt of sin that it is impossible to repay. But when you humble yourself before him and plead for mercy, he forgives you of all your sins. The entire debt is forgiven.

You would think that the slave would be so grateful that he would forgive all his debtors as well—that the forgiveness he received would be extended to others he needed to forgive. But this was not the case. Instead, the slave found a fellow slave who owed him a hundred denarii, which was about fifteen dollars. This was a significant amount for what a slave made in wages, but it was minuscule in light of the amount he had been forgiven.

The fellow slave threw himself on the floor, just like the slave himself had done before the king. He even said the same words that the slave had said to the king, "Have patience with me, and I will repay you." It would seem that these words would jog his memory—that maybe he would remember the forgiveness he had received so mercifully from the king.

But instead of forgiving him the debt, he seized the fellow slave and choked him. With his hands firmly grasped around the fellow slave's neck, he squeezed off his air supply. As the man fell to his knees, gasping for air, the slave screamed at him, "Pay back what you owe me—now! Pay me now, I said!"

Since the fellow slave could not repay the debt, the slave threw him in the dungeon. We have no record that the fellow slave has ever been released. He is still in prison, chained to the walls, waiting to be set free.

Perhaps you are choking some people right now. In your mind, your hands are around their necks, and you are screaming at them to repay the debts against you. When they can't, you throw them into the dungeon—the dungeon of your soul.

How many people are locked up in that dungeon? Every fellow slave that you refuse to forgive is imprisoned inside of you. There they are. You can see them now. They hang there, chained to the walls of your dungeon. Some have been imprisoned only for a few days. Others have been locked up for months. And some have been in your dungeon for years.

Every time you recall a hurtful memory, you make a trip down the stairs into your dark dungeon where all those unforgiven people are. You pull out your whip and lash those prisoners chained to the walls, making them pay for their crimes against you.

Your father is chained to that wall. He has been down there ever since you were a child. You pull a list out of your pocket of the mistakes he made as a parent. After you read the list aloud to him, you yell, "You did all these things to me and I'm going to make you pay!" You take your whip and lash him for each offense as he hangs helplessly on the wall.

Then you move on to the next person. She talked about you behind your back. She was a vicious gossip who hurt you deeply, so now it's time for her to pay and your turn to get even. You pull out your whip and beat her unmercifully until she is unconscious.

You go from prisoner to prisoner until every person in the dungeon of your soul has been brutally punished. Then you turn to look around the room to make sure you have not forgotten anyone who hurt you. Everyone has been accounted for, so you put your whip under your arm and walk back up the stairs. This is your secret world, the dungeon of your soul. No one outside knows what you do down there.

Although you should feel relieved after serving justice to these people, you don't. Instead, you feel a sharp pain inside your stomach. It is almost as if, instead of whipping them, you were whipping yourself on the inside.

You admit that no real satisfaction is found in tormenting those people. The constant thinking about them because of what they have done is wearing you out. You can't sleep. You toss and turn all night. Deep down you know you must forgive and release those prisoners in your dungeon, but you don't know how to do it.

Before you can be set free, you must ask yourself, "Am I willing to let go of my past hurts? Am I willing to release those who have hurt me? Or do I want to keep them imprisoned a little longer?" Several things are necessary when it comes to forgiving those who have hurt us.

First

We base our forgiveness on what God has done for us, rather than on what the person has done to us.

We may think that what the person did to us is too big a debt to forgive. Nearly everyone uses that as an excuse. But whatever a person has done to us is insignificant compared to the debt God has forgiven us. It's like the fifteen dollar debt compared to the fifty million dollar debt. The two don't even come close in comparison.

The first principle of forgiveness is this: I cannot give away something I haven't first received. I can't give you fifteen dollars unless I have first received fifteen dollars. I also can't give forgiveness to others unless I have first received forgiveness from God. If he has given me fifty million dollars, then it will be very easy for me to give away fifteen dollars. Forgiveness is not based upon how much someone else owes us, but upon the abounding mercy God has granted us through Christ's death on the cross.

Second

We must let God heal our past wounds.

Unforgiveness means we desire to hurt the people who have wounded us. It's like the little boy who was sitting on a park bench in obvious agony. A man walking by asked him what was wrong.

The boy answered, "I'm sitting on a bumble bee."

"Then why don't you get up?"

The boy replied, "Because I figure I'm hurting him more than he is hurting me!"

The healing process begins when we get up off the park bench. God will only heal our wounds when we stop inflicting pain upon the one who hurt us. If we don't let God heal our wounds from the past, those hurts will turn into hate. The seed of unforgiveness will sprout into the root of bitterness (Heb. 12:15), and the hurt we submerge within us will become a land mine. Then when someone places the slightest pressure on our area of hurt, we explode! We must get up off the park bench and ask God to heal us of our hurts inside. And then we must let him do it.

	We need to feel compassion for the person who hurt us.
Third	

The king felt compassion for the slave. Forgiveness proceeds out of compassion, not anger. We might think that we can't forgive because we hurt too much, but the pain won't go away until we forgive. It's impossible for us to forgive if we still feel hate for the person, so we must change the way we view the offender. Every time Jesus felt compassion for someone, he saw a real need inside the person. In order to have compassion for people, we must look through the eyes of Jesus at their real needs.

Many people hurt others because they themselves hurt inside. Hurt people hurt others through releasing their hostility upon them. They, too, have a need for their inner wounds to be healed. Sometimes people don't realize how they hurt others. When Jesus had his hands and feet nailed to the cross, he said, "Father, forgive them; for they do not know what they are doing" (Luke 23:34).

Did they know what they were doing? In one sense, they did. They had crucified criminals hundreds of times. But in the spiritual realm, they were blind; they didn't know what they were doing.

Many people who have hurt us are also blind to the injury they have inflicted. We must compassionately pray for the Father to forgive them for what they have done.

	We choose to pay off the debt the person owes us.
Fourth	

The king forgave the slave of his debt. That didn't mean the debt disappeared. It meant the king decided to pay off the slave's debt rather than make the slave pay. It cost him something to forgive the slave, but somebody had to pay the debt. It could not be ignored.

People owe different kinds of debts. Some owe the debt of money. Maybe someone has borrowed money and hasn't paid it back, just like in this parable. Some owe the debt of gratitude. We have done things for people, and they haven't thanked us for it, but they should. Some debts are apologies that people owe. They have done something wrong and owe us an apology, but they have yet to apologize.

To forgive people of these debts, we must quit expecting them to repay their debts to us. Instead, we choose to pay off their obligations for them, just like the king did. We must take our hands off their necks. We must stop choking them, trying to get them to repay. And we must make a deliberate decision to pay off the debt ourselves and never again ask them to repay it.

We stop replaying the hurt on the screen of our minds.

Fifth

Whenever we are hurt by someone, we record the incident on the video tape in our minds. Every time we recall an injury, we hit the "play" button on the VCR in our minds and watch the hurt happen again. The remembrance of the event will instantly bring back the painful feelings we experienced. And every time we watch the "rerun" of the offense, we get wounded one more time! The person may have caused harm only once, but because we keep replaying the tape, we experience the hurt a hundred more times. Our own unforgiveness causes the pain to be multiplied much worse than the original wounding.

When we forgive, we choose to stop recalling the past. Forgetting doesn't mean we lose our remembrance of past events, but that we choose not to remember them. Because we have forgiven them, we make a definite decision to not call up hurtful memories in our minds.

If a person wants to delete a computer file, he clicks the Delete button. Instantly the screen displays this message: "Caution: You are about to delete a file. Are you sure?" The reason this warning appears is because once a document is deleted, it can't be recalled. The typist must click on the button a second time to delete the file completely.

Many people have clicked on the button the first time to delete the "past hurts" file, but haven't clicked on it the second time. Because they have clicked on the delete button the first time, they think they have forgiven that hurt. But they aren't really sure if they want to completely delete the files by clicking the second time.

We must click the delete button a second time. We must erase the video tape. Once the "wounded memory" tape is erased and the "past hurts" files are deleted, they cannot be recalled again.

| Sixth |

We must release the person from our prison.

The king forgave and released the slave from the debt. We need to release the person who has offended us. Let him go! Unforgiveness will keep us chained to whomever we don't forgive. If we don't release him, we will take the unforgiven person with us wherever we go.

When we go to bed at night, the unforgiven person is there to keep us awake. When we go on vacation, the unforgiven person travels with us to our destination. We can't get away from him. Wherever we look, he is there ruining the trip.

The only way to get unchained is to forgive and release the person who has offended us. Unless we unlock the chains and release him, we will remain chained to him until we go to our grave!

You need to make one more trip down into that dark dungeon. Walk down the stairs one more time. As you open the windows, the light shines brightly inside. The prisoners squint as they see you approach, expecting you to beat them again.

But this time it is different. Instead of pulling out your whip, you pull out the key of forgiveness. You walk over to your father, the gossip, and everyone else in your dungeon, unlock their chains, and announce to them:

> "I'm letting you out now. I'm not going to whip you any more. I'm setting you free. I release you from the prison that I have kept you in. But before you leave, I plead with you, will you forgive me for keeping you imprisoned for so long and torturing you for all these years?"

You watch them walk up the stairs and leave your dungeon. It is empty now. All that is left are the unlocked chains hanging on the walls and a peace that surpasses all understanding. It's been years since the dungeon has been empty. You can't explain it, but that sharp pain in your stomach is gone. You are no longer tormented inside. Peace floods your soul. You get the feeling it wasn't them whom you set free. It was you!

Releasing Your Prisoners

- Make a list of the people in the dungeon of your soul. Be honest, and don't overlook anyone.

- Jesus didn't just die for your sins on the cross. He also died for the sins committed against you by people who have hurt you. Picture in your mind Jesus dying on the cross for those sins people have committed which have hurt you so deeply. Since Jesus died for those sins, you must let go of them.

- Individually forgive and release each person out of your dungeon. In prayer to God, declare out loud each person's name, and announce you are setting them free. God may also lead you to speak to some people face-to-face.

- Destroy the mental tape of a time someone hurt you so that you can't replay it. If Satan tries to remind you of the hurt, announce out loud, "I have forgiven (person's name), and he/she is no longer in my prison. Thank you, Jesus, for setting me free from unforgiveness!"

CHAPTER 6

When You Can't Forgive Yourself
Canceling Guilt Trips

> But the chief priests and the elders persuaded the multitudes to ask for Barabbas, and to put Jesus to death. But the governor answered and said to them, "Which of the two do you want me to release for you?" And they said, "Barabbas." Pilate said to them, "Then what shall I do with Jesus who is called Christ?" They all said, "Let Him be crucified!" And he said, "Why, what evil has He done?" But they kept shouting all the more, saying, "Let Him be crucified!" And when Pilate saw that he was accomplishing nothing, but rather that a riot was starting, he took water and washed his hands in front of the multitude, saying, "I am innocent of this Man's blood; see to that yourselves." And all the people answered and said, "His blood be on us and on our children!"
>
> (Matthew 27:20–25)

WHEN PILATE TURNED JESUS over to the multitudes to be crucified, no doubt he felt extremely guilty. He didn't want to do it. He couldn't find anything wrong with Jesus, but the pressure to please the crowd was too great. So he bowed to peer pressure, released the criminal, and sentenced the innocent man to be crucified. Then Pilate went over to a bowl of water, washed his hands in front of the multitude, and told them, "I am innocent of this Man's blood."

Innocent? If he really thought he was innocent, why did he wash his hands? People don't wash their hands unless they are dirty. Pilate's problem was he tried to wash his hands rather than his heart. Hands don't sin. Hearts do. The washing of hands will never cleanse a guilty conscience.

Pilate, after delivering up Jesus to be crucified, was trying to find a method to remove his guilt. I am certain that when he went to bed that night, he did not have a clear conscience.

You know what guilt is. It is your refusal to allow Jesus Christ to pay for your sins. It is manifested by those nagging thoughts that accuse us when we have done something wrong.

One little boy was asked to define guilt. He said he wasn't quite sure what it was, but he thought it had something to do with feeling bad when he kicked girls.

God has put a conscience within us that works like an alarm clock. Romans 2:15 tells us that our consciences bear witness with thoughts that either accuse us or defend us. Whenever we sin against God, our consciences alert us to the fact that we have done wrong even if we say we are innocent.

In a San Diego courtroom two men were on trial for robbery. A witness to the crime was asked, "Were you at the scene when the robbery took place?"

The witness replied, "Yes."

"And did you observe the two robbers?"

Again, the witness said, "Yes."

The prosecuting attorney turned up the intensity and with a booming voice asked, "And are those two men in the courtroom today?"

Before the witness could answer, the two defendants raised their hands![1] Although they claimed to be innocent, their consciences gave them away.

Pilate claimed innocence, but his conscience was eating away at him. He tried to excuse his guilt by washing his hands of it. And just like Pilate, we try to remove our guilt using wrong methods. Here are some of those bad methods, exposed.

Method # 1 Blame It On Someone Else

This is the method Pilate used. Pilate said to the crowd, "This is not my fault. It's *your* fault." The Blame-It-On-Someone-Else Method simply shifts the blame off yourself onto someone else. To err is human. To blame it on someone else is also human.

One day when my son Scott was two years old, I heard him crying. I went into his room and my daughter Hannah, who was four, was there also. A plastic bat was lying on the floor.

"What happened to Scott?" I asked her.

Hannah answered, "He hit his head."

"On what?"

She pointed toward the bat on the floor and said, "The bat."

"Where was the bat?"

She said, "In my hand." We learn the Blame-It-On-Someone-Else Method at such an early age.

This method is not new. It goes all the way back to the Garden of Eden. After Adam sinned against God, he felt guilty. He needed some advice, so he made an appointment with psychiatrist Sigmund Freud.

Adam said, "I feel so guilty. What should I do?"

Freud answered, "It's simple. Blame it on your mother."

"But I don't have a mother."

"Oh yes. That's true," Freud said. "Then . . . blame it on your wife. Where did you get her?"

"God gave her to me."

Freud pounded his desk and said, "Now we're getting somewhere! You see, God is really the one to blame for this whole thing. If he hadn't given her to you, she wouldn't have given you the fruit, and you wouldn't feel guilty."

God asked Adam, "Have you eaten from the tree of which I commanded you not to eat?" Adam answered, "The woman whom Thou gavest to be with me, she gave me from the tree, and I ate."

Then the Lord asked Eve what she had done. She got in on the blame game, too. She said, "Don't blame me. The serpent made me do it." Like a hot potato, Adam tossed it to Eve, who tossed it to the serpent. But God didn't ask the serpent because he knew he didn't have a leg to stand on! Neither do you when you try to shift the blame.

The Blame-It-On-Someone-Else Method: blame it on God. Blame it on your wife. Blame it on your mother. But whatever you do, don't blame yourself.

When you blame others, you are attempting to transfer the guilt off yourself to someone else. You will never get rid of your guilt using this method.

| Method #2 | **Run and Hide** |

This is the method Peter used. Jesus told Peter he would deny him three times before the cock crowed twice.

Peter answered he would never do anything like that. But he did. At the exact moment he denied Jesus the third time, the cock crowed and Matthew 26:75 says he went out and wept bitterly. He went into hiding. He was using the Run-and-Hide Method to deal with his guilt.

We will respond in one of two ways when we sin. We can either run from God and hide, or we can run to God and receive cleansing. For the moment, Peter tried to run from God. His shame was too great to face his Savior whom he denied.

Maybe you have felt this way too. You believe you cannot face God because of what you have done. So you run away from church. You run away from Christian fellowship and the support system that you need. You try to hide from God, just like Peter did.

This is exactly where Satan wants you. As long as you are on the run, Satan's work on you becomes easy. If you are not a Christian, his job is to keep you from a relationship with God. If you are a Christian, his job is to keep you from having fellowship with God. The Run-and-Hide Method is the way Satan wants you to respond to your guilt.

| Method #3 | **Cover It Up** |

This is the method Judas used. The person who uses this method pretends that nothing is wrong. He will cover up what he has done and push it down inside of himself. Some call this being in denial. Denial is refusing to admit there's a problem.

I heard about a lady who was pregnant and on a strict diet. She made her husband a coconut-cream pie, and after a couple of days, he'd only eaten half of it. One day she was cleaning the table and decided to sneak a bite. One bite led to another, and before long she had eaten the rest of the pie. She felt guilty about cheating on her diet and knew she either had to admit it or cover up what she had done.

There was only one thing she could do. She baked another coconut cream pie and ate half of it to make it look like the original pie. If we don't *own up* to the things we do, we are forced to *cover up.*

That's what Judas did. He had an amazing ability. He betrayed the Son of God and then sat down and ate with him, acting like everything was just fine. He betrayed Jesus for thirty pieces of silver and then went to the upper room for the Last Supper with him.

As they were eating, Jesus said, "Truly I say to you that one of you will betray Me." Then all of the disciples asked, "Surely not I, Lord?" Finally it was Judas' turn. He asked, "Surely it is not I, Rabbi?" Judas never could call him "Lord." To Judas, Jesus was only a rabbi, or teacher. With a sheepish look on his face, he asked, "Who, me?"

Judas thought if he acted innocently, then his guilt would go away. It didn't. His guilt eventually drove him to suicide. The Cover-It-Up Method doesn't work either.

| *Method # 4* | **Get Some Professional Help** |

I am both amused and disturbed when I watch a talk show, and people from the television audience call in to the program. Usually, a panel of "experts" intends to help people with their problems. The host of the show stands in the studio audience and says to the TV camera, "We have a caller from Dallas. Are you there?"

The caller responds, "Yes, I have a question. I feel terribly guilty for the things that I have done. I am depressed and don't know what to do. Can you help me?"

The host of the show usually says something like, "I'm sorry to hear that. Have you been feeling this way for a long time?"

The caller answers, "Yes, for several years now."

The host briefly discusses the problem with the "experts" who give their opinions and then ends the conversation with, "It sounds to me like you need to get some professional help. Thank you for calling." This is another way of saying, "We don't know how to help you!"

Now, I want you to know that I am not against counseling. As a pastor, I counsel people all the time. However, it is of the utmost importance that you choose the right counselors. "Blessed is the man who does not walk in the counsel of the wicked" (Ps. 1:1).

The problem is some people think the answer is in counseling rather than in having an inward change of heart. That is why they go for years and never really receive healing. It makes them feel better because they are making an attempt to do something about their problems. But many counselors never address the root of the problems. They only deal with surface issues.

Suppose you go to a medical doctor, and he examines you. His tests reveal you have a tumor. He says to come back next week.

When you go to his office the next week he says, "The tumor is slightly larger than it was last week. I don't want you to become alarmed because this is to be expected. I will prescribe some medication to calm your nerves. Make an appointment with the receptionist to see me again next week."

The next week he takes more x-rays and tells you, "The tumor is slightly larger than it was last week. You will experience some slight discomfort, but I will prescribe pain medication to help you cope with it."

This goes on for several weeks. He diagnoses the problem, talks about it, and prescribes medication to help you cope with it, but he never solves the problem. He never operates to remove the tumor.

You would say to yourself, "Hey, wait a minute. I think this doctor is making his living off of my *not* getting well!"

Many people have gone to counseling for years and have never received healing for their guilty consciences. One man who visited a psychiatrist regularly confessed, "I must be the only guy who ever spent fifteen thousand dollars on a couch—and I still don't own it!" Counseling will never cure the guilt problem.

The Only Cure for the Guilt Problem

The answer to the guilt problem is found in Matthew 27:25: "His blood be on us and on our children!" There it is. That's the answer. The multitude gave Pilate the solution to the guilt problem, and they didn't even realize it. The cause of Pilate's guilt was to be the solution. His guilt was caused because he delivered Christ to be crucified. The blood shed at the crucifixion was his remedy. But the remedy must be received in order for the guilt to be removed.

Guilt comes as a result of sinning. When we are cleansed from our sin, we are declared "not guilty" by God. We don't need our guilt relieved. We must have it removed. Guilt can only be removed when it encounters something more powerful than itself. The only thing more powerful than guilt is the blood of Jesus.

> The blood of Jesus His Son cleanses us from all sin . . . If we confess our sins, He is faithful and righteous to forgive us our sins and to cleanse us from all unrighteousness. (1 John 1:7, 9)

> How much more will the blood of Christ . . . cleanse your conscience from dead works to serve the living God? (Heb. 9:14)

First

Admit what you have done.

No more covering up. No more pretending. It's time to "'fess up". David said, "I acknowledged my sin to Thee, and my iniquity I did not hide; I said, 'I will confess my transgressions to the Lord'; and Thou didst forgive the guilt of my sin" (Ps. 32:5).

A prince traveling through France visited the arsenal of Toulon, where prisoners were kept. Because of his nobility, he was given permission by the commandant to release one of the condemned men. He went from cell to cell and inquired why they were there.

Each prisoner declared his innocence, saying he was falsely accused and did not deserve to be there.

Finally he came to one man who said, "My lord, as much as I long to be free, I am guilty. I have committed many crimes and have nothing to say except that I deserve to be here."

The prince then yelled with a voice heard by all the prisoners, "You despicable wretch! What a pity you should be among so many 'honest' men. By your own confession you are bad enough to corrupt them all. You shall not stay with them another day!" Turning to the officer, he said, "This is the man. Release him at once!"[2]

When we try to justify ourselves, our sin remains. But when we confess our sins, it puts us in position to receive forgiveness. Confession does not cleanse us from all sin. It only opens the way to receive the cleansing. It is the blood of Jesus that cleanses us from all sin. We don't need to confess our sins a thousand times. We need to confess them once and thank God a thousand times for forgiving them.

One lady called in to a Christian radio program and said, "I had an abortion seventeen years ago, and I have asked forgiveness from God every day since then." She wanted to know if God would ever forgive her. She asked if she were going to hell for it.

The talk-show host said, "How would you like it if someone who did something wrong to you comes knocking at your door the next day to ask for forgiveness. You forgive the person and everything is cleared up on your part.

"But the next day, the person shows up at your door and asks forgiveness again.

"You remind her that you already forgave her the day before.

"She leaves, but returns the next day, knocks on your door and again asks forgiveness.

"Again you remind her, 'I forgave you two days ago. Don't you remember? Don't you believe what I said?'

"This goes on day after day for seventeen years! Wouldn't you be frustrated because she didn't trust your word?"

The lady on the phone said, "I never thought about it that way before."

The host then said, "When you asked Jesus to save you, he forgave you of all your sins. Confession means 'to say the same thing.' You need to say the same thing as what God says about your sins— he died for every one of them."

When we confess our sins, we not only admit we have done them, but we agree with God that Jesus died for them. Confession declares that the blood of Jesus is more powerful that the guilt that haunts us.

	Receive the cleansing.
Second	

The work has been done on the cross. The blood has been shed. The price has been paid. The only thing left is for you to receive the forgiveness.

I could offer to give you a hundred dollar bill by holding it out with my hand. But until you reach out and take it from me, it will never be yours. The same is true with God's forgiveness. Until you receive it, it's not yours.

When you reach out and receive his forgiveness, the blood of Jesus cleanses you from all unrighteousness. Once the sin is removed, you don't need to feel guilty, because Jesus paid for your sins.

But what about the haunting thoughts of guilt that come after you have confessed your sins and received forgiveness? We must not forget that Satan is the accuser of the brethren and a liar. Times will come when he will try to convince you that you are not forgiven.

In Richard Hoefler's book *Will Daylight Come?*, a little boy visiting his grandparents was given his first slingshot. He practiced in the woods, but he could never hit his target.

As he returned to Grandma's backyard, he spied her pet duck. On an impulse, he took aim and let fly. The stone hit its target, and the duck fell over dead. The boy panicked. He took the duck and hid it in the woodpile, only to look up and see his sister watching him. Sally had seen it all, but she said nothing.

After lunch that day, Grandma said, "Sally, help me wash the dishes, please."

Sally told her, "Johnny told me he wanted to help in the kitchen today. Didn't you, Johnny?" Then she whispered to him, "Remember the duck!"

So Johnny washed the dishes.

Later Grandpa asked if the children wanted to go fishing.

Grandma said, "I'm sorry, but I need Sally to help make supper."

Sally smiled and said, "That's all taken care of. Johnny wants to do it." Again she whispered, "Remember the duck."

Johnny stayed home while Sally went fishing with Grandpa.

After several days of Johnny doing both his chores and Sally's, he could not stand it anymore. He decided to confess to Grandma that he had killed the duck.

"I know, Johnny," she said, giving him a hug. "I was standing at the window and saw the whole thing. Because I love you, I forgave you. I just wondered how long you would let Sally make a slave of you."[3]

The spirit of condemnation is when the voice of Satan comes to the child of God and whispers, "Remember the duck! Remember what you did in the past." Satan is trying to make a slave of you even though God has already forgiven you.

If you have confessed your sins and received God's forgiveness, he has forgiven you. Now forgive yourself.

Removing Your Guilt

- What wrong methods have you tried to use to remove your guilt?

- Have you been honest in confessing your sin to God?

- Have you received the cleansing that only the blood of Jesus can provide?

- Read chapter 24, "When You're Not Sure You're Saved."

CHAPTER 7

When You Are Disappointed
God's Recipe for Leftovers

Now Lot, who went with Abram, also had flocks and herds and tents. And the land could not sustain them while dwelling together; for their possessions were so great that they were not able to remain together. And there was strife between the herdsmen of Abram's livestock and the herdsmen of Lot's livestock. Now the Canaanite and Perizzite were dwelling then in the land. Then Abram said to Lot, "Please let there be no strife between you and me, nor between my herdsmen and your herdsmen, for we are brothers. Is not the whole land before you? Please separate from me: if to the left, then I will go to the right; or if to the right, then I will go to the left."

(Gen. 13:5–9)

ONE OF MY LEAST favorite meals is leftovers. Maybe it's the aging process that bothers me. After food has been in the refrigerator for a while, it looks and tastes different. Call it personal preference if you will, but to me fresh tastes better than wilted. Sometimes it's hard to remember when we had the original meal. "Did we have this last Wednesday or Wednesday a week ago?" I believe it was Erma Bombeck who said her mother served her family nothing but leftovers for thirty years. She said the original meal was never found. A rule of thumb in our family is, if no one can remember the original meal, it goes down the disposal.

Did you know God has a recipe for leftovers? He doesn't want you to throw your leftovers away. He has a plan for them. Let me explain what I mean. Leftovers are those situations that are less than ideal. You end up with what appears to be second best, or what is left over.

Maybe your husband ran away with another woman, leaving you to raise three children by yourself. Perhaps you are a victim of circumstances. You may have had a very rough childhood or come from a broken family. You haven't had the opportunities other people have had. Or maybe the other person got the promotion instead of you. Leftovers. You are disappointed because your expectations have not been met, so life offers little hope.

Tired of eating leftovers? Well, you need to understand God doesn't want to just bless your leftovers. Sometimes he actually ordains them.

Leftovers: Second-Choice Casserole

In Genesis 13, Abram's herdsmen and Lot's herdsmen argued because their herds became too large and the land could no longer sustain them.

Abram told Lot, "I don't want strife between you and me, so I'll give you the first choice of the land for your flocks and herds. I'll take what's left over."

This was unusual because Abram had the right to choose first. He was the elder, the one who helped Lot get established in his livestock business. Yet Abram gave Lot the right to choose first.

Why? Because Abram believed leftovers were ordained by God. Even though someone else got to choose first, God would bless whatever was left over. What would normally be destined for the garbage disposal is salvaged by God and prepared as another meal. After he adds his spice to the leftovers, scraps become sacred. Trash turns into treasure and burdens into blessings.

When Abram surrendered the first pick to Lot, he had unwavering faith God controlled events that were totally out of his hands. And this was no small decision. Although he didn't know it at the time, the entire future of the nation of Israel was at stake on the outcome of this decision.

> And Lot lifted up his eyes and saw all the valley of the Jordan, that it was well watered everywhere—this was before the Lord destroyed Sodom and Gomorrah—like the garden of the Lord, like the land of Egypt as you go to Zoar. (Gen. 13:10)

Lot saw the green valley of Sodom and Gomorrah and thought, "This green pasture would be great for all my livestock. Plenty of water there, too. That's the best choice. I'll take it." So, without even considering what would happen to Abram, he selfishly chose Sodom.

At first, it looked like Lot had made the best choice. When someone else chooses first, he appears to get the upper hand. But the game isn't over after the first inning. The first choice is not always the best or the blessed.

Lot believed the greener grass in Sodom would be best for his livestock. But he forgot to think about what was best for his family. He was more concerned with making a profit off his cattle than what would profit his wife and children.

Not long after Lot arrived in Sodom, he was kidnapped by armies that had invaded Sodom. Abram had to go and rescue him (Gen. 14:1–16). Then he found out that because the people in Sodom were exceedingly wicked, God was going to destroy the city (Gen. 19). Lot never thought his dream home could turn into such a nightmare. When you choose your own way, it never turns out like you think it will.

> And the Lord said to Abram, after Lot had separated from him, "Now lift up your eyes and look from the place where you are, northward and southward and eastward and westward; for all the land which you see, I will give it to you and to your descendants forever."
>
> (Gen. 13:14–15)

After Lot made his choice of land, God said He would give what was left over to Abram and his descendants forever. The leftovers turned out to be the promised land! God loves to bless a submissive and yielding spirit. Abram had that kind of spirit. He didn't want strife with Lot, so he yielded the first choice.

He didn't angrily relinquish his rights to Lot. He had no bitterness. No regrets. No hand wringing. He wasn't even the least bit disappointed when Lot apparently picked the best piece of property. He simply trusted the Lord to bless his submissiveness. Author Andrew Murray has rightly said, "God reserves the very best for those who leave the choice with him."

God then told Abram, "All the land which you see, I will give to you . . ." How do you see your leftovers? Maybe someone in your life has disappointed you. Sometimes disappointments can actually be blessings in disguise.

A good friend of mine was engaged to be married. When his fiancé broke off the engagement, he sank into depression. Not long after the breakup, he met someone else. That someone else became his wife. They have now been happily married for over twenty years. What looked like the greatest disappointment in his life was divinely engineered to point him to God's best choice. He now thanks God for not giving him what he thought was best.

You can become bitter for receiving leftovers, or you can see God giving you a promised land. If you look with the eye of faith, you will see that leftovers are really blessings ordained by God.

Leftovers: Canaanite Crumb Cake

In Matthew 15:21–28, a Canaanite woman begged Jesus to heal her demon-possessed daughter. The first time she asked, Jesus gave her no answer. Most people would have gone home disappointed and dejected, thinking he wouldn't grant their request. But this woman knew no answer didn't necessarily mean a "no" answer. Because she refused to leave, Jesus' disciples tried to send her away. The welcome mat was not out for this Gentile woman.

Jesus told her, "I was sent only to the lost sheep of the house of Israel." That's good news for Jews. But if you were a Canaanite woman, that's not what you wanted to hear. Because she was a Gentile, she was not a part of the house of Israel. Even though she was excluded, she persisted.

Jesus then added, "It is not good to take the children's bread and throw it to the dogs." The children were the Jewish people, while the dogs were the Gentiles. That meant no plates were set for Gentile people at the Jewish table. It appeared to everyone but her that Jesus wasn't going to heal her daughter.

Rather than giving up on her request, the Canaanite woman seized upon his illustration. She answered, "Yes, Lord; but even the dogs feed on the crumbs which fall from their masters' table." She wasn't asking to sit at the table; she was asking for the opportunity to sit under the table. Yes, she was a dog. She was a bulldog! Her tenacity made her refuse to take no for an answer.

My little dog Bandit has become an expert in begging. When we sit at the table to eat, he sits on the floor next to me, staring at my face. If I ignore him, he uses another tactic. He will reach up with his paw and touch me on the leg, then resume his sitting position. I will glance down at him and notice tears forming in his eyes. This usually touches my heart, causing me to at least consider feeding him something. If that doesn't work, he resorts to a third tactic. He sits on his back legs and lifts his front paws in the air, assuming the look of a prairie dog. Sometimes it becomes obvious that he wants the food on our plates more than my children do! But no matter how pitifully he begs, I will never take food away from my children to give to my dog. However, when my kids are finished eating, Bandit has the right to the leftovers.

When Jesus told this Canaanite woman he couldn't take away the children's bread to throw it to the dogs, she replied, "Yes, Lord; but even the dogs feed on the crumbs which fall from their master's table." She, like Bandit, understood the Master rules the table, and the food is for the children. Her attitude was, "You don't have to throw me anything. I'll eat whatever falls from the table. I'll take the leftovers."

Because she was not of the Jewish race, this Gentile woman didn't have the opportunities to receive from the Messiah like the Israelites had. But she had a much greater understanding than the Jews concerning God's ability to bless. All she needed was, not an entire meal, but one small crumb. She knew one touch from the Master's hand would transform a crumb into a healing for her daughter. She had the ability to see that leftovers are really camouflaged miracles.

Jesus wasn't trying to discourage her faith through his answers. He was trying to develop it. Because she passed each test, Jesus told her, "O woman, your faith is great; be it done for you as you wish" (Matt. 15:28). Her daughter was immediately healed.

Perhaps, for whatever reason, you haven't had the opportunities others have had. You find yourself under the table, begging for scraps. Learn a lesson from this Gentile woman. Don't complain because you can't sit at the head of the table. Grab the leftovers, then ask God to bless them.

Most people don't view leftovers as something to be coveted. Only a few people, like this Canaanite woman, have the faith to see that God has a recipe for them.

Leftovers: Andrew's Fish and Chips

In John 6, a great multitude followed Jesus and they became hungry. In an attempt to solve the problem, Andrew found a boy with five barley loaves and two fish (6:8–9). Jesus took the loaves and fish, blessed them, miraculously multiplied the food to feed five thousand people, and had enough left over to fill twelve baskets. He then instructed the disciples, "Gather up the leftover fragments that nothing may be lost" (6:12). He didn't want them to be thrown away because he planned on serving them again.

Don't throw your leftovers away. Trust God to do something good with them.

As a senior at Wheaton College, Ken and several friends took an aptitude test for medical school. All of his friends, including his brother, passed the test. Ken failed it. He was depressed by this closed door.

However, this closed door pointed him to the open door of Christian ministry. Ken Taylor went on to paraphrase the *Living Bible* and start Tyndale House Publishers. He might have never accomplished these things had it not been for an early failure in his life. God had plans for his second choice, not his first.

Ken wrote about that early failure: "It was a long time before I came to realize that I was being given clear guidance about what God wanted my future to be. I should have been grateful instead of disappointed."[1]

It doesn't matter how your leftovers got to be leftovers—whether you made a mess out of your own life or whether you are a victim of circumstances. What does matter is whether or not you allow God to bless your leftovers. Just like Jesus blessed the fragments of bread, he can bless the fragments of your life. God will take you in your present situation, and if you will surrender your circumstances to him, he will turn your leftovers into a gourmet meal.

Blessing the Leftovers

- Write on a piece of paper the leftovers you have received. Rather than complaining about them, commit your leftovers to God, and ask him to bless them. It may help to pray this prayer:

Heavenly Father,
I ask you to forgive me for being angry and bitter about my circumstances. I know you have the ability to take any situation and work it into your will. I realize that my attitude may have hindered your working in my life. I surrender my leftovers to you right now, and I ask you to bless them. Thank you! In Jesus' name, Amen.

- Read chapter 15, "When You Feel Like Complaining" and chapter 21, "When Bad Things Happen."

CHAPTER 8

When You Need to Make a Change
Breaking Out of Comfort Zones

And in the fourth watch of the night He came to them, walking on the sea. And when the disciples saw Him walking on the sea, they were frightened, saying, "It is a ghost!" And they cried out for fear. But immediately Jesus spoke to them, saying, "Take courage, it is I; do not be afraid." And Peter answered Him and said, "Lord, if it is You, command me to come to You on the water." And He said, "Come!" And Peter got out of the boat. . . .

(Matthew 14:25–29)

ALL OF US ARE SURROUNDED by comfort zones, those invisible barriers that make us feel cozy and secure. Comfort zones develop after we have done things a particular way for a certain amount of time. Unfortunately, they can make us feel so comfortable we may never want to change the way we do things.

Change is the greatest enemy to a comfort zone. The only people who like change are babies with dirty diapers. Sometimes it's easier to keep doing the same things over and over again than to make adjustments in our lives.

Two construction workers had taken a lunch break and opened up their lunch boxes. One of them looked inside his and said, "Not baloney again! I can't believe it. I hate baloney. This is the third time this week I've had baloney. I can't stand baloney!"

The other one said, "Why don't you ask your wife to make you something different?"

He replied, "I don't have a wife. I made these myself."

The fact is, most of the baloney in our lives we put there ourselves. If we ever want life to be any different from the same old baloney we keep serving ourselves, then we must break out of doing the routine.

Comfort zones are not completely bad. They can build security within us. That's definitely better than insecurity. However, security is like money. It is a wonderful servant, but a terrible master. Healthy security can be found in a loving home, but a different kind of security is found in a prison.

In a penitentiary the inmates don't have to make decisions. Food and shelter are provided. They never have to worry about making house payments or where the next meal is coming from. One of the main reasons prisoners commit crimes after they have been released is so they can go back to the penitentiary where it's secure. The prison, which is designed to be punishment to them, becomes their comfort zone.

That is the danger for us also. We can become imprisoned by our own comfort zones. They can keep us from experiencing all that God has for us and can hinder us from growing as Christians.

Imprisoned by Stage Fright

When a crab grows, it breaks out of its hard shell and begins the process of forming a new one. Its life span is marked by passing through successive shells. The crab grows when it is in-between shells. It will continue to grow as long as it dares to break out of its shell. When it stops breaking through shells, the crab ceases to grow and eventually dies. The last shell becomes the crab's coffin.

For me, life has been a continual process of breaking through shells. From grade school to beyond high school, I had a terrible case of stage fright. A person with stage fright doesn't want to be noticed. His worst nightmare is being the center of attention.

When I was in second grade, I needed to go to the rest room but didn't want to ask the teacher for permission. Not wanting to call attention to myself or my problem, I refused to raise my hand and decided to "hold it." I couldn't hold it for long . . . so I went in my pants. After I had finished the job, the teacher asked each student to come up to her desk to show her our work. It was pretty hard to cover up the obvious.

In fifth grade, I faced another crisis. My part in the Christmas play was to walk across the stage. I didn't have to say any words, just walk. Sounds simple enough, but I dreaded it for weeks. The ten seconds it took to walk in front of the audience seemed like an eternity.

In high school, I avoided the stage at all costs. Then as a senior, as fate would have it, I was appointed to read the class poem at the senior banquet. As I held the paper, I could barely read the poem because my hands were shaking so much.

After graduating from high school, I thought all possibilities of being on stage were now behind me. But during my last year in college, God interrupted my plans for the future and called me to preach. What a cruel trick, calling someone with stage fright to do that job. Not only would I have to be on stage, I would also have to speak on it. Definitely outside my comfort zone.

My first few attempts at preaching were tormenting. Not just for me, but for everyone in the congregation as they watched me sweat, fidget, and stumble through the messages. Then, bless their hearts, people told me how wonderful it was! Thank God he forgives truth-stretching to beginning preachers. Because I would have preferred a torture chamber over preaching a sermon, I even wondered about my calling.

Eventually, as you will discover in a moment, I broke out of my shell. But along the way, I had to learn a few things. Here are some principles I have learned concerning breaking out of comfort zones.

Comfort-Zone Principles

Principle # 1	We break through comfort zones when we do something that makes us feel uncomfortable.

God places many of his blessings outside of our comfort zones, then asks us to come get them. If we ever want to receive some things we've never had before, we've got to do some things we've never done before. That means we will have to break through some comfort zones. Peter was about to break through one by stepping out of the boat and walking on the water.

Any science student will tell you water won't hold up a person who tries to stand on it. But this time, it was going to be different. The law of gravity would be suspended. Peter forgot about what he had learned in science class and thought, "If Jesus is walking on the water, then it is possible for me to do it, too."

The comfort zone Peter had to break through was the rim of the boat. In order for him to walk on to the water, he had to step over it. He had to decide to leave the security of the boat for the insecurity of the water. Breaking through a comfort zone begins with a decision to let go of our security blanket in exchange for something that looks frightening.

Perhaps you need to do something you have never done before. The security blanket is keeping you inside the boat. To break through your comfort zone, you must be willing to leave your boat and take a step over the rim.

Principle # 2	**We break through comfort zones by refusing to listen to our fears.**

A spy was once captured and sentenced to death by a general in the Persian army. Before the execution, the general went through an unusual ritual. He gave the criminal a choice between the firing squad or a big, black door.

This spy was given the same two choices. He deliberated for a long time, then finally decided the rifles would be the instruments of his death. Moments later, he was executed by the firing squad.

The general turned to his aide and said, "They always prefer the known way to the unknown. It is characteristic of people to be afraid of the undefined."

"General, what is behind the big, black door?" the aide asked.

"Freedom," the general answered. Behind the black door is a passageway that leads outside, but only a few have been brave enough to see what was behind it."[1]

Fear is the big, black door that keeps us trapped inside our comfort zones. In order to be free from what imprisons us, we must be brave enough to open the door.

Why We Stay in the Boat

Different fears will keep us inside the boat. Before Peter stepped over the rim, a lot of thoughts must have run through his mind.

Fear of Criticism asks, "What will the other disciples think of me if I get out of the boat?" The biggest critics we have will be those who stay inside the boat—the ones who don't take the risks. We must not allow peer pressure to keep us in our comfort zones. We should not be governed by the fear of what people think of us. Our actions should be determined by what God wants us to do.

Fear of Failure asks, "What if this doesn't work?" Many people haven't taken the risk of breaking through their comfort zones because of the fear of failure. The possibility of failing can make us afraid of being embarrassed in front of others if we aren't immediately successful. In order to keep safe from failure, we stay inside the boat.

But failure is not falling down, it's staying down. Proverbs 24:16 says, "For a righteous man falls seven times, and rises again." If we are in bondage to this fear, we will never succeed because we never attempt anything new or different. We must take some risks in life if we are to ever accomplish anything significant.

Most of us know Babe Ruth set a record with 714 home runs in his baseball career. But few remember he struck out 1,330 times on the way to that record. Most people know Jonas Salk discovered the polio vaccine, but few realize he failed two hundred times before he found the right one.

Nearly everyone who watches professional basketball agrees Michael Jordan is one of the greatest players of all time. But most people don't realize he failed to make the basketball team his sophomore year in high school. He didn't quit playing because of one failure.

Henry Ford went bankrupt five times before he finally succeeded. Thomas Edison failed over ten thousand times in his attempts to find the correct filament for the light bulb. When an aide urged him to quit after several hundred failures, he replied, "Why quit now? We know of at least a hundred things that won't work."

Learning from our failures is part of the process of being successful. None of these people could have accomplished what they did if they had listened to the fear of failure.

Fear of the Unknown asks, "I wonder what is going to happen to me if I step out of the boat?" Fear of the unknown keeps a lot of people in the boat. We want to know what we are getting into when we try something new. But that's not always possible. Sometimes we must take a step into the unknown.

An old mariner's chart of the east coast of North America and adjacent waters, drawn by an unknown cartographer in 1525 and now in the British Museum, has some interesting and fearful directions on it. The map maker wrote across the great areas of then unexplored land and sea the following inscriptions: "Here be giants," "Here be fiery scorpions," "Here be dragons." At some time in its career, the chart fell into the hands of the scientist, Sir John Franklin. He scratched out the fearful old markings and wrote across the map, "Here is God."[2]

You can imagine the fear the early explorers must have felt when they read that map. "I'm not going into that area. No way!" The fear of the imaginary dragons kept them from discovering new worlds. Only those who refused to obey their fears would dare to venture into those uncharted waters.

Peter could step out of the boat onto uncharted waters because he could say, "Here is God." He was not going to allow the imaginary dragons to keep him inside the boat. Are the imaginary dragons keeping you in the boat?

Principle # 3	We break through comfort zones by taking a step of faith.

Peter and the other disciples huddled together in the U.S.S. Comfort Zone. A storm was rocking their boat when Jesus walked toward them on the water. Sometimes God has to rock the boat to get us out of our comfort zones.

At first, the disciples thought they had seen a spirit. After all, isn't it easier to believe a spirit can walk on water than it is to believe a man can do it? But if any one could do it, it would have been Jesus. The way to find out was simply to ask if it was he.

Doubting Thomas no doubt would have said, "Lord, if it is you, make a bridge appear on the water between you and me." My suggestion would have been, "Lord, if it is you, stop this storm!" But impetuous Peter said, "Lord, if it is you, tell me to come."

Jesus answered, "Come."

Why did Peter ask Jesus to command him to come? Because in order to get out of the boat and break through his comfort zone, he had to hear a word from God. "So faith comes from hearing, and hearing by the word of Christ" (Rom. 10:17). When Peter heard Jesus say, "Come," he received the word, and it produced faith. If we are going to break through our comfort zones, we also need to hear from God, just like Peter did.

When Peter saw by faith he actually could walk on water, he made a commitment with both of his feet to step over the rim. Unbelief keeps both feet inside the boat. Doubt takes one step out of the boat and keeps one foot in. But faith steps completely out of the boat. Peter totally committed himself to his decision by putting both feet out onto the water.

Faith in action will always shatter the stronghold of fear. In order to break through our comfort zones, we must take a step of faith with both feet through the fear barriers that keep us inside the boat.

Principle # 4	**We break through comfort zones in order to fulfill God's will.**

Now this is important. When Jesus told him to come, Peter understood it was God's will for him to get out of the boat. We don't get out of the boat just so we can break out of a comfort zone. We get out in order to get into God's will.

After God called me to preach, I enrolled in Southwestern Baptist Theological Seminary. One Sunday night I was invited to preach at First Baptist Church, Olney, Texas. Just minutes before church was to begin, I was as nervous as a mouse at a cat convention. Because of my stage fright, the mere thought of speaking to all those people was terrifying. Finally, I cried out to God, "Lord, why did you call me to preach? I hate this. I can't go the rest of my life feeling this way. If you want me to preach, you are going to have to change me."

Then I heard God clearly speak to my heart, "Quit thinking about what the congregation thinks of you, and start thinking about what they need to hear. I have a message for you to deliver."

Instantly, I was set free from my stage fright. My nervousness vanished as I felt God's peace calm my spirit. No longer was I afraid to stand in front of the congregation because now I had a new sense of purpose. I had heard from God, which produced the faith to do his will. My desire to fulfill his will gave me the courage to break through my comfort zone. I stood before the people that night, having been set free from fear and trembling, and boldly preached the message they needed to hear.

The same thing happened to Peter when he heard Jesus say, "Come." Peter was freed from his fears because he knew he was obeying the will of God. He understood it was better to walk on the water with Jesus than to remain in the boat. We cannot make the changes we need until we understand this very important principle: Being in God's will is more fulfilling than staying inside our comfort zones.

Principle # 5	**We break through comfort zones to experience freedom on the other side.**

As Peter got out of the boat and walked on the water, he was thinking, "One small step for man, but one giant leap through my comfort zone." After taking a couple of steps, Peter noticed how the wind was blowing the waves. His mind reverted back to his science class where he learned the density of a man on top of water is greater than the density of water under his feet. A few quick calculations proved to be his downfall.

His faith converted into doubt, causing him to quickly plunge underneath the water. Not only had he forgotten how to walk on the water, he had also forgotten how to swim in it! Fear can paralyze us, not from just doing new things, but also from doing familiar things.

I'm sure a couple of disciples in the boat were quick to point out his inability to make it from point B to point J. "You just can't trust what Jesus says," Judas would say. Thomas would add, "I knew he wouldn't make it. It's impossible to walk on water."

After Peter began to sink, Jesus asked, "O you of little faith, why did you doubt?" If Peter only had little faith, then those in the boat must have had no faith. At least he got out of the boat.

Yes, Peter sank after he took his eyes off Jesus and looked at the storm. He didn't sink because Jesus deceived him or because it was impossible to walk on water. He sank because he focused on his circumstances rather than Jesus.

When we break through a comfort zone, we may sink if we take our eyes off Jesus. But remember, he didn't let Peter drown. Jesus stretched out his hand and lifted Peter up, and he will do the same for us.

Although Peter sank, he wasn't a failure. Those few steps made history. Twelve men have walked on the moon, but Peter walked on the water. That's something only Jesus has done.

Whenever we first break through a comfort zone, we will probably feel uncomfortable at first. But not long after we make the change, we experience a new-found freedom on the other side. Then we wonder why we didn't break through sooner.

You have probably been to a swimming pool where people in the water are having a great time. Someone yells, "Come on in. The water's fine."

You put your toe in the pool, then shrink back, thinking the water is too cold. But as you stand by yourself, you notice how much fun the people are having. So you decide to join them and dive into the pool. For a few seconds the water is cold, but it soon feels refreshing. You spend the rest of the day in the swimming pool, not even thinking about the few uncomfortable seconds when you first jumped in.

You broke through a comfort zone. It was uncomfortable at first, but you found freedom and enjoyment on the other side.

What comfort zones do you need to break through? God may be prompting you to do something you have never done before. Perhaps you need to make a career change. Maybe you need to teach a Bible study, start a new ministry, or reach out to someone you don't know. Jesus is standing outside your comfort zone right now, calling for you to come. How will you respond?

Now is not the time to cling to the rim of the boat. It's time to walk on the water!

Stepping Out of the Boat

- What "boat rim" do you need to step over?

- List the different kinds of fears that are keeping you in the boat.

- In what ways can you take a step of faith through your comfort zone?

- Read chapter 14, "When You Need to Make a Decision."

CHAPTER 9

When You Are Depressed
The Elijah Complex

Then Jezebel sent a messenger to Elijah, saying, "So may the gods do to me and even more, if I do not make your life as the life of one of them by tomorrow about this time." And he was afraid and arose and ran for his life. . . . But he himself went a day's journey into the wilderness, and came and sat down under a juniper tree; and he requested for himself that he might die, and said, "It is enough; now, O Lord, take my life."

(1 Kings 19:2–4)

ELIJAH CHALLENGED the 450 prophets of Baal on Mount Carmel and prayed down fire from heaven. God sent fire and consumed the sacrifice. Then Elijah went to the brook Kishon and slew the false prophets. What an act of faith! What an example of courage!

Not long after this, Elijah got a fax from Jezebel. You would think she would be afraid of a man like this, but she wasn't. She sent word she was going to make sure he was dead within twenty-four hours. When Elijah got the message, butterflies began to flutter inside his stomach. His knees grew weak and wobbly. He lost his senses and ran for his life. What an act of unbelief! What an example of cowardice!

How could he go from feeling so high to so low in so short a period of time? Just hours before this, he was victorious on Mount Carmel. Now he was hiding and depressed in the wilderness.

You have heard of the inferiority complex. Elijah was suffering from what we might call "The Elijah Complex." The Elijah Complex is when we lose all sense of God's presence, protection, and provision.

Life becomes meaningless. When we are in that situation, we feel forsaken, hopeless, and depressed. Elijah was at such a low point he wanted to die.

How did he lose his perspective? Can it happen to us?

Here are some thought patterns that can cause you to acquire the Elijah Complex.

> **Thought # 1** | **Your problem appears to be bigger than God.**

At this point in Elijah's life, Jezebel looked bigger than God. He lost his perspective because he got his eyes off God and on his problem. Then Satan put the problem under the microscope and magnified it. He always makes the problem look bigger than it really is. Elijah saw Jezebel through the microscope, and she looked like a scene from the movie *The Attack of the Fifty-Foot Woman*.

During the Civil War, Gen. Robert E. Lee had a shortage of soldiers. His army could be devastated if the Union army discovered this weakness. Since he could not increase the number of soldiers, he decided he could make his army look larger than it actually was.

He loaded troops on trains and transported them to different places. At every train station, the same Confederate soldiers were unloaded from the trains. It appeared that new troops were being transported in to be added to the Rebel army.

The Union forces became confused and afraid because they believed the South had a much larger army than they actually had. General Lee hadn't made his army any larger or more powerful. He was simply using a psychological tactic to discourage the Union army. And it worked.

Years ago I counseled a depressed woman who thought no one had bigger problems than she. In reality, her situation was not nearly as bad as she perceived it. She had good health, and all her family's needs had been met. But her perspective of life was so warped she could only see huge problems. Rather than seeing a big Jesus and a little devil, she saw a big devil and a little Jesus. People can view a glass of water that is half filled differently. Positive people see it as half full. Negative people see it as half empty. This woman didn't see the glass as half empty, but as totally empty!

When I counsel people like this, I try to get them to change their outlook so they will view life in a different way. Changing their perspectives from negative to positive doesn't happen overnight. It's a gradual process that takes place day by day through the renewing of the mind (Rom. 12:2).

If you have the Elijah Complex, you must look at the big picture, not just the details. Rather than just seeing problems, start counting blessings. View the glass as half full, not half empty. See a big Jesus and little devil. The only one who can change your thought patterns is you. You decide how you view the size of your problems.

Our difficulties are never as large as they appear to be. Satan tries to magnify them in our minds in order to discourage us. Don't let him do it. Our problems will never become bigger than God!

| *Thought* | **You see yourself as the only one with problems.** |
| *# 2* | |

Elijah told God, "I alone am left"(19:10). He had spiritual claustrophobia. A person with claustrophobia gets into an elevator and panics because he thinks the four walls are closing in on him. They aren't really closing in, but he thinks they are. Elijah felt closed in. He thought he was the only one with problems.

Peter wrote a group of Christians who thought they were the only ones who were experiencing trials. He told them to resist Satan, "knowing that the same experiences of suffering are being accomplished by your brethren who are in the world" (1 Pet. 5:9). He told them that, because it helps to know when trials come, we are not alone.

When Elijah thought he was the only one left, God told him there were "7,000 in Israel, all the knees that have not bowed to Baal and every mouth that has not kissed him" (1 Kings 19:18). Not only was God aware of what Elijah was going through, but he also knew exactly how many others were having the same experiences as his servant Elijah. God was aware of their problems back then, and he is also aware of the struggles we are experiencing right now.

| Thought # 3 | **You lose hope for the future.** |

Elijah requested that "he might die"(19:4). He was fleeing from death, yet he prayed for death. Sometimes we do not pray wisely when we have the Elijah Complex. Elijah was bewildered in the wilderness. He had lost hope for the future and had slipped into depression.

The irony of the situation was that Elijah prayed for death, yet he never died. He was caught up alive in a whirlwind to heaven without tasting death (2 Kings 2:11). Little did he realize during his time of depression the great plans God had for him. Depression will always blind us to hope for the future.

Have you ever wondered why you become depressed? I would like to give you a little test to help you analyze yourself.

The Thought-Analyzer Test

1. When I am happy, I have been thinking _____ thoughts.
2. When I am sad, I have been thinking _____ thoughts.
3. When I am angry, I have been thinking _____ thoughts.
4. When I am depressed, I have been thinking _____ thoughts.

The answers are:
1. happy
2. sad
3. angry
4. depressing

It is so profoundly simple that it is simply profound. The way we think will affect the moods we are in. Thoughts do affect emotions. My thoughts tell my emotions what to do. Emotions simply respond to the information that is fed to them.

For example, if I go to a horror movie, I experience fear even though I know what I am watching is not real. If I watch a sad movie, I may cry because my emotions have been touched by my thoughts. A comedy can put me in a jovial mood. Thoughts have a powerful effect upon emotions.

If I have been depressed, it is because I have been thinking depressing thoughts. Although some depression is caused by poor diet and lack of exercise, the vast majority of cases are caused because people have been dwelling upon depressing thoughts. I cannot dwell upon negative thoughts without becoming depressed.

That is the problem. But it is also the solution to the problem. If thoughts determine emotions, then my depression can be reversed by changing the way I think. Feelings follow thoughts like a caboose follows a locomotive. If my "thought locomotive" goes into the valley, then my "feelings caboose" will follow it down into the valley. But if the locomotive goes up a mountain, although the caboose lags behind the train at first, it will eventually follow it up the mountain.

If my emotions are to be turned around, then my thought process must be reversed. Rather than thinking depressing thoughts, I choose to think joyful thoughts. At first I may not feel like rejoicing, but thinking joyful thoughts eventually makes me joyful. Thinking positively releases chemicals called endorphins into our bodies that correct the chemical imbalances caused by depression. Although God didn't explain to us the medical reasons for rejoicing, he did tell us "a joyful heart is good medicine" (Prov. 17:22).

I don't have to dwell on the negative. I can choose to dwell on the positive. A cartoon depicted a man hanging by chains on the wall of a dungeon. He was skinny and had long hair and a long beard. He had obviously been hanging there a long time.

A psychiatrist was sitting in a chair in front of him with a pad and pen and was taking notes as he listened to the man.

The man hanging on the wall, grinning from ear to ear, said, "Call me weird, but I feel good!" It is possible to feel good in spite of the circumstances.

We can see whatever we want in our circumstances. Two young boys were raised in the home of an alcoholic father. As young men, each went his own way. Years later a psychologist, who was analyzing the effects of alcoholism on children, searched out these two men.

One had turned out to be like his alcoholic father. The counselor asked him, "Why did you become an alcoholic?"

The son answered, "What else would you expect if you had a father like mine?"

When the psychologist found the other son, he was amazed to discover he had never taken a drink in his life. He asked, "Why did you decide to never drink alcohol?"

The son answered, "What else would you expect if you had a father like mine?"[1]

The two boys grew up under the same circumstances but had turned out completely different. Why? Because it is not what we go through that determines what we become. It is how we respond that determines what we become.

The first son claimed to be a victim of circumstances. The second son used his situation to motivate him out of a life of alcoholism. He was a victor over his circumstances. Are you a victim or a victor? You have the choice.

Here are several positive steps you can take to improve your perspective when you are depressed.

First — Put your hope in God.

David was once depressed and in despair. He said in Psalm 42:5, "Why are you in despair, O my soul? And why have you become disturbed within me? Hope in God." If you have lost hope, you will find it if you look to God. James 4:8 tells us to "draw near to God and He will draw near to you." This verse isn't talking about our distance from God, but intimacy with him. A man and wife can be standing side by side, yet be far away from each other in their hearts. We must draw near to God in our hearts.

A man in a rowboat was caught in a current and floated downstream toward a waterfall. As he was drifting away, he saw a large rock on the river bank. The rock provided security and stability for the man who was about to lose hope. He took a rope, threw it around the rock, and pulled the boat toward it. As he drew near to the rock, the rock drew near to him.

When we call out to God for help, we are throwing out the rope to the Rock. "To Thee, O Lord, I call; my rock" (Ps. 28:1). As we draw near to God's throne of grace, the Lord will draw near to us. It is only at the throne of grace that we can find grace to help in our time of need (Heb. 4:16).

	Sing in the dark.
Second	

The second thing David said was, "and His song will be with me in the night." (Ps. 42:8). If you are going through a dark time, sing in the dark. Put on a tape of praise music and sing along with it. Continue singing to the Lord until your depression leaves.

Some of the most beautiful singing canaries in the world have come from the Harz Mountains of Germany. But during World War I, it became impossible to obtain these little warblers. So a dealer in New York came up with the idea of training an American finch to sing like the European variety. He had the songs of these famous birds recorded and mailed to his home. When they arrived, he played them over and over each day in the room where he kept his own canaries.

At first, his efforts met with little success. Then one day he made a startling discovery. He found that if he covered their cages and completely shut out the light, his American birds soon sang like the birds on the recording. They learned to sing in the dark.[2]

Just like the birds, we need to learn to sing in the dark times that we experience. We may not see what lies ahead because our vision is restricted by the darkness of trial and despair. But that is the best time to sing. It will help us endure the dark times until the morning light arrives.

	Rejoice in the Lord.
Third	

Philippians 4:4 commands us to "rejoice in the Lord always." That includes during times of depression. Telling a depressed person to rejoice is like asking a man with broken legs to dance. You may not feel like doing it, but you must obey because rejoicing is one of the main factors involved in being healed from depression. Remember, changing your thought patterns from negative to positive is the key to turning your emotions around.

| **Fourth** | **Reach out and help other people.** |

Dr. Viktor Frankl was an Austrian physician who was imprisoned in one of Hitler's death camps. He and his fellow Jewish people suffered unbelievable atrocities. Over a period of time, he discovered a unique phenomenon. In his book *Man's Search for Meaning*, he said those people who kept their strength and sanity the longest were those who tried to help other prisoners and share what little they had. Their physical and mental condition seemed to be strengthened by their friendliness, compassion, and focus on something other than themselves.[3]

Depressed people are consumed with thoughts about themselves. This inward thinking process will cause a person to sink continually deeper into depression. The way out is to turn your eyes from inward to outward. Rather than thinking about yourself, reach out to other people and meet their needs. If you do this, you will find your depression will lift.

| **Fifth** | **Change the way you view your problems.** |

Philippians 4:8 tells us to let our minds dwell on good things. We may not choose our circumstances, but we can choose the way we view them. We can decide whether to focus our attention on the positive or the negative.

When Moses sent the twelve spies into the promised land (Num. 13), all of them viewed the same set of circumstances. They observed that the land flowed with milk and honey, but they also noticed giants were in the land. When they returned, ten of the spies were fearful of the giants. The other two, Joshua and Caleb, were excited about the land God had promised to them. Even though they all had seen the same thing, ten chose to focus on the giants and two chose to focus on the promises.

Several years ago my mother-in-law Barbara sank into deep depression. Her mother had been deeply depressed and eventually committed suicide. Now Barbara was afraid the same thing might happen to her, but she kept her feelings of despair to herself. Week after week her depression got worse and wouldn't leave. She realized this wasn't the kind of depression most people experience but had reached the point of being a serious problem. The weeks turned into months, and she was losing all hope of being cured.

During this time, Barbara and her husband Neil drove from Texas to Kansas to visit us. As she watched the miles go by, the weight of her deep depression caused her to sink even lower. She had always trusted the Lord but for some reason had not handed this problem over to him. At that point, she prayed, "Lord, I don't think I can get out of this on my own. You will have to do it. Please help me."

That Sunday morning, they visited our church before returning home. I preached a message on David and Goliath, "Killing the Giants in Your Life." During the sermon, I told the congregation, "Just as God gave David the ability to defeat the giant, he can give you victory over the giant in your life." At that moment, Barbara decided to slay the giant of depression which had been defeating her. By the end of the message, she realized the weight of the depression had lifted. She felt free for the first time in months.

At first, she was hesitant to tell anyone, thinking it might come back. But it has been over five years since that happened, and the giant of depression is still in the grave. Barbara was set free from her depression because she saw that God's promise was bigger than her problem.

Changing the way we see our circumstances is critical to overcoming depression. A little boy was playing outside and was stung by a bee. He went into his house crying and said to his mother, "I hate bees! I wish God had never made them."

The mother eased his pain, then sat him down at the table and gave him some toast and honey. The little boy said, "This is great!"

"You really do like honey, don't you?" the mother responded.

"Like it?" the little boy replied, "I love it!"

The mother then said, "The same bee that stings also produces the honey you are enjoying right now."

Her son thought for a minute and said, "I never realized there was a good side to that bee!"

We can view a bee as an enemy that stings or as a friend that produces honey. And that's the way it is with everything in life. We can choose to look at the plus side in every situation, or we can choose to look at the minus side. The difference will be one of living a life of depression or a life of rejoicing.

Lifting Your Depression

- Rather than thinking depressing thoughts, verbally rejoice in the Lord. Listen to uplifting Christian music, and sing praises to God.

- Turn your thinking outward by reaching out to others. Visit a lonely person or someone in the hospital. Take food to a needy person.

- Write down positive things in your situation that you can dwell upon. Post it on your mirror or another visible place as a reminder.

CHAPTER 10

When You Feel Like Quitting

Preventing Burnout

And let us not lose heart in doing good, for in due time we shall reap if we do not grow weary.

(Galatians 6:9)

BURNED-OUT LIGHT BULB doesn't produce light. Neither does a burned-out Christian. Burnout is a modern-day term for "growing weary." God promises we will reap the harvest if we don't burn out.

On February 2, 1985, during the Daytona 500 Auto Race, the $250,000 car driven by professional driver Donny Allison was only on its third lap when it rolled to a stop on the infield side of the track. Nothing was mechanically wrong with the vehicle. Nor was anything wrong with the driver. Someone had forgotten to put fuel in the tank! An innocent but costly mistake. The performance of the race car and the skill of the driver were completely nullified, simply because the car hadn't received the fuel it needed to finish the race.

It is so easy to quit. All we have to do is keep giving out until the tank is empty. Then when the fuel gauge reads "E," we quit. We go from giving *out* to giving *up*. Burnout occurs when we give out more than we take in. Cars that aren't refueled will run out of gas. Wells that are not replenished will run dry. Batteries that are not recharged will have no power. We are not any different. A Christian that is not refueled, replenished, and recharged will burn out.

Burnout doesn't happen overnight. It's a process that occurs over a period of time. It begins by burning the candle at both ends. That works fine for a while, but then a series of events brings us to the point of exhaustion. We become sapped of strength. Our motivation to continue quickly evaporates. We can't stand the thought of one more obligation, so we resign. It happens every day in jobs, marriages, and churches.

As Rick Warren, senior pastor of Saddleback Valley Community Church in Orange County, California, has said, "If you are burning the candle at both ends, you are not as bright as you think you are." We can, however, learn to burn the candle wisely. Burnout can be prevented if we watch for red flags. These flags, listed below as parts of the stages of burnout, can warn us trouble is coming if we don't take action immediately.

Stage # 1	**We become disillusioned** *Result: Losing vision* *Red Flag: Dreading the future*

When we become disillusioned, we lose our vision. Disillusionment comes when the picture in our minds of the way things ought to be doesn't match the way things really are. That ideal mental picture is shattered by the reality of the situation. The bubble bursts. The dream dies. The vision vanishes. And then we become disillusioned.

Dr. Howard Hendricks has said people get married with pictures in their minds of perfect marriages. Then after a few trials, they discover they aren't married to perfect pictures, but to imperfect people. When this realization occurs, they will either tear up the pictures or they will tear up the partners.

But we don't just have pictures in our minds of what marriage ought to be. We have pictures of what everything ought to be. When we draw these perfect pictures in our minds, we exclude the flat tires, dirty diapers, broken water pipes, unreasonable employers, overdue bills, and disagreeable people that will mess up our pictures. We leave them out because these nuisances are unpleasant to think about. However, all these things are part of the reality of life. When reality clashes with fantasy, something must give. If reality destroys the pictures, disillusionment will occur.

Stage # 2	**We become discouraged**
	Result: Losing heart
	Red Flag: Significant decrease in motivation

When we become discouraged, we lose heart. Disillusionment in our minds can bring discouragement to our hearts. Our motivation for completing a task dwindles. If a football team ever loses heart during a game, they won't win. All they will think about is getting the game over and going to the locker room because discouragement destroys their motivation to continue.

When Joshua sent the soldiers to Ai shortly after they had conquered Jericho, the sons of Israel thought victory would come easily. They only sent three thousand men to Ai to fight and were defeated. The picture in their minds of victory was shattered, bringing discouragement to their hearts. As a result, Joshua 7:5 says "The hearts of the people melted and became as water." When they became discouraged, they lost their courage. They lost heart, so their motivation to gain victory evaporated. We always give up in our hearts before we give up in our actions.

Jesus said to not lose heart in prayer (Luke 18:1). We may have prayed for something for years, but nothing has happened. So we become discouraged and quit.

One wealthy woman phoned the manager of a concert hall and asked, "Have you found a diamond pendant? I think I lost it in your building last night."

The manager said, "No, we haven't found it, but we will look. Please hold the line."

After several minutes of searching, someone found the diamond pendant. The manager rushed back to the phone and said, "We have good news for you. We found it! Hello…hello…"

The woman who called had hung up. She never called back, and the jewelry went unclaimed. If we lose our patience while waiting, we can become discouraged and hang up before the answer comes.

Don't give up. The answer is on its way!

Stage #3	**We become discontented** *Result: Losing joy* *Red Flag: Restlessness and complaining*

When we become discontented, we lose our joy. Discontentment and joy cannot reside together within the same heart. One will drive the other out. Have you ever met joyful, discontented people? No, because they don't exist.

If we allow discontentment to enter our hearts, we will become unsettled and restless. Nothing will satisfy or make us happy. We will become so irritated with our present circumstances that we will do anything to get away from them. Discontentment is now controlling us, rather than God. At this stage, we are in serious danger of stepping out of God's will.

Discontentment disrespects God's will.

Quitting becomes more dominant in our thoughts than whether or not we are in God's will. Once we quit something the first time, it becomes that much easier to quit the next time. Then when things get a little tough in the next situation, we decide to quit again.

After we quit a second time, we will search to find another problem-free environment in which to live. But sooner or later, trouble will arise in that place too. By now quitting has become a habit, making it easy to resign and look for something better. We have developed a quitting mentality and have never seriously considered whether or not it was God's will to make those changes.

Discontentment disregards the consequences.

Discontentment doesn't permit us to think about what will happen to us if we quit. Many discontented people have quit a job, only to find they can't find another. They disregarded the consequences of their actions. Wrong decisions can bring disastrous results. Discontentment will always blind us to the consequences that we must face as a result of giving up too soon.

Discontentment distorts our view of life.

Once discontentment enters our hearts, it affects our entire perspective of life. The pure in heart will see God (Matt. 5:8), but the defiled in heart will have blurred vision. Discontentment contaminates our perspective causing us to see everything in a negative light. No matter where we go or what we do, we will not be happy. Nothing will satisfy because everywhere we go, we are there. Our distorted perspective ruins everything we see.

A little boy sneaked into the bedroom where his grandfather was sleeping. He put some limburger cheese in his mustache, then slipped out of the room.

A little while later, his grandfather woke up. He sniffed a few times and said, "This room stinks." He got up and went into the living room and sniffed again. He muttered to himself, "This living room stinks!" Then he walked into the kitchen and said, "This kitchen stinks, too!" Finally, he walked outside to get some fresh air. After drawing a deep breath, he yelled out in disgust, "This whole world stinks!"

Some people have limburger cheese in their attitudes. Wherever they go, they think the world stinks. But it isn't the world that stinks. It's their attitude!

We become disassociated
Result: Losing rewards
Red Flag: Deciding to quit

When we disassociate ourselves from the situation that bothers us, we lose our reward. The reward for the farmer who has plowed, fertilized, sowed, watered, and waited is the harvest. God will reward our labor if we endure to the end. "We shall reap if we do not grow weary" (Gal. 6:9).

One of the largest gold mines in the world was discovered just six inches deeper from the place where the last crew quit digging. By quitting too soon, they lost the reward of their labor. When we quit, we forfeit the harvest. The harvest comes at the end of the season, but if we quit before then, all the work we have done will have been in vain.

How to Prevent Burn-Out

Is every hard worker doomed to burn out sooner or later? Not if you carry out these simple preventive steps.

	Rest from your labor.
First	

"Six days you shall labor and do all your work, but the seventh day is a sabbath of the Lord your God; in it you shall not do any work." (Ex. 20:9–10)

God commands us to rest from our labors. This command is just as valid as the command to work. God knew we needed a day to cease from our labors and become refreshed. If we don't take regular breaks from our labors, we can become addicted to our work, turning us into workaholics.

One workaholic stood at a busy intersection holding a sign that read, "Will Work for the Fun of It." Although God wants us to enjoy our work, he also wants us to enjoy our rest. I have found in counseling people that those who burn out seldom take time off. They work like buzz saws seven days a week and rarely vacation. This not only cheats themselves but also their families who need time away, too.

I know I must not only take a day off once a week, but I also need to take a vacation with my family. My wife and I are constantly talking about church activities and our phone continually rings. Time away helps give our minds a vacation, too. We find when we return from our trip, we are refreshed both physically and mentally, which helps us do a better job in what God has called us to do.

	Reduce your workload.
Second	

"Let us also lay aside every encumbrance." (Heb. 12:1)

Many people burn out because their work loads are too heavy. In the old West, cowboys put their branding irons in the campfire to heat them up so they could mark their cattle. If too many irons were put in, they would put out the fire.

Too many irons in the fire will put out your fire, too. The branding irons we have today are all the duties and responsibilities that weigh us down in our daily walk. While some responsibilities are important and necessary, others aren't. The energy it takes to heat the unnecessary irons can encumber the high-priority irons. That's why God says, "Let us also lay aside every encumbrance." We must pull a few unnecessary irons out so the fire will continue to burn.

The ship HMS *Queen Mary* had to be brought into dry dock to clean off the barnacles. A barnacle is a small crustacean that grows on the hull of a ship. It isn't very big by itself, but enough of them can cause major problems. The ship had accumulated so many tiny barnacles that it slowed down the huge ship, causing it to drag.

Just like too many barnacles can put drag on a ship, too many responsibilities can drag us down. God doesn't expect us to do everything, just the things he has planned for us. That's why we need to re-evaluate everything we are doing. We must ask God what we need to let go of and what he wants us to continue to do. If we don't let go of some things, we will eventually let go of everything because we will burn out.

> **Third** **Regulate your schedule.**
>
> "Live one day at a time." (Matt. 6:34 TLB)

Because the race of life is a marathon, we must learn how to pace ourselves. We must "run with endurance the race that is set before us" (Heb. 12:1). Long-distance runners have learned to endure by pacing themselves so they won't burn out before the finish line. The secret to enduring the race of life is to regulate our schedule by living just one day at a time.

Two men each had fifteen logs to build their own campfires on a cold night. The first man threw all of his logs on his campfire at one time. It made a dandy bonfire but burned out long before the night was over. The other man added logs to the fire every few hours. His campfire continued to burn throughout the night. He had learned to wisely distribute his energy resources.

Some people start running the race in a big flash but burn out quickly because they haven't learned how to endure. Winners, on the other hand, have learned how to regulate their pace.

A boating accident once occurred far from shore. Everyone drowned except for one woman who swam to safety. She was able to keep swimming by constantly repeating to herself, "Just one more stroke. Just one more stroke." When people found her on the shore, she was half conscious and still muttering the phrase, "Just one more stroke...just one more stroke."[1] Even though she was far from shore, she covered that great distance by swimming one stroke at a time.

A thousand-mile journey can only be walked one step at a time. A thousand-page book can only be read one page at a time. And you can only run the race of life one day at a time.

Fourth	**Refuel your spirit.** Be filled with the Spirit. (Eph. 5:18)

It's not enough to get refueled physically through food, or mentally through rest and recreation. We must also refuel our spiritually empty gas tanks. Our spiritual batteries must be recharged. Usually when a person burns out, he has been trying to live the Christian life by the flesh rather than by the Spirit.

I once came to a point where I grew weary of trying to live the Christian life. I prayed, "Lord, I can't live this way anymore. If you want me to live like you want, you are going to have to do it. I give up. I ask you to fill me with the Holy Spirit right now. Amen."

After praying, I didn't feel a thing. But faith is based upon God's Word, not our feelings. I decided if I was asked if I was filled with the Holy Spirit, I would declare I was, even though I didn't feel like it.

Over the next few days, something changed. It became fun again being a Christian! I had power that I hadn't experienced before. I was filled with joy and zeal. Witnessing became a privilege rather than a duty. Within a few days, I led four people to a saving knowledge of Jesus Christ. I had a hunger to read my Bible as never before. What happened? God had filled me with the Holy Spirit, just like I had prayed!

You have probably been in a restaurant where the waitress has asked, "May I warm up your coffee for you?" The cup is half-full and cold after sitting on the table for a while. When she pours the new coffee in, she refills and warms up the cup.

Maybe you are spiritually cold and empty. It doesn't have to stay that way. Quit trying to do it with your own power and strength. Ask God to fill you with the Holy Spirit right now.

	Renew your vision.
Fifth	Where there is no vision, the people perish. (Prov. 29:18 KJV)

The late Supreme Court Justice, Oliver Wendell Holmes, was on a train when the conductor came through collecting tickets. Holmes, unable to locate his, became quite distraught.

The conductor said, "Mr. Holmes, don't worry. When you find your ticket, just mail it in. We trust you."

"My dear man, that's not my problem," Holmes replied. "I need my ticket to tell me where I'm going!"[2]

Vision is the ticket that tells you where you are going. Without it, you have no destination. You are simply wandering through life.

If you have become disillusioned through losing your vision, you must do everything you can to regain it. Vision is the God-given ability to anticipate crossing the finish line. It gives hope for the future and a motivation to continue running the race of life. When you renew your vision, you will be motivated out of inspiration rather than out of desperation. People without vision will drop out of the race, but people with it will finish victoriously.

Although you may be on the verge of burning out, don't throw in the towel yet. The race is still before you. It's not the early bird that gets the worm. It's the one that keeps on digging.

Refueling the Tank

- Are you showing signs of burning out?

- Make a list of all your responsibilities. How can you lighten your load of unimportant things so you won't burn out?

- In what ways are you being refueled spiritually?

CHAPTER 11

When You Are Criticized
Coping with Criticism

And why do you look at the speck that is in your brother's eye, but
do not notice the log that is in your own eye?

(Matt. 7:3)

CHARLES SPURGEON AND D. L. Moody were two of the greatest
preachers during the nineteenth century. Although Moody
had never met Spurgeon, he greatly admired the Englishman
and arranged to meet him in London. After he traveled across the
Atlantic, Moody found Spurgeon's residence and knocked on the door.
Spurgeon answered with a cigar in his mouth. Moody was aghast.

"How could you, a man of God, smoke that?" asked Moody.

Spurgeon took the cigar from his mouth, put his finger on
Moody's huge stomach, smiled, and said, "The same way that you, a
man of God, could be that fat!"[1]

It's easy to see the faults in others, but difficult to see them in
ourselves. Faults are like the headlights in a car—those of others seem
more glaring than our own. Because our faults are easily seen by others, it doesn't take much for us to become targets of criticism.

When I first began preaching, I was pretty naive. I thought if I
accurately preached God's Word, everyone would agree with me. I
believed a church should be one big, happy family that could easily
resolve its differences.

My unrealistic view of life was shattered one Sunday morning.
After I had preached my sermon, I greeted people as they left the
church. A man walked up to me visibly upset. He obviously did not
appreciate something I had said in my message. With his fists
clenched, he was trying to restrain himself from punching me.

Through gritted teeth, he said, "You called me an idiot from the pulpit!"

At first I thought he was joking. Of course, I had not called him an idiot, but this man was so angry he thought I really had said it. Shaking my head in disbelief, I said, "You must be pulling my leg. Are you saying I called you an idiot while I was preaching?"

He answered, "Yes! You called out my name in front of everyone and said I was an idiot!"

As I looked at his doubled fists, I knew this was no joke. It appeared as though he was going to hit me in the face at any moment. I wasn't sure whether it was scriptural to block the punch or if I had to offer my cheek as a target. But instead of hitting me, the man bolted out of the door, never to return again.

Maybe you have been in a similar situation. You have been accused of something you didn't do, but no matter how hard you try, you can't convince the other person of your innocence. So you must learn how to live under the scrutiny of judgmental eyes.

Here are a few lessons I have learned about criticism:

- People often become critical based upon wrong or misleading information.

- I cannot escape criticism by trying to please my critics.

- If I try to defend myself against criticism, I waste a lot of energy and accomplish little.

- If Jesus couldn't please everyone, why do I think I can?

- The more spotlight placed upon me, the bigger the target of criticism I become.

- Wherever there is light, there are also bugs.

- God will use my critics to reveal things in my life that need to be changed.

We must learn to discern when criticism is and isn't valid. And because criticism can be so devastating, we must also learn how to cope with it.

Why People Criticize

When we are being judged, we usually don't stop to consider the reasons for the criticism. We would like to retreat inside a cave and hibernate rather than deal with it. But God will allow criticism to come to us, whether justified or not, to refine us in his crucible. Believe it or not, correctly handling criticism is one of the quickest ways to become like Jesus. If we can understand the reasons why people criticize, we can learn how to handle fault-finding correctly.

Reason # 1 **Some people criticize because they have critical spirits.**

Jesus said a critical person can't see the log in his own eye, yet he will point out specks in other people's eyes. He can't see any faults within himself, yet he will nitpick about the smallest details in everyone else's life.

A judgmental person is very quick on the flaw. He inspects for specks. He has unreal expectations of what he wants from us, so we will never be able to live up to his standards. He will drag us into his court of judgment, and without a trial, sentence us to a life of condemnation without parole.

A man and his wife once pulled into a gas station to refuel their car. As the tank was being refilled, the station attendant washed the windshield.

When the attendant finished, the driver of the car said, "The windshield is still dirty. Wash it again."

"Yes, sir," the attendant answered. As he scrubbed the windshield a second time, he looked closely for any bugs or dirt he had missed.

When he finished, the driver became angry. "It's still dirty!" he yelled. "Don't you know how to wash a windshield? Do it again!"

The attendant cleaned the windshield a third time, carefully looking for any place he might have missed, but could find no messy spots anywhere.

By now, the driver was fuming. He screamed, "This windshield is still filthy! I'm going to talk to your boss to make sure you don't work here another day. You are the lousiest windshield washer I have ever seen!"

As he was about to get of the car, his wife reached over and removed his glasses. She carefully wiped them with a tissue, then put them back on his face. The driver embarrassingly slumped down in his seat as he observed a spotless windshield.

Critical people view others through their own dirty glasses. The dirt on their hearts causes them to see everything from an unclean, critical perspective. They become angry at what they perceive to be dirt on other people, when in reality they are looking at others through the dirt on their own hearts. Their critical spirits cause them to continue to find fault in others until the filth in their hearts has been cleansed.

Reason # 2	**Some people criticize because they don't know the whole story.**

Because the critical person is looking for specks, he usually doesn't take time to observe the big picture. A situation can't be correctly understood until it is seen in its entirety. Since the critical person refuses to see the whole, he misinterprets the part. He takes things out of context, reads between the lines, and jumps to wrong conclusions because he hasn't taken time to know the whole story. He refuses to see life from any perspective other than his own.

An old poem shares good advice for all of us:

> Don't find fault with the man who limps
> Or stumbles along life's road,
> Unless you have worn the shoes he wears,
> Or struggled beneath his load.

> There may be tacks in his shoes that hurt,
> Though hidden away from our view,
> The burden he bears, if placed on your back,
> Might cause you to stumble, too.

> Don't sneer at the man who is down today,
> Unless you have felt the blow
> That caused his fall, or felt the shame
> That only the fallen know.

You may be strong, but still the blows
That were his, if dealt to you
In the self same way at the self same time,
Might cause you to stagger, too.

Don't be too harsh with a man who sins,
Or pelt him with words or stones,
Unless you are sure, yes, doubly sure,
That you have no sins of your own.[2]

Before I became one, I heard about the stress upon pastors and their families. But to be quite honest, I was suspicious. The ministry didn't look any more difficult than any other job, I thought. Maybe even a little easier.

When I became a pastor, I understood why ministers burn out more than any other profession. The burden of carrying people's problems, the phone constantly ringing, weekly pressure to prepare new sermons, numerous decisions to make, and stress from dealing with disgruntled people opened my eyes. I didn't know the whole story about the pressure pastors experience until I became one.

I'm sure you have your own story to tell about how difficult your situation is. But people cannot completely understand what you are going through until they experience the same thing. After walking in your shoes for a while, they might not be so critical.

Reason # 3	**Some people criticize because it makes them feel better about themselves.**

The critic usually has a terrible self-image. His inability to accept himself as God created him causes him to view himself in a distorted, unhealthy way. He feels inferior to others, and considers everyone else a threat to his self-worth. In order to elevate himself and look better in comparison, he resorts to belittling and criticizing, pointing out real or apparent flaws in others.

King Saul was insecure and felt threatened by David. After David had killed the giant Goliath, women danced in the streets and sang, "Saul has slain his thousands, and David his ten thousands." Jealousy and anger filled Saul's heart, and he looked at David with suspicion from that day onward (1 Sam. 18:6–9).

The next day, an evil spirit came upon Saul. His insane jealousy opened him up to the influenced of this demon, which eventually took control of him. The next time Saul saw David, he hurled a spear at him, trying to pin him against the wall (1 Sam. 18:10–11).

Critical spirits will always try to pin people against walls. But this wasn't just a one-time event. The evil spirit caused Saul to try to kill David throughout the rest of his life. Saul never wanted to be compared to David, because he thought it would make him look inferior. The only solution, in Saul's mind, was to destroy the person who was a threat to his self-image.

Have you criticized someone because you felt threatened? Perhaps the competition is a rival in your school or someone whose business is more successful than yours. Don't let your self-worth be determined by comparing yourself with him. Comparison with others will only cause you to feel proud or discouraged. Neither pride nor discouragement are from God.

Reason # 4	**Some people criticize because it's easier to complain about problems than to solve them.**

Some people have enough steam to blow the whistle, but not enough steam to pull the train. They blow off steam by whining and complaining, rather than trying to be part of the solutions.

Years ago a lady who used to go to my church was known for her persistent complaining. One day she said, "Our church doesn't have enough fellowships. You should rent the YMCA for the church to have a fellowship night." Several other times she came to me complaining, "When is the church going to rent the YMCA? We don't have enough fellowship around here." Her continual reminders prompted me to think we should probably rent it, although I didn't appreciate the spirit in which her suggestions were made. So we rented the YMCA, organized games and events, and promoted them within the church.

On the big night, everyone in the church showed up at the YMCA, everyone, that is, except the critical woman and her family. I phoned her from the YMCA asking if she or someone in her family was sick.

"No," she replied, "we're just tired and won't make it tonight."

My eyes were opened to the truth that some people have enough steam to blow whistles, but not enough steam to pull trains. I have discovered that the people most critical of problems usually have no intention of becoming part of solutions.

| *Reason # 5* | **Some people criticize because the person is godly.** |

And indeed, all who desire to live godly in Christ Jesus will be persecuted. (2 Tim. 3:12)

For every godly action, there is an equal and opposite criticism. Jesus was perfect, and we think he would have been exempt from criticism. If anyone could have straightened out the critics, it was Jesus. But instead of worshipping him, the critics hated him without a cause (John 15:25), nailing him to a cross.

Jesus promised us that the world would also hate those who followed him (John 15:18–19). Add to that group a small but vocal minority of cynical people who reside within nearly every church. Percentage-wise they are few, but they can stir up an angry mob in an instant.

We wonder how someone can regularly attend church and be so critical. The reason is because if you are living for Jesus Christ and doing his will, Satan isn't happy about it. He will incite critical people wherever he can find them to discourage you because he wants to stop your work for the Lord. Like it or not, that's just the way it is.

| *Reason # 6* | **Some criticize because a real fault needs correcting.** |

Undoubtedly, we heartily agree with the first five reasons but will dismiss this last reason. Not so fast, my friend. As much as we hate to admit it, we do have faults. These are blind spots we can't see, so sometimes God brings someone who cares about us to lovingly reveal them. At other times, God allows critics to hatefully expose them for us. That doesn't mean everything they say is true, but there may be a grain of truth within their judgments. We must not confuse those who are sincerely concerned about us with those who are critical, but God will use both to reveal matters that need correcting.

I'm not your typical pastor. I'll take blue jeans and tennis shoes over a suit and tie any day. I also like to have fun. That's usually not included in most pastors' job descriptions. I love to imitate voices on our answering machine at home, and from time to time I change the recording. Barney Fife, James the English butler, and Elvis Presley all have taken turns answering our phone when we're not home.

One month, it was Elvis' turn. When people called our house, they heard this recording, which sounded exactly like Elvis' voice: "Hello. This is Elvis Presley. I've been hangin' out at the Crockett's house, and they aren't here right now. So leave a message. Thank you very much." People loved it. The messages left on our answering machine were preceded with everything from giggles to outrageous laughter.

One day a woman called who was experiencing a minor crisis, and Elvis answered the phone. Needless to say, she was not impressed. She laughed at the recording when she called at an earlier time, but this time she was in no mood for humor.

A couple of days later, I received a letter from her explaining how upset she was with the recording and requesting we change it.

My wife's first reaction was, "Do we have to give up our fun just because we are in the ministry? Everyone else in the church can have fun with the recordings on their answering machines."

After a few moments of contemplating the situation, I said, "You know, Cindy, she's right. If we make ninety-nine people laugh and hurt one person that hears it during a time of crisis, then I need to remove my imitations from the answering machine." God had used this woman to correct me in order to reveal something I needed to see.

How to Respond to Criticism

Now that you know why criticism comes your way, you might want to try these steps for handling critics.

| *First* | **View your critics as being sent by God.** |

When King David came to Bahurim, behold, there came out from there a man of the family of the house of Saul whose name was Shimei, the son of Gera; he came out cursing continually as he came. . . . Then Abishai the son of Zeruiah said to the king, "Why should this dead dog curse my lord the king? Let me go over now, and cut off his head." (2 Sam. 16:5, 9)

When Shimei cursed David, Abishai wanted to cut off his head. But David told Abishai to leave him alone because "the Lord has told him [to curse]" (2 Sam. 16:11). Why did David tell Abishai to not take revenge? Because he viewed his critics as being sent by God.

I don't think David actually believed God had caused Shimei to curse him, but that the Lord had allowed the criticism to occur for a reason. Shimei used his hands to cast stones at the king (v.13), but David also saw God's hand in the situation.

When someone criticizes us, the first thing we should ask is, "Lord, what are you trying to teach me through this?" It will help us handle the criticism if we view the person as being sent by God to teach us something rather than seeing him as someone to afflict us.

Criticism is the mildest form of persecution. Jesus clearly taught us how to respond to our critics when he said, "Blessed are you when men hate you, and ostracize you, and cast insults at you, and spurn your name as evil, for the sake of the Son of Man. Be glad in that day, and leap for joy, for behold, your reward is great in heaven; for in the same way their fathers used to treat the prophets" (Luke 6:22–23).

Receiving hate, ostracism, and insults from others is not a joyful experience in itself. But what did Jesus say to do? Lose our joy? No, leap for joy! Why? Because our reward is great in heaven. Jesus said our critics are actually helping us gain eternal rewards. When the apostles were flogged for speaking the name of Jesus, they rejoiced that they had been considered worthy to suffer for his name (Acts 5:40–41).

We can look at our critics in one of two ways. We can see the hate and insults, which will cause us to react in anger and vengeance. Or we can see God's hand allowing the criticism to help us gain eternal rewards, which will motivate us to leap for joy.

Second

Find the grain of truth in the criticism.

Many times a grain of truth is buried in what the critic is saying. Shimei accused David of being judged by God for the bloodshed on the house of Saul. He assumed the Lord had given the kingdom to Absalom because David was evil (2 Sam. 16:8). That's why Shimei was so arrogant. He thought David was out of the way for good and would never be king. He was wrong.

Most of what he said wasn't true, but there was one truth mixed in with his lies. David was a man of bloodshed. Because of this, Solomon was assigned to complete the task of building the temple (1 Chron. 22:7–8; 28:3).

When we are being criticized, we can use the critics to our advantage. Whenever Gen. Dwight D. Eisenhower was about to implement a plan, he showed it to his greatest critics. They, of course, usually tore his plan apart, explaining that it would never work.

Someone asked him why he wasted his time showing it to a group of critics instead of to advisors who were sympathetic to his ideas.

He answered, "Because my critics help me find the weaknesses in the plan so I can correct them."

In the same way, God uses the judgmental person to reveal our blind spots so we can make the necessary changes. If we truly want to be pleasing to the Lord, we will accept the exposure of our faults so we can correct them, even if the revelation comes from a hateful person.

Third

Don't counter-criticize your critics.

Jefferson Davis, President of the Confederate States of America during the Civil War, once asked Gen. Robert E. Lee to give his opinion of another military officer.

General Lee praised the man and told what a wonderful job he had done.

A man who was present overheard him and said, "General, don't you know that the man of whom you speak so highly is one of your bitterest enemies and misses no opportunity to slander you?"

Lee answered, "Yes, but the President asked my opinion of him. He didn't ask his opinion of me."[3]

When we receive criticism, it's easy to lower ourselves to the critic's level and counter-criticize. David could have had Abishai cut off Shimei's head, but he didn't. Instead of returning insult for insult (1 Pet. 3:9), we must learn to absorb criticisms and false accusations without retaliating.

When Jesus stood before Caiaphas, many false witnesses testified against him (Matt. 26:60). Isn't it interesting that even though Jesus was perfect, they were able to find so many false witnesses? These deceitful people were probably anxiously waiting in line for their turn to slander Jesus and distort the facts. According to Jewish law, it only took two witnesses to make an accusation fly in court. Even then, the witnesses' stories didn't match (Mark 14:59).

Then the high priest asked Jesus to defend himself against the accusers. Jesus didn't say, "Well, let me tell you something. These guys are a bunch of liars! I'm innocent, I tell you! Please believe my side of the story!"

Instead, Jesus kept silent. He didn't defend himself against the false accusations, because no matter how good an argument he had, they would not have received it. Their minds were already made up against him.

Jesus didn't counter-criticize his critics. "He did not revile in return; while suffering, he uttered no threats, but kept entrusting himself to him who judges righteously" (1 Pet. 2:23). He did this as an example for us to follow in his steps (1 Pet. 2:21).

	Don't allow critics to discourage you.
Fourth	

If we know that we are in God's will and have corrected exposed faults, then we must not allow the critics to discourage us. We must continue in the work that the Lord has called us to do.

Christopher Wren, who rebuilt St. Paul's Cathedral and much of London after the Great Fire of 1666, was invited to design a new town hall in Windsor. When he submitted his plans, a member of the town council insisted that the roof required better support and wanted extra pillars added.

Wren, the greatest architect in the region, argued that his planned structure was perfectly safe.

But the politician was adamant and spread alarm throughout the community, pressuring Wren to add the supports.

Many years later, when both the builder and politician were dead, repairs and cleaning were performed on the hall. The workmen were surprised to find that, invisible from the floor below, the extra columns Wren put in were two inches short of touching the roof![4] He knew his building would stand, in spite of what the critics had said. He refused to allow them to shake his confidence in what he knew was true.

Perhaps criticism has discouraged you. It has kept you from doing what you know is true. The bottom line is you must please God, not men. On the Judgment Day, it won't be the critics evaluating your life. It will be God Almighty.

Coping with the Critics

- Ask God what he is trying to teach you through the criticism you are receiving.

- Correct any faults the critics expose.

- Pray for every person who is criticizing you.

CHAPTER 12

When You Are Tired of Waiting
Giving Birth to Ishmael

And after Abram had lived ten years in the land of Canaan, Abram's wife Sarai took Hagar the Egyptian, her maid, and gave her to her husband Abram as his wife. And he went in to Hagar, and she conceived. . . . And Abram was eighty-six years old when Hagar bore Ishmael to him.

(Genesis 16:3–4, 16)

BRAM, WHO IS BETTER known as Abraham, wasn't getting any younger. He was eighty-five years old and had been drawing Social Security for over two decades. Ten years had passed since God first promised him he would have a son, but the stork had still not arrived. He had thought about adopting Eliezer to be his heir, but then God told him his heir would come from his own body (Gen. 15:2–4).

So his wife Sarai, whose name was later changed to Sarah, did what most of us do when we get tired of waiting for God to answer our prayers. She decided to figure out a way to fulfill the promise of God. She went to Abram one day with her handmaiden and said (in so many words), "Abram, God said the heir would come through your body, but he didn't say anything about my body. Let's use Hagar to fulfill God's promise. I've been barren for years, and I'm tired of waiting for the Lord to come through. After all, doesn't God expect us to do our part in fulfilling the promise?"

So Hagar conceived and gave birth to Ishmael. He was such a cute baby. Little did Abram and Sarai know the problems this baby would create in the generations to come. One of Ishmael's descendants was Mohammed, who started the religion of Islam. From that cute, innocent-looking baby, a whole race of people followed who are still fighting the Jewish people in the Middle East.

Whenever we grow impatient and refuse to wait for God's timing, we give birth to another Ishmael. And although our Ishmael looks innocent when he is first born, he will grow up and return to haunt us.

Do you ever get tired of waiting for God to answer your prayers? Waiting can be frustrating. One man had a neighbor with a rooster that crowed three times a day and only three times. The man went to his neighbor and asked him to get rid of it.

The neighbor answered, "He only crows three times a day. Is that too much?"

"No, that isn't too much. But you don't know what I go through waiting to get that third crow over with!"

We are a little like that when we wait for God to answer our prayers. We believe he will send an answer, but it drives us crazy not knowing when it will come.

I would rather chop wood than wait. I worked in a drugstore when I was in high school. When business was slow, I looked at the clock and it read 1:35. An hour later, I looked at it again, and it read 1:45. Ten minutes can seem like an hour when we are waiting.

One afternoon I took my children to the movies. My son Scott, who was seven years old at the time, was anxious for the movie to begin. As the different advertisements appeared on the screen, Scott leaned over and whispered, "Dad, when's the movie going to start?"

"In a few minutes."

One minute later he again asked, "Dad, when is it going to start?"

"In just a little bit."

After he asked the third time, I said, "Scott, don't ask me that question again. Just sit there and wait."

My son, who was a quiet and obedient child, fidgeted and tried to be patient. Finally, he leaned over and whispered a different question. "Dad, can you make time go faster?"

This little boy didn't have any control over when the movie started, but he thought his father could shorten the waiting period by speeding up time. Many times we say to God, "Father, can you make time go faster? I'm so tired of waiting. I'm anxious for my prayer to be answered. Please make it arrive sooner."

Are you trying to talk God into speeding up time? Here are some of the tell-tale symptoms that reveal our impatience.

Symptom # 1	**Trying to help God**

Abram and Sarai tried to help God. He had promised them a son, but there was one problem. He didn't tell them how long they would have to wait.

Abram probably thought, "I only have to wait nine months." So he got out the calendar and marked off the days. Nine months later, Sarai wasn't even showing. Not even a little bulge.

One year passed. Then two. Then five years went by. Eight years, then ten. Abram was eighty-five now, and Sarai was at the ripe old age of seventy-five. After a decade of waiting, it was time to do something. They knew God had promised a son, but it was difficult for them to comprehend how a baby could be born from a barren womb.

They decided God needed a little help in accomplishing this. Hagar offered her help. Abram offered his help. And Sarai reluctantly offered to stand on the sidelines. We always get into trouble when we try to help out God.

Henry was walking down the street when he saw his neighbor Mr. Smith trying to get a washing machine through the door of his house. He went over to the doorway and said, "Here, let me help you."

After thirty minutes of struggling, Henry said to Mr. Smith, "I don't think we'll ever get this washing machine into the house."

Mr. Smith responded, "Get it in? I'm trying to get it out!"

When we try to help God, we often find ourselves struggling against him. We think we are helping, but we are only making things more difficult. Abram and Hagar wound up with a baby named Ishmael as a result of helping out God. We will also end up with an Ishmael in our lives if we don't wait on God's perfect plan and timing.

Overstepping the boundaries

In 1 Samuel 10:8 and 13:8–12, Samuel told Saul to go to Gilgal and wait seven days until he arrived. Then he would sacrifice a burnt offering to the Lord.

Saul waited seven days but thought he couldn't wait any longer. He had some good reasons for not waiting. The Philistines were getting ready to attack, and his own people were deserting him. Rather than wait for Samuel, Saul sacrificed the burnt offering. He overstepped his boundaries as king. He went beyond what he was instructed to do.

As soon as he finished, Samuel arrived. The prophet told him that because he did not wait and disobeyed, God rejected him as king. Saul thought Samuel was going to be late, but in reality Saul was impatient and sacrificed prematurely.

We grow impatient because we think God is late. The reality is that we are just too early. So we overstep our boundaries and do forbidden things, justifying those things in our minds. The Philistines are coming. The people are scattering. Samuel hasn't arrived, so we take matters into our own hands. And we always lose because of it.

An unmarried person can sometimes become impatient while waiting to get married. Many singles are tempted to panic when another birthday passes, and they still haven't tied the marriage knot. The single person may overstep the boundaries and start hunting for a companion in the wrong places, such as singles bars. Often he or she will meet someone who is interested, but for all the wrong reasons. The person the single meets usually isn't a Christian and isn't the mate in God's perfect plan.

If we want God's provision, we must obey his instructions and wait for his timing. That means we need to seek Christian fellowship (2 Cor. 6:14) and patiently wait for him to bring the right person.

My sister-in-law Brenda married when she was eighteen years old and has had a wonderful marriage for nearly twenty years. On the other hand, a Christian man I know had to wait a lot longer for the right person. When people asked him if he ever wanted to get married, he would say, "Yes, but God hasn't shown me the right one yet."

The Lord finally did bring him the right woman, and he got married at age thirty-eight. Both received their spouses in God's perfect timing. One had to wait twenty years longer than the other, but learned to be content until God brought his wife to him. The Lord will always reward those who patiently wait for him to provide.

Symptom #3	**Becoming restless and irritable**

If we don't *rest* in the Lord, we become *restless.* We become impatient with others. We may even be on the verge of panic. We have expected God to fax the answer to our prayer, but he seems to be using the pony express to deliver it to us. We believe God has forgotten about our request or maybe he just doesn't care. This frustration will manifest itself by our irritable behavior.

Single people sometimes become restless and irritated when someone they know gets married. But God has a different timing for everyone's marriage, and the timing for someone else's marriage is not necessarily the perfect timing for yours. The same holds true when we are waiting for an answer to prayer. God will do it in his time. Restlessness occurs when we want God's timetable to match ours, rather than ours matching his.

Why Should We Wait on the Lord?

God does not want us to wait on him because he likes to see us squirm. He has good reasons for us to wait. Satan always puts his best up front so people will grab it quickly. Those who want instant gratification usually don't want to wait for God's provision.

On the other hand, God usually gives his best much later. He is more concerned about us receiving his best rather than when we will get it. It doesn't bother him to let us go through a waiting period before he provides.

Why does he do this? Doesn't he care about the way we feel? Of course he does. But there are several reasons why he wants us to wait.

Reason # 1

We may not be ready for what God has for us.

God uses the waiting period for us to straighten out our priorities so the right ones can rise to the top of our list. Sometimes waiting periods are designed to get *us* ready for what he has planned. If we are not ready, we might not appreciate it at best or even destroy it at worst.

My daughter Hannah was anxious to drive when she was eleven years old. But I couldn't give her my car keys at that age because she wasn't ready. The car was ready for Hannah, but she wasn't ready for the car. Even though she thought she was ready to drive, I knew better. If she had started driving prematurely, she would have certainly been in a wreck and possibly injured. It wasn't until she turned sixteen and completed a driver's training class that I handed her the keys.

Some people are anxious to get married, but they aren't ready. They haven't prepared themselves to be the perfect mates for their spouses-to-be. Their attitudes may be discontentment and complaining, and they haven't made themselves as healthy and attractive as they can be. Perhaps they are irresponsible or in debt financially, and are not ready for the demands of marriage. Marriage will not solve any of these problems. It will only compound them.

An unprepared single person getting married is as dangerous as my daughter driving the car at eleven years old. It's a formula for disaster! If this describes you, don't let your anxiousness to get married blind you to the preparation you need to do. God is waiting for you to get ready for what he has planned.

Reason # 2

What God has planned for us may not be ready.

God may still be in the process of preparing what we are praying for. He may be doing some things "behind the scenes" that we are not aware of. The people, events, and situations involved in God's plan may not yet be in place. We must wait for his timing to bring these things together.

The greatest musicians in the world may come together to play the most beautiful song in the world. But if the musicians' timing is off because they are not watching the conductor, it will be total confusion. Timing can make the difference between something being beautiful or chaotic.

When God's time is right, the people, events, and situations will converge beautifully. "There is an appointed time for everything" (Eccles. 3:1) and "He hath made every thing beautiful in his time" (Eccles. 3:11 KJV).

| *Reason # 3* | **God is using the waiting period to develop patience within us.** |

Patience means "to abide under" or "to stand up under pressure." When you begin exercising on a weight-training program, lifting seventy-five pounds might be difficult at first. You may have to struggle to lift it over your head. But as you continue to work out, you get stronger. You will improve to the point of being able to lift one hundred pounds.

You continue to make progress until you can lift 150 pounds over your head. Now anything under 150 pounds is no longer difficult for you because you have developed the quality of patience. You have developed the ability to "stand up under pressure."

God uses waiting periods to develop patience within us so life can actually become easier. When we wait on the Lord, he will renew our strength (Isa. 40:31). Abraham grew in strength as he waited all those years (Rom. 4:21). Patiently waiting on the Lord will not drain our strength but will renew it.

| *Reason # 4* | **God wants to do a greater miracle for us.** |

In John 11, Jesus arrived at Bethany two days after Lazarus had died. Mary and Martha thought Jesus had made a mistake by not showing up according to their timetable.

If Jesus had arrived sooner, he would have healed Lazarus. By purposely delaying his arrival, he demonstrated an even greater miracle. He raised him from the dead! God's delays are not his denials. Sometimes he wants to do something greater than we expected.

Our church needed to purchase land. We had prayed eleven years for God to show us the right place. The only problem was over that eleven-year period, the price of land was escalating. Every piece of property we looked at, God would close the door. We originally wanted four acres of land, but as the church grew, we looked for eight, then ten. Some land was selling for as much as forty-five thousand dollars per acre, and we couldn't afford to buy ten acres in town.

I prayed, "Lord, I know you have some land for us. Please show us where it is."

God immediately put "Eighth Street" in my mind. At first, I wasn't sure if this was God speaking or my own thoughts. But every time I prayed, "Eighth Street" would pop into my mind. I asked a realtor in our church to check out any property that might be for sale on Eighth Street.

He came back reporting, "A piece of property on Eighth Street just became available this week. People have been trying to buy this land for years, but it hasn't been for sale until now, and we are the first in line. Two land developers also want it, but the owners said they will let us have the first option to buy at a reduced price."

For the eleven years we had been looking for land, this property was not for sale. The moment it opened up, God told us where it was! We now own twenty-two acres, having paid a total of fifty-five thousand dollars. We waited eleven years for God to provide, and he did a much greater miracle than we ever expected.

How Do We Wait on the Lord?

David knew what it was like to wait on the Lord. He penned the following words of wisdom for all of the future generations, instructing us in how to wait:

> Trust in the Lord, and do good; Dwell in the land and cultivate faithfulness. Delight yourself in the Lord; and He will give you the desires of your heart. Commit your way to the Lord, Trust also in Him, and He will do it. . . . Rest in the Lord and wait patiently for Him. (Ps. 37:3–5, 7)

Notice the four things he tells us to do when we are waiting.

- *First, trust in the Lord* no matter what circumstances may look like. He has not forgotten your request, because he is faithful.

- *Second, delight yourself in the Lord.* Have you ever noticed how time flies when you are having fun? Two weeks of vacation seem like two days, while two days of misery seem like two weeks. To delight yourself in the Lord means to find your pleasure in God.

- *Third, commit your way to the Lord.* Jesus committed his spirit into the Father's hands. Committing your way to the Lord means you put your life, your plans, and your future in God's hands.

- *Finally, rest in the Lord* as you patiently wait. Don't worry or fret if everyone else has already received answers to their prayers but you haven't. When you rest, you remove the deadline you have placed on God. All stress is gone. You can't and won't worry when you are resting.

Abraham and Sarah finally lived to see the promised son born. He was one hundred years old, and she was ninety when she gave birth to Isaac. Twenty-five years had passed since God first made the promise to them.

Even though your situation looks impossible, just remember circumstances don't matter to God. Neither does time. All he has to do is speak the word, and it will happen. So don't jump the gun and give birth to another Ishmael. Wait for the Isaac that God has promised for you.

Learning to Wait Patiently

- Place your situation in God's hands, and ask him to handle it.

- Remove the deadline you have placed on God while you wait for his answer.

- Learn to rest in the Lord as you patiently wait.

CHAPTER 13

When You Are Afraid
No Fear!

And when he was entered into a ship, his disciples followed him. And, behold, there arose a great tempest in the sea, insomuch that the ship was covered with the waves: but he was asleep. And his disciples came to him, and awoke him, saying, Lord, save us: we perish. And he saith unto them, Why are ye fearful, O ye of little faith? The he arose, and rebuked the winds and the sea; and there was a great calm.

(Matthew 8:23–26 KJV)

ONE OF THE RECENT fads has been that of wearing No Fear shirts. They are T-shirts with different slogans written on the backs, making a challenge to the person reading them and ending with the words "No Fear." I once went to a clothing store and asked the salesman if he had any *No Fear* shirts.

He pointed to a whole section of shirts hanging on the walls and displayed on circular racks.

As I looked through the the shirts, I wrote some of the sayings on a piece of paper. About fifteen minutes later, the salesman came over and asked, "Uh, could I help you?"

I told him, "No, thank you. I am a pastor and I'm preparing a sermon on fear." The salesman walked away with a bewildered look on his face.

Here are slogans from a few of the shirts:

It must be hard living without a spine. No Fear
Wanna impress me? Step on the Ice. No Fear
It's not whether you win or lose. It's whether I win! No Fear

If you aren't living on the edge, you're taking up too much space. No Fear

You do not greet death, you punch him in the throat repeatedly as he drags you away. No Fear

Then there was the imitation No Fear shirt a friend told me about. He said the shirt had no slogan, just a picture of a pistol with No Fear under it.

When someone proudly displays a No Fear shirt, what is he trying to say? He wants to convince everyone that he's not afraid. Actor Dean Martin once said, "Show me a man who doesn't know the meaning of the word *fear*, and I'll show you a dummy who gets beat up a lot." When we deal with our fears in the wrong way, it's likely we'll get beaten up.

The world deals with fear quite differently from the way a Christian should handle it. The world says you don't have to be afraid because you are one tough dude. But God says you don't need to be afraid because he is with you (Joshua 1:9).

Fear Isn't Logical

Fear isn't logical. If it were, we could talk ourselves out of it. There is no rhyme or reason to fear because it affects people in many different ways. What one person is afraid of, another person isn't.

Some people are tormented when they must fly on an airplane.

In an interview done aboard *Air Force 1*, President Ronald Reagan was asked if he had overcome the fear of flying.

"Overcome it!" he retorted. "I'm holding this plane up by sheer will power."[1]

Heavyweight boxer Carl "The Truth" Williams had a boxing match scheduled in Japan. Because he had a fear of flying, he traveled there via ship. A boxing ring was set up on the ship so he could train for the upcoming fight. "I flew as a young pro and a member of the U.S. Boxing team," he explained. "But even then, I had to get drunk to get on the plane."[2]

Here was a man who was afraid to fly, but not afraid to fight. Most people would be afraid to fight, but not afraid to fly. Because fear isn't logical, it takes something beyond logic to get rid of it.

Fear affects people in different ways because there are different kinds of fears. We can have more than one fear in our lives. In Psalm 34, David said the Lord delivered him from all his fears. When we read Psalms, we find he was afraid of losing his life. Even though David was a man after God's own heart (1 Sam 13:14), he still had to be delivered from fear.

Job was another godly man who experienced fear. He was blameless and upright, fearing God and turning away from evil. Yet after disaster struck, he said the things which he feared the most had come upon him (Job 3:25–26).

What do you fear the most? Are you being controlled and tormented by any of the fears listed below?

- *Fear of the future*: the fear that believes the worst will happen

- *Fear of death*: the fear of your destiny beyond the grave

- *Fear of starvation*: the fear that God will not provide for you

- *Fear of losing your job*: the fear that any day the boss will let you go

- *Fear of not getting married*: the fear that God will not bring a spouse to you

- *Fear of rejection*: the fear that you will not be accepted by someone

- *Fear of failure*: the fear that what you attempt will end in disaster

- *Fear of evil*: the fear that harm will come to you or someone you love

How Fear Affects You

Fear is **F**alse **E**vidence **A**ppearing **R**eal. Most fears are our imaginations out of control. Because fear involves torment (1 John 4:18), it will rob us of our peace and joy. It can also force us to make wrong decisions which keep us from reaching our full potential. Like the man with one talent in Matthew 25:25, fear will cause us to hide our talents and not take any risks.

Until fear is driven from our lives, we will be manipulated by its treacherous control. It will dominate our thinking and dictate to us what we can and cannot do. Faith comes by hearing what God has said (Rom. 10:17), but fear comes by believing what Satan tells us. That's why we must refuse to listen to the dictates of our fears.

In the war of the Rhine in 1794, the French took over an Austrian village without striking a blow. Here is how they did it.

Two companies of French foot soldiers were ordered to attack the Austrian village at ten o'clock at night. The six hundred Austrian soldiers who were guarding the city found out about the surprise attack and prepared to defend their village. Communication was to be relayed to the Austrian troops through a trumpeter who would signal when the French attacked.

Little did they know the French had sent their trumpeter, Joseph Werck, under the cover of darkness, to take his position among the Austrian soldiers. At ten o'clock, Werck blew his trumpet for the Austrian soldiers to rally, and then he sounded retreat a few moments later. The Austrian soldiers immediately rallied together, then retreated from the battle, allowing the French to capture the village without any opposition![3]

Just as the Austrians were defeated by listening to the deceptive command of the French trumpet, we can be defeated by following Satan's fearful orders. He cannot overcome the child of God (1 John 4:4), so the only way he can defeat a Christian is to get us to defeat ourselves. Fear is his trumpet sound, commanding us to retreat.

Satan blows his trumpet, and a man loses his confidence and runs from responsibility. He blows it again, and a young woman worries, while an elderly woman is gripped with the fear of being robbed. He sounds it a third time, and a lonely child is seized with terror. He tries to control everyone in the world with his trumpet. Everyone, that is, who is willing to listen.

How to Deal with Fear

You don't have to listen to Satan's trumpet. Here are a few ways to turn a deaf ear to it.

First

Seek the presence of the Lord and trust him.

In Psalm 34:4, David said, "I sought the Lord, and He answered me, and delivered me from all my fears." Psalm 23:4 says, "I fear no evil; for Thou art with me." God told Joshua that he did not have to fear because "the Lord your God is with you wherever you go" (Josh. 1:9).

When we are afraid, we want a secure presence with us. One elderly woman was waiting for a bus in a crime-ridden area when a rookie policeman approached her and asked, "Would you like me to wait with you?"

She answered, "No, thank you. I'm not afraid."

The policeman responded, "Well, I am. Could I wait with you?"

Having the presence of someone with us can help us when we are afraid. When we become aware of the presence of God with us, our fears will leave.

Because the perfect love of God casts out all fear, the one who is afraid has not been perfected in love (1 John 4:18). The disciples were afraid during the storm on the Sea of Galilee because they had a selfish love. Their own safety and survival were their primary concerns. They didn't seem to care that the Messiah was also in the boat and that his life could be in danger. So they cried out, "Save us, Lord; we are perishing!"

Even though the Lord was in the boat, their selfishness blinded them to the fact God was with them. They didn't realize that Jesus' presence on board was enough to guarantee their own protection. The Father would not allow Jesus to sink to the bottom of the Sea of Galilee when it was predetermined that he would die on the cross for the sins of the world (Acts 2:23). Jesus was so assured the Father was in control of the storm that he slept through it.

After the disciples woke him, Jesus asked, "Why are you fearful, O ye of little faith?" Fear had filled the void where faith should have been. Faith and fear cannot coexist together. To overcome fear, we must fill the void with faith. When we are full of faith, then we have No Fear.

Jesus then spoke to the winds and the sea, and they became perfectly calm (v. 26). The disciples were amazed that he could control the storm. He had demonstrated to them he was in charge, whether he was sleeping or awake.

We must also understand he is in control of the storms that come our way. The lesson God wants us to learn is not how to speak to the wind but how to sleep through the storm. If God does not calm the storm we are going through, he will calm us in the midst of the storm.

Whenever we are gripped by fear, we must decide to put our faith in God. "When I am afraid, I will put my trust in Thee" (Ps. 56:3). We also need to believe God not only cares for us but that he controls every storm we encounter.

| | **Face up to your problem.** |
| *Second* | |

I once knew a lady who was terrified of flying. She would fly out of necessity, but would never look out a window. The fear of flying kept her in torment.

On one of her flights, she was almost in a state of panic. She resolved to do something she had never done before, to look out the window. As she opened her eyes and leaned over to peep out, something happened when she viewed the clouds and mountains. She later told me, "It was so beautiful out there! I never realized what I had missed all those years by not looking out the window."

She overcame her fear by facing up to what frightened her. Fear is like a bully that challenges everyone to fight him. But whenever someone stands up to him, he backs down. Because fear tries to intimidate people into running away, we can only overcome it by standing up and calling its bluff.

| | **Stand on God's promises.** |
| *Third* | |

Most fears are direct challenges to what God has promised in his Word. We have a choice of whether we are going to live in fear or believe God's Word. David chose to believe what God had said: "I fear no evil; for Thou art with me" (Ps. 23:4). "You will not be afraid of the terror by night, or of the arrow that flies by day" (Ps. 91:5).

I once went on an overnight camp-out at a nearby lake with a couple of elders in our church. Before we left, we failed to check the weather report. We were having a great time of fellowship at sunset when we noticed the clouds grew very dark and the wind blew.

Within minutes, we were in the middle of a terrible storm. The rain poured heavily with winds blowing forty to forty-five miles an hour. Lightning struck within yards of us every few seconds. Psalm 91:5 refers to the "terror by night." This was it! The pup tent where we were huddled together offered zero protection.

For a few moments, I thought we had a good chance of making pages one and two of our local newspaper (the headlines and obituary). "Local Pastor, Elders Struck by Lightning, see Obituary page A2." Fear overtook us as we realized that we might never see our families again. I had never experienced a situation where I was this close to dying.

Then the Lord reminded me of the disciples in the boat when the terrible storm hit. We were acting just like the disciples did when they woke up Jesus and shouted to him they were about to die. They didn't believe God was in control of the storm. And now that we were in the same boat, neither did we! We were looking at the storm rather than trusting in his sovereignty.

I told the other men the disciples must have felt this way during the storm on the Sea of Galilee. I asked, "Are we going to trust God to protect us or not? He knows whether this is the time we're supposed to die."

A supernatural peace came over us, even though lightning was striking within yards of our tent. We rejoiced through the rest of the storm as we realized God's presence with us. When the storm had passed, we had learned through personal experience something we had only known in theory before. Many different kinds of storms will come our way, but if we will simply put our trust in God, we will have No Fear!

Facing Your Fears

- Make a list of your fears.

- Create an awareness of God's presence, and allow him to fulfill his promises to you.

- Pray about different ways to exercise your faith over your fears.

- Read chapter 8, "When You Need to Make a Change" and chapter 23, "When You Are Afraid of Dying."

CHAPTER 14

When You Need to Make a Decision
The Deciding Factor

"For I know the plans that I have for you," declares the Lord, "plans for welfare and not for calamity to give you a future and a hope. . . . And you will seek Me and find Me, when you search for Me with all your heart."

(Jeremiah 29:11, 13)

ORMER PRESIDENT RONALD REAGAN says he learned the need for decision-making early in life. An aunt had taken him to a cobbler to have a pair of shoes made for him. The shoemaker asked young Reagan, "Do you want a square toe or a round toe?"

Reagan hemmed and hawed.

So the cobbler said, "Come back in a day or two, and let me know what you want."

A few days later, the shoemaker saw Reagan on the street and asked what he had decided about the shoes.

"I still haven't made up my mind," the boy answered.

"Very well," said the cobbler.

When Reagan received the shoes, he was shocked to see that one shoe had a square toe and the other a round toe.

"Looking at those shoes every day taught me a lesson," said Reagan years later. "If you don't make your own decisions, somebody else will make them for you!"[1]

God wants to help us make the right decisions. To find his will, we must obey what he tells us to do.

Where there is a will, there is also a won't. We usually want to obey the parts of God's will we like. For the parts we don't like, we pray, "Thy will be changed" rather than "Thy will be done." In order to make the right choices, we must believe he has the very best planned for us.

God's will isn't revealed as a blueprint we see all at once, but as a scroll that is unrolled a little at a time. He does this so we will learn to trust him day by day. Jesus told his disciples, "I have many more things to say to you, but you cannot bear them now" (John 16:12). Because he loves us so much, he doesn't disclose any more than we can handle. He reveals his will one step at a time through the decisions we make every day.

Because God speaks in various ways, it would be wise for us to examine the different ways he has spoken to his people because he will probably choose similar ways to speak to us. Several guidelines need to be considered when making a decision. Different ones will apply to various situations you encounter, so you must choose those that best fit your circumstances.

Guideline # 1	**Consult God's Word.**

Forever, O Lord, thy word is settled in heaven. . . . Thy word is a lamp to my feet and a light to my path. . . . Thy word is truth. (Ps. 119:89, 105; John 17:17)

When we come to a crossroad in our lives, we must decide which road to take. In the movie *The Wizard of Oz*, Dorothy followed the yellow brick road easily until she came to a crossroads. Then she didn't know which way to go because the road split in several directions. A scarecrow in the cornfield next to the road offered his advice. The only problem was—he didn't have a brain!

What do we do when there is no more yellow brick road to follow? Anytime we come to a crossroads, we need something to point us in the right direction.

The Bible is the first place we must go to find the direction we need. It is the clearest revelation we have of God's will; therefore, it is the most important. God has already spoken to us concerning his will in many areas. His Word speaks to us concerning salvation, morality, marriage, divorce, attitudes, and numerous other topics. It also gives examples of how others made decisions and what happened as a result. The decisions we make should never contradict God's Word. Therefore, all of the following guidelines are based upon Scripture.

Guideline # 2	**Pray for God's wisdom.**

But if any of you lacks wisdom, let him ask of God, who gives to all men generously and without reproach, and it will be given to him. But let him ask in faith without any doubting, for the one who doubts is like the surf of the sea driven and tossed by the wind. For let not that man expect that he will receive anything from the Lord. (James 1:5–7)

If we need wisdom, we should ask God. God always knows what to do when we don't. If we don't understand that principle, we'll panic and try to figure out what to do on our own. This verse says when we ask for wisdom, God gives it generously every time to everyone.

Why, then, does it seem like he sometimes doesn't answer? Because people doubt that he will answer. The problem is not on the giving end; it is on the receiving end: "who gives to all men generously. . . . For let not that man expect that he will receive anything from the Lord." The problem is not in the shipping department. It's in the receiving department.

Your local radio station is sending out radio signals right now. You don't hear anything because you need a radio to pick up the signals. The station gives out the signals, while the radio receives them.

Two things are involved in receiving God's wisdom signals:

First, we must have a radio. The Holy Spirit who indwells all believers acts as the radio receiver within us. He is the one who knows the thoughts of God. "For who among men knows the thoughts of a man except the spirit of the man, which is in him? Even so the thoughts of God no one knows except the Spirit of God. Now we have received, not the spirit of the world, but the Spirit who is from God, that we might know the things freely given to us by God" (1 Cor. 2:11–12).

Second, we must listen by turning to the right station. We must "tune in" to what God is saying. We can't keep turning the dial every two seconds because we don't hear anything. When we pray for wisdom and thoughts enter our minds, we shouldn't dismiss them as being our own. God will speak his wisdom as thoughts and ideas in our minds. But if we doubt that he will speak to us, we won't receive anything from the Lord.

| *Guideline # 3* | **Gain insight through wise counselors.** |

For by wise guidance you will wage war, and in the abundance of counselors there is victory. (Prov. 24:6)

Sometimes we should seek advice from other people. We don't need to ask advice on every decision, but we do on major decisions. Waging war falls into the category of major decision-making. It would not be wise to choose our friends to be our advisors simply because we like them. Our counselors need to be qualified before they should be allowed to advise us.

Here are suggestions on how you can select qualified people as your advisors.

Choose godly counselors.
How blessed is the man who does not walk in the counsel of the wicked. (Psalm 1:1)

It is extremely important that our advisors love God and have a relationship with him. This will be evidenced by good fruit in their lives. Godly counselors are stable examples of godly living. They put into practice what they preach and have a track record of making good decisions. More than likely other people have gone to them for advice; ask those people if they received good counsel. If the counselors meet these criteria, they will be able to hear God's voice and confirm what he has been speaking to you.

Choose wise and knowledgeable counselors.
> For by wise guidance you will wage war. (Prov. 24:6)

An advisor should not be the nearest warm body that has an opinion. We must choose someone with knowledge concerning the problem we are dealing with. It will help if that person is experienced and has already traveled down the road we are about to walk.

If you were about to wage war, which Norm would you choose to advise you—Gen. Norm Schwarzkopf, who led the troops to victory in the Persian Gulf war? Or Norm Abrams, the carpenter on the television show *This Old House?* Norm Schwarzkopf, of course. But if you wanted to remodel your house, you would choose Norm Abrams. Your counselor should be knowledgeable and experienced in his field of expertise.

Choose caring counselors.
> Faithful are the wounds of a friend, but deceitful are the kisses of an enemy. (Prov. 27:6)

The wounds of a friend are those truthful statements that may hurt, but we need to hear them. The kisses of an enemy are insincere and deceitful statements that point us down the road of destruction. Some people don't want to see us succeed. Others like to hand out advice, but aren't concerned about the consequences if we follow their counsel. We must choose people to advise us who truly care about what happens to us down the road.

I once had to make a decision concerning the direction of our church and decided I needed some counsel. Although I didn't know him very well, I went to a Christian man outside of our church who had counseled many churches. When I explained our situation, this man became upset and condescending. I could sense he felt threatened by the decision we were trying to make, and God made it clear we shouldn't follow this man's advice. He wasn't a caring counselor.

On the other hand, on several occasions I have gone to a pastor friend in town who has always given me excellent advice. He doesn't feel threatened by our church because he is interested in expanding the kingdom of God. He's a caring counselor whom I can trust. What a difference in attitude between these two men!

Choose a multitude of counselors.
> In abundance of counselors there is victory. (Prov. 24:6)

We should select our multitude of counselors after they have met the above qualifications. That means we must exclude many people who want to tell us what to do.

Two bums, both broke and destitute, were sitting on a park bench. One said, "I'm a man who never took advice from anybody."

The other bum said, "Shake, old buddy. I'm a man who followed everybody's advice!" If we are not selective in choosing our counselors, it will lead to our ruin.

After our counselors have been qualified, we should pick several to advise us. One counselor might see one area clearly, but another will see something different from another angle. We won't be able to understand the complete picture until we view it from all angles. The purpose for the multitude of counselors is not to get a popular-opinion poll but to receive a greater variety of wisdom. Although we may receive counsel from several people, we must remember that the final decision is our responsibility, not theirs.

| Guideline # 4 | **God will speak to your heart.** |

When we ask Jesus to save us, he enters in and dwells in our hearts (Eph. 3:17). He can now direct us from inside and lead us into his will in two ways:

First, he will put desires in your heart.
> Delight yourself in the Lord; and He will give you the desires of your heart. (Ps. 37:4)

He will put the desires in our hearts to want what he wants. This doesn't mean that everything we want is his will. It means when we are submitted to doing his will, he will prompt our heart, our "wanter," in the direction we should go.

Eight years after Cindy and I bought our first house, we had a desire to buy a larger one. We made a list of everything we wanted in a house and asked God if he wanted us to move, to show us one with everything on our list. If we couldn't find the house, we would be content to stay where we were.

After looking for several weeks at every house on the market, we couldn't find a single one that matched the desires of our hearts. So we thanked God for the home we were in and gave up our search.

Not long after we stopped looking, I received a business call from a lady in town, whom I didn't know. During the course of our conversation I asked where she lived. When she told me, I said, "I'd love to live in that neighborhood."

She said, "I wish someone would buy the house next door to us. The owner lives in Oklahoma, and renters are in the house. Although it's not listed on the market, he's wanting to sell."

We made an appointment to see the house. It was the only one in town that had everything on our list. It was also the lowest priced out of all we had seen. After going through the normal channels of house hunting and coming up with nothing, God directed us to our new home through a random phone call. And it all began with a desire he put in our hearts.

Second, he will put peace in your heart.
        Let the peace of Christ rule in your hearts. (Col. 3:15)

If we have no peace in our hearts, God may be saying that what we are asking for is not in his will, or we may simply need to have some of our questions answered. Once we have received the answers, peace should come. If we still have no peace after receiving the answers, our decision is probably not his will or the timing is wrong.

It is not wise to make decisions if we are experiencing turmoil inside our hearts. This lack of peace may be the Holy Spirit warning us that what we are desiring isn't right for us. On numerous occasions, I was about to make a decision, but the lack of peace in my heart kept me from doing it. I have learned not to make decisions if my heart is unsettled. The peace of God in our hearts will point us to the things that are in His will.

| Guideline #5 | **God may speak through a sign.** |

A "sign from God" is when he does something in an unusual way to confirm his will. He gave signs to Moses, Hezekiah, Gideon, and others. Signs can be divided into two categories: those God initiates and those we ask for.

Remember in chapter 12 when I prayed for land for our church and God put "Eighth Street" in my mind? I asked a realtor in our church to find out what was available on that street and bring back a report to our board.

During the meantime, I drove there and spotted some property on the north end of the street on the east side, which I assumed was the property that might be available. A few days later, a man in my church told me he saw in a dream that our new building was going to be built on Eighth Street.

I was surprised to hear this, because no one in the church knew we were looking there. I asked him, "Was the property you saw at the north end of Eighth Street on the east side?"

He answered, "No, it was south of the property on the west side."

When the realtor came back with his report, the land available was the exact location the man had seen in his dream! We wouldn't have bought this property just on the basis of his dream alone, but God had given him the dream as a sign of confirmation to our board. This was a sign we hadn't asked for, but one which God initiated.

A word of caution here. Generally speaking, most dreams are not God revealing something to us. But from time to time, he does use this avenue to confirm what he has revealed through the other guidelines mentioned in this chapter.

Another kind of sign is one we ask for. Gideon wanted to know if it was God's will to go to battle, so he put a fleece of wool on the threshing floor. He asked the Lord to confirm his will by making the morning dew to be on the fleece and for the ground around it to remain dry. The next night, he asked for the opposite to happen, for the fleece to remain dry and for the dew to be on the ground (Judg. 6:36–40). God answered both of his requests.

Although it may be comforting to have a sure statement like this concerning God's will, signs are often followed by a severe testing of faith. Gideon had to go to battle against the Midianites with his army whittled down to three hundred men. If we ask God for a sign, we must be prepared to have our faith tested.

What I am about to tell you, I wouldn't advise. But it's true (Kids, don't try this at home!). When I first met Cindy, I asked God if she were going to be my wife. I believed he told me yes, and I wanted him to confirm this by giving me a sign. I prayed, "Lord, if Cindy is supposed to be my wife, I'm going to put my finger down in the Bible, and I'm asking you to speak to me through that verse."

I closed my eyes, randomly flipped open my Bible, and put my finger on Genesis 29:19 (KJV), "It is better that I give her to thee, than that I should give her to another man." If God were going to speak to me through a verse, that would be the perfect one. I thanked him for showing me his will. You may call it a coincidence, but I call it a sign from God.

Several months after this, my faith underwent a severe test. Our relationship fell apart and we went our separate ways. Circumstances told me that we weren't meant for each other and we would never get married. But I couldn't forget the verse I had put my finger on. I had asked God to reveal and confirm his will, which he had done. He had given me the sign because he knew I needed to know his will regardless of how circumstances appeared.

God used the time of separation to refine our faith and bring us closer to him. Then he brought us back together, and our relationship became even better than before. Oh, and by the way, we have been happily married for over twenty years.

Just because we ask for signs, that doesn't mean he will give them (Matt. 12:38–39). Some people continually ask God for signs so they will know what to do. Becoming dependent upon signs before doing God's will is dangerous (1 Cor. 1:22). Although he may give signs, don't let this be the only factor you consider in making a decision.

| Guideline # 6 | **Look for open and closed doors.** |

He who is holy, who is true, who has the key of David, who opens and no one will shut, and who shuts and no one opens, says this: "I know your deeds. Behold, I have put before you an open door which no one can shut." (Rev. 3:7–8)

It's always easier to choose between two open doors than it is to wait when no doors of opportunity are open. When doors are closed, we need to keep knocking as we patiently wait. One thing is certain: if we are willing to do God's will, he will open the doors that need to be opened. He has the ability to open doors for us that no one can shut. To protect us, he also has the ability to close doors so we won't go through them.

Just because a door is open doesn't mean we are to go running through it. Not every open door is God's will for us to go through. Many times a door we desire to walk through is closed, but God will open it later. We must let the Holy Spirit lead us through the right doors in his timing.

| Guideline # 7 | **Gather all the facts about the decision.** |

"For which one of you, when he wants to build a tower, does not first sit down and calculate the cost, to see if he has enough to complete it?" (Luke 14:28)

It sounds pretty obvious that we should gather all of the facts before we make a decision, but you would be surprised how many people don't do this. Some people think it is a lack of faith to see if we can afford the item before we purchase it. But Jesus is the one who told us to do this. Here's what he said to do:

Sit down.

He didn't say, "First, rush to do it while you are still on an emotional high." He told us to first sit down because people can get excited about building something. Adrenaline and emotions can eliminate common sense (which is not too common nowadays). Many people become very excited about buying a new car without thinking about the payments, taxes, and insurance. Soon after the purchase, the emotions settle down, but the constant reminder of the payments every month puts the owners in financial bondage. Sitting down settles our emotions so we can think clearly.

Calculate the cost.

Get out a calculator, a pencil, and a piece of paper, because we need to do some figuring. Do we have enough resources to finish the job? If we don't, then we shouldn't start. Either it shouldn't be done, or should be done at a later time. Decisions should not be based upon the amount of our excitement but on the amount of our resources.

If we don't have adequate means, the job will not be completed. Should we get into insurmountable debt to finish the project? No! "Otherwise, when he has laid a foundation, and is not able to finish, all who observe it begin to ridicule him." (Luke 14:29). The man shouldn't have tried to build the tower to begin with.

"Counting the cost" means:

- Do all your homework before the decision is made.

- Collect all information about the decision.

- Explore all possible avenues and options.

- Look at the situation from every angle.

- Consider all possible outcomes of the decision.

- Leave no stone unturned. Check out everything.

If we do all of these things, we will be able to evaluate the long-term big picture rather than how the situation looks at the present moment. It will also keep us from being unpleasantly surprised after the decision is made.

If you are thinking about moving to another city, have you counted the cost? Many people make a major move because one factor is appealing. Perhaps the scenery is beautiful or living closer to a family member is convenient. Lot decided to move his family to Sodom because the valley looked green from a distance (Gen. 13:10–11). He made a major decision based upon just one factor, rather than considering all the things involved.

He should have made a visit to the city first to see what kind of people lived there. If he had done that, he would have known it was not the place where God wanted him to be. Many people decide to move to another city in the same way that Lot chose Sodom: "It sure is pretty there!" That's not a good enough reason to move.

If you are going to move, are you and your spouse in agreement? Have you checked out the job situation? Have you talked to the person who left the job you are about to take? Why did he or she leave the job? What are the churches like? How about the schools? Are they good or filled with problems? Are the people friendly? What is the crime rate? What is the unemployment rate? How much do houses cost? What is the cost of living? If you don't get answers to these questions before you move, you will find out the answers after you move. And then it's too late.

Counting the cost means you take inventory of what you are giving up versus what you will receive. Every decision is an exchange: what you have, for what you will get. You are sacrificing one thing to receive something else. That's why you need to list the advantages and disadvantages of both situations. Assign a value to each item. Don't forget to include all those things you take for granted. It is so easy to overlook them when you take inventory, but you will surely miss them when they are gone. Esau took his birthright for granted, gave it up, but later cried trying to get it back. Here is an example on how to list the advantages and disadvantages of two situations:

My situation now		*Place where I want to move*	
+3	great church family	?	unsure of church
+3	Christian school	-2	bad schools
+2	nice house	+4	larger house
+1	low payments	-1	higher house payments
+1	good salary	+2	salary increase
-1	little chance for promotion	+1	chance for promotions
0	normal cost of living	0	normal cost of living
?	other factors	?	other factors
total 9		4	

According to this incomplete chart, it is better to stay in your situation than move. However, the church situation and other factors can change the reading on the chart. For example, a good church (+3) where you want to move could change the total from 4 to 7. I am convinced that finding a good church needs to be a high priority in making a move. I have seen too many families destroyed by moving to a good job but never being able to find a good church. As a result, their spiritual lives dry up, causing problems for them in other ways as well.

"Other factors," which is left blank, can also change the reading. Friendships, conveniences, social life, and other things also need to have an assigned value. Only you will be able to assess these.

This chart is only one guideline when making a decision. It helps you to clearly evaluate what you are exchanging so you know what you are giving up and what you are receiving in return. However, if God should clearly reveal to make a change, you need to do so regardless of what the chart reads. You simply need to understand you are going to make sacrifices in order to do God's will.

Guideline # 8	**Be sensitive to God's timing.**
	He has made everything appropriate in its time. (Eccles. 3:11)

God has a plan, but he also has a timing. In making decisions, there are two reasons why people miss God's timing. Some people decide too quickly, while others wait too long.

> I will instruct you and teach you in the way which you should go; I will counsel you with My eye upon you. Do not be as the horse or as the mule which have no understanding, whose trappings include bit and bridle to hold them in check. (Ps. 32:8–9)

Because the horse runs ahead, the bit and bridle is used to slow him down. The mule, on the other hand, is so stubborn that the bit and bridle is used to pull him. The person who runs ahead of God can be compared to the horse, while the person who delays in making a decision is like a mule. Both will miss God's timing.

Esau was like the horse because he decided too quickly to sell his birthright. If he had waited two days in making the decision, he would not have done it. Felix the governor, on the other hand, was like the mule because he took too long to decide. Paul told him about Jesus, but Felix became frightened and responded, "Go away for the present, and when I find time, I will summon you." Felix left Paul imprisoned for two more years (Acts 24:24–27). There comes a time when we must decide to decide.

Guideline # 9	**Begin to make plans in the direction you are being led.**

The mind of man plans his way, but the Lord directs his steps. (Prov. 16:9)

Do you remember the incident in *Alice in Wonderland* where Alice is talking to the Cheshire cat perched in a tree? Alice is confused about her direction. She asks the cat, "Would you tell me, please, which way I ought to go from here?"

"That depends a great deal on where you want to go," replies the Cheshire cat.

"I don't much care where," says Alice.

"Then it doesn't matter which way you go."[2]

If we don't care which way we go, then we don't need to make any plans. But God's Word says that it does matter, and we are to plan. Notice the two elements mentioned in the verse—our part and God's part. Our responsibility is to make the plans. God's responsibility is to direct our steps.

How do we begin making plans? "Commit your works to the Lord, and your plans will be established" (Prov. 16:3). If we put our works in God's hands, he will lead us in making our plans. But we shouldn't plan until after we have gathered all of the information concerning the decision and have received the green light.

If God's going to direct our steps, why plan? Here are some reasons.

Plans give you direction.

When we plan the way, the Lord will direct our steps. He gives our plans direction. A powerful railroad train has the ability to carry a lot of cargo and people, but it can't do anything without the railroad tracks. The tracks give the train direction, and they always lead to a destination. Tracks are nothing more than plans to direct the train.

If you were to enroll in college and major in civil engineering, the college has planned the courses you must take to receive the degree. The courses are the "tracks" to point you in the right direction.

Plans keep you from getting diverted.

By taking the required courses to get a civil-engineering degree, you have eliminated all the other courses being offered at the college. Whenever we make plans, the options are narrowed down to one direction. Once we eliminate all other avenues, we can concentrate and become focused. The plans will keep us from getting diverted or sidetracked to other roads.

Plans help you reach your destination.

The college planned the courses you needed for four years in order to receive your degree. Once you have passed all of them, you have reached your goal of becoming a civil engineer. But what if the college hadn't told you which courses they required for the degree? You would have wandered aimlessly through, trying to guess which were the correct courses. You could spend your whole life in college and never graduate!

Imagine going on a cruise to an island. After you have been out on the ocean for a week, you say to the captain, "It sure seems like we should have arrived by now. When do we plan to arrive?"

The captain answers, "Plans? I don't make plans. I just trust God to guide the boat through the wind and waves to the right destination."

That sounds ridiculous, but many people drift through life in the same way. They make no plans, yet believe they will reach their destination on time.

If we fail to plan, we plan to fail. Making plans will cause us to act rather than react. Without plans, we will bounce around like a ball in a pinball machine, merely reacting to every circumstance until we finally run out of energy. If we travel through life in this manner, we will never reach our destination.

Guideline # 10

Walk in the light you have.

Thy word is a lamp to my feet, and a light to my path. (Ps. 119:105)

When God directs us, he will shine light on the right path. Sometimes the light is bright, but at other times it is dim. We must walk in the light we have, even if it is only a flicker. We may have only enough light to take one step, but if we will take that step, God will give us enough light to take the next one.

A father was teaching his daughter to drive. Before they got into the car, the daughter asked the father numerous questions about what to do in specific situations. She became annoyed when he couldn't answer her questions.

"If you will start driving the car, I will instruct you as you go," he said. "But I really can't instruct you in a way you'll understand until you start driving down the road!"

In the same way, our heavenly Father says, "I will instruct you and teach you in the way which you should go" (Ps. 32:8). If we walk in the light we have, then God will instruct us step-by-step down the road.

Guideline # 11

God may lead without you knowing it.

Sometimes we get the idea that God can't lead people without them knowing they are being led. But a careful examination of the Scriptures reveals this is not the case. These people were led by God without their knowing it:

- Abraham's servant was led to Rebekah (Gen. 24:1–24).

- Saul was looking for lost donkeys and found Samuel (1 Sam. 9:3–20).

- Abraham didn't know where he was going, but God led him to the promised land (Heb. 11:8).

- The four lepers were led to the enemy's camp (2 Kings 7:4–8).

- The Ethiopian eunuch was led to a desert road to meet Philip (Acts 8:26–39).

This is very important to remember: *Many times God will lead us to places through his sovereignty, and we will not be aware that he is leading us.* If God can lead people who are not seeking him (like Saul), then won't he lead his own children who are seeking him? We must learn to rest in his sovereignty. He is ruling the universe and in control. Our responsibility is to seek first the kingdom of God and his righteousness (Matt. 6:33), and he will take care of the rest.

Guideline # 12	**Make your decision, and don't look back.**

"No one, after putting his hand to the plow and looking back, is fit for the kingdom of God." (Luke 9:62)

Once we start walking in the direction of the decision we have made, it is important that we not look back. We must examine all avenues *before* we make the decision. We have to do our questioning before we decide. But once we decide, we are not to think about it anymore.

Don't continue to question yourself as to whether or not you have made the correct decision. Instead, pray, "Lord, I believe that you are leading me in this decision, and I am trusting you to direct me every step of the way."

Jesus clearly instructed us in Luke 17:32 to not look back when he said, "Remember Lot's wife." She is remembered for only one thing. As she was leaving Sodom when God was judging the city, she looked back after being warned not to. She did so because her heart wasn't totally in her decision. Even as she left, a part of her was still in Sodom. It is important, after making a decision, that we not leave a part of our heart in what we are leaving behind. We must commit to our decision with our whole heart.

Whenever we make a decision, we have chosen to give up one thing to get something else. It will help us to remember that whatever we receive in the exchange will also have its problems.

When Israel was set free from Egyptian bondage, they were glad to be set free from slavery. They exchanged the bondage in Egypt for freedom in the wilderness. But when things got rough, some wanted to go back to Egyptian bondage. They had left a part of their hearts in Egypt, and that part was calling them to return when things became uncomfortable. They had made the same mistake as Lot's wife by looking back instead of looking forward.

If God leads you to make a decision, then don't look back to your previous situation. Close the back door of your mind. Looking back and doubting yourself will only cause problems after you have already made the correct decision. Spend your time looking forward to the good things God has planned for you.

Deciding to Decide

- What decisions have you been putting off that you need to make?

- When making major decisions, follow the principles outlined in this chapter.

- Close the back door of your mind on past decisions.

- Read chapter 8, "When You Need to Make a Change."

CHAPTER 15

When You Feel Like Complaining
The Empty-Net Syndrome

Now it came about that while the multitude were pressing around Him and listening to the word of God, He was standing by the lake of Gennesaret; and He saw two boats lying at the edge of the lake; but the fishermen had gotten out of them, and were washing their nets. And He got into one of the boats, which was Simon's, and asked him to put out a little way from the land. And He sat down and began teaching the multitudes from the boat. And when He had finished speaking, He said to Simon, "Put out into the deep water and let down your nets for a catch." And Simon answered and said, "Master, we worked hard all night and caught nothing, but at Your bidding I will let down the nets."

(Luke 5:1–5)

SIMON PETER HAD BECOME a victim of the Empty-Net Syndrome. The Empty-Nest Syndrome occurs when the last child leaves home, the parents are left alone, and the "nest" is empty. The Empty-Net Syndrome occurs when you've fished all night long on the Sea of Galilee and have returned to the dock with empty nets.

Simon had worked hard that night but had nothing to show for it. No fish in his nets meant no money in his pocket. Although he wouldn't admit it, he was angry at God. After all, shouldn't he have caused the fish to be there to catch? Isn't he supposed to reward patience and hard work? So how do you explain the empty nets?

What Simon Peter failed to realize was that God had purposely kept the fish from entering the nets that night. Believe it or not, it was his will for the nets to be empty. God had divinely ordained empty nets in order to accomplish a much greater purpose in Peter's life. As a matter of fact, if the nets had been full that day, the course of history would have been changed—in the wrong direction!

How could an apparent failure possibly be in God's will? Well, let's think about what would have happened if their nets had been full instead of empty.

If they had netted a huge catch that day:

- They would have missed meeting Jesus. They would have been too busy unloading their fish to take to the marketplace.

- Their boats would not have been available for Jesus to preach from. Jesus wanted to use a boat to preach to the multitudes on the shore so more could hear his words. There's no telling how many lives were changed who heard him speak that day.

- There would have been no need to have the miracle Jesus performed. "We already caught our fish, Jesus. We don't need you to provide for us."

- Peter might have continued to fish for fish instead of fishing for men.

No, it clearly was God's will for them not to catch any fish that day.

God has plans for our empty-net days too. We probably won't understand why we have not been successful. We will not be able to see any good reason for it. No voice from heaven will be heard to explain why our work has not been rewarded.

So how are we going to view those days? Will we see them as being God's will, just like the days when our nets are full? Or are we going to complain about not getting our catch?

God is testing us on empty-net days to see how we will respond. We can choose to either be an *optimist* or a *pessimist*. Let's suppose an optimist and a pessimist were helping Simon that day. Both view the same circumstances but have different responses. Which one can you identify more closely with? For the next few pages, let's take a look at the odd couple in action after the nets come up empty.

The pessimist says: *"We wasted the day because we didn't catch anything."*
The optimist says: *"God had a reason why we didn't catch anything."*

When the nets come in empty, we scratch our heads and wonder why. We need to realize God has reasons that aren't always obvious.

Charles Francis Adams, Abraham Lincoln's ambassador to Great Britain, kept a diary during his lifetime. One day he wrote, "Went fishing with my son. A day wasted."

His son Brooks Adams also kept a diary. His note concerning the same day when he was eight years old said, "Went fishing with my father; the most glorious day of my life!" Through the next forty years Brooks made constant references in his diary concerning that special day and the influence it had on him.[1]

So was it a wasted day? They made no references as to how many fish they caught. God's purpose for that day was not to catch fish, but for a father to spend time with his son. The father had missed it. He didn't seize the opportunity of the moment. He couldn't see what God had planned for that day.

When you have an empty net, do you look for God's purpose? Sometimes there is a divine purpose for the things that don't happen.

The pessimist says: *"The fish aren't out there. It won't do any good."*
The optimist says: *"I will trust and obey, though I don't understand."*

"Put out into the deep water and let down your nets for a catch."
(Luke 5:4)

These fishermen were exhausted and ready to go home and sleep. They had just returned from ten to twelve hours of throwing out those same nets and pulling them in, throwing them out and pulling them in. They hadn't even caught a minnow. And then after they had finished washing out the nets, a stranger tells them to go back and throw out their nets again.

The pessimist says, "Again? Go out after we have been out all night? We haven't been back thirty minutes, and he wants us to go again. If this stranger knew what he was talking about, why didn't he tell us to go back out before we washed the nets?"

The optimist says, "What does this mysterious stranger know that I don't? I listened to him speak from the boat as I was washing my nets. His words penetrated my heart. He was speaking with an authority I never heard before. And even though hundreds, maybe thousands of people were present, it was as if he were only speaking to me."

So with the optimist and the pessimist on board, Simon Peter sets sail to throw out the nets one more time.

The pessimist says: *"Look at the nets!"*
The optimist says: *"Look at the fish!"*

> And when they had done this, they enclosed a great quantity of fish; and their nets began to break. (Luke 5:6)

The pessimist says, "The nets are breaking! Jesus, you're making my life miserable. Now I've got to spend all my time repairing my nets. I've got enough to do without having to repair these stupid nets!"

The optimist says, "Look at all the fish! I can sell them and buy new nets and a new boat. Thank you, Jesus!"

The nets represent the things we want to hold on to. The fish represent what God wants to give us. Some people would prefer to keep their nets unbroken than to receive a miraculous provision from God.

The pessimist complains when the nets are empty and complains again when the nets are full. We can always choose what we want to see. A pessimist sees a difficulty in every opportunity. An optimist sees an opportunity in every difficulty. We can either rejoice over the fish or complain over the nets.

The pessimist says: *"God is sinking our boats!"*
The optimist says: *"God is blessing our boats!"*

> They signaled to their partners in the other boat, for them to come and help them. And they came, and filled both of the boats, so that they began to sink. (Luke 5:7)

Can't you hear the pessimist whining? "These nets are so heavy! My back is killing me! Call a doctor. I think I threw my back out. I'll sue!"

The optimist says, "This is great! I've never seen a haul like this before! Only God could do this. We need help!"

When God starts blessing our boat, we'll need to make adjustments: Repair the nets. Hire more help. Clean up the boat.

As our church has grown, we've had to hire more nursery workers. We need more space, so we need to build a new facility. These are good problems, the kind we want to have. We can either complain about our boat sinking or rejoice over God's provision.

The pessimist says: *"I'm not a bad person!"*
The optimist says: *"I'm a sinful man!"*

> But when Simon Peter saw that, he fell down at Jesus' feet, saying, "Depart from me, for I am a sinful man, O Lord!" (Luke 5:8)

We might think the optimist would say he was not a bad person, not the pessimist. But that's not true. The optimist realizes his true condition before God. The pessimist tries to cover up his spiritual condition.

Simon Peter had called Jesus "Master" before he performed the miracle. Now he calls him "Lord." Simon had seen something beyond the miracle. He wasn't thinking about all the fish that had jumped into the net. He was thinking about the Lord who caused them to jump into the net. He said to himself, "If the Lord has control over the fish in the sea, then he needs to have control of my life as well. If he really is the holy Lord, then I must be a sinful man! I never realized my true condition until now."

The pessimist says: *"I am losing my fishing business!"*
The optimist says: *"I am gaining eternal life!"*

> And Jesus said to Simon, "Do not fear, from now on you will be catching men." And when they had brought their boats to land, they left everything and followed Him. (Luke 5:10–11)

After the boats returned to land, these fishermen left *everything* and followed Jesus. They left their boats, the source of their livelihood. They forsook their nets, the tools of their trade. They abandoned their tremendous haul of fish, which would have brought in more money than they ever dreamed of. All those thousands of fish—they left every one of them behind. What have you left behind to follow him?

God had a purpose for their empty nets. And it was not to make them frustrated and angry. Now he had a purpose for their full nets. And it wasn't so they would have an abundance of fish. It was to prove he could provide for them wherever and whenever he wanted to.

Why would they leave their boats and fish after they had brought in the largest catch they had ever experienced? Because they discovered something better. They found a new reason to live. From now on they would fish for men, not fish.

What about the loss of income? No problem. They were convinced if Jesus could provide that many fish, then he could provide all their other needs as well.

Many people haven't figured that out yet. They are still laboring in their own strength, pulling in empty nets and complaining about them.

So which are you? The pessimist or the optimist?

Seeing the Positive

- How did you respond the last time you pulled in an empty net?

- If Jesus tells you to throw out your net again, will you obey even if you don't understand?

- What does it mean to have *good* problems?

- Read chapter 7, "When You Are Disappointed."

CHAPTER 16

When You Are Middle-Aged
Calming Mid-life Crisis

The glory of young men is their strength, and the honor of old men is their gray hair.

(Proverbs 20:29)

THE GLORY OF A YOUNG man is his health and physical strength. The honor of an old man is his wisdom and experience. But what about the middle-aged man? Is the benefit for his age a balding head and pot belly? Let's hope not.

Someone once said that youth looks forward, old age looks backward, and middle age looks worried! Mid-life can be a traumatic time for many people. During this period, many are thrown into a tailspin called *mid-life crisis.*

Mid-life is the group, generally speaking, between the ages of thirty-five to fifty years old. Mid-life is when:

- You know all the answers—but nobody asks you the questions.

- You are too tired to work—but too broke to quit.

- Your work is less fun—and your fun is more work.

- Your narrow waist and your broad mind change places.

- You have more hair growing in your ears than on your head.

- You read the obituary page every day to see if anyone your age has died.

Just like adolescence is a transition from childhood to adulthood, mid-life is a transition from being a young person to an old person. Because the aging process is both stressful and difficult to accept, this middle age time bomb needs to be defused.

149

What Causes Mid-Life Crisis?

Factor # 1	**The Aging Factor: The realization you are getting old.**

In Psalm 37:25, David said, "I have been young, and now I am old." It didn't happen overnight. He wasn't young one day, then woke up the next day as an old man. It happened gradually.

When I was a child, I desperately wanted to be older. When I was eight, I couldn't wait to be twelve. When I was twelve, I couldn't wait to be sixteen. And when I was sixteen, I wanted to be twenty. And when I turned thirty, I wanted to be twenty! I stepped on the accelerator of life until I reached age twenty-one. Then when I hit the brakes, I discovered they didn't work and the accelerator was stuck!

Rick Majerus, the men's basketball coach at the University of Utah, commented about his mid-life experience, "Everyone's worried about the economy this year. Hey, my hairline is in recession, my waistline is in inflation, and altogether, I'm in depression." The day will come when you, like Coach Majerus, will look in the mirror, see a receding hairline, wrinkles, or gray hair and think, "I'm not just getting older. I'm getting old. I thought that only happened to everyone else. But it's happening to me, too. I'm never going to be young again."

Welcome to mid-life! The negative impact the aging process makes on your face and body can also be a shock to your mind and emotions. Part of calming mid-life crisis is accepting in your mind what is taking place in your body. The crisis begins when you refuse to accept the fact you are aging.

A young man walked up to a woman and asked, "How old are you?"

The lady responded, "Young man, my age is my own business!"

The man said, "Well lady, it looks like you've been in business a long time!"

Many people during mid-life want to look younger than their age. One lady asked her friend, "I don't think I look forty years old, do you?"

Her friend answered, "No, but you used to!"

It is difficult for the middle-aged person to accept the fact that he is becoming more "mature" in his appearance. One of the factors contributing to mid-life crisis is realizing we are looking old—and that others are also aware of the fact.

| Factor # 2 | **The Time Factor: Time seems to pass more quickly.** |

Not only are you getting older, each year seems to pass a little faster than the year before. You are getting older faster. When you were a child, one year seemed to take forever to pass by. But when you reach age forty, one year seems to take only a few months. Each year goes by a little faster the older you get.

I call it the theory of relativity. Even though a year is 365.25 days, each year seems to pass more quickly from our perspective. One year is one-fifth of a five-year-old's life. But that same year is one-seventieth of a seventy-year-old's life. This truth can't be explained by the hands of a clock: time actually passes more quickly the older we get.

A lot of film is wound around a video cassette's spindle before you start watching it. When the movie begins, the tape unwinds slowly. As the movie nears its end, the tape around the spindle unravels at a increasingly faster rate, even though the film you are watching is moving at normal speed.

The years of your life are like that tape. When your life begins, the tape unravels slowly. But as you near the end of your life, the tape unravels faster and faster—even though the movie of your life is being played at normal speed. Mid-life brings the realization that time is unwinding at a faster pace each year, and unfortunately, you can't hit the pause button.

| Factor # 3 | **The Boredom Factor: Life becomes monotonous.** |

Solomon recognized life can become routine when he penned these words:

> That which has been is that which will be, and that which has been done is that which will be done. So, there is nothing new under the sun. (Eccl. 1:9)

Lots of exciting changes take place between babyhood and child-hood, such as learning how to walk and talk. Exploring this new world is quite an adventure. Even more changes take place during the adolescent years. Dating, school activities, and learning to drive a car can bring excitement to life.

Then you get out "on your own" and get a job. At first, this, too, is exciting. But things soon become monotonous. You get up, go to work, and come home. By the time you reach age forty, you have been getting up, going to work, and coming home for two decades. Life becomes routine and boring. The boredom factor can contribute to mid-life crisis.

| Factor #4 | **The Failure Factor: Goals you haven't reached.** |

As you were growing up, you were going to be a millionaire by age thirty. You are now forty and just trying to get the bills paid each month. You were going to be a star quarterback in the NFL. But instead of playing professional football, you are watching it on television on Sunday afternoons.

The goals you set for yourself were never accomplished. The dreams died a long time ago. The motivation you had for reaching those goals has also disappeared. You may even conclude that you are a failure in life. This lack of motivation or purpose in life can be a primary cause for mid-life crisis. The middle-ager may panic and search for a new reason to live.

| Factor #5 | **The Reflection Factor: Regrets over past decisions.** |

If you are a mid-lifer, you have had plenty of time to reflect upon the decisions you've made thus far in your life. You've reviewed your marital and career choices and may have concluded your dis-satisfaction is due to wrong decisions you've made. You may think you married the wrong person, chose the wrong career, or moved to the wrong city. You won't listen to anyone who tries to convince you these things aren't true, because in your mind you are convinced they are.

In order to correct these perceived mistakes, you attempt to rewind the video tape. You try to start life over again by making drastic changes to bring excitement back to your life. You may change vocations. You may want to move to a new location or leave your spouse and family.

If you allow the crisis to take hold of you, you'll act as if you have lost your mind. None of your decisions will make sense to a normal person. But the one undergoing mid-life crisis is not normal. You are experiencing a form of temporary insanity that has distorted your view of life.

The good news is that the crisis won't last forever. There is light at the end of the tunnel, but you must follow it to find your way out.

How do you follow the light? Here are a few concrete steps you can take to escape your sense of crisis.

First	**Don't panic!**

A person going through mid-life crisis is tempted to panic. If you do, you are almost guaranteed to make bad decisions. It is not wise to make any if you are either on an emotional high or an emotional low. Decisions made on an emotional roller-coaster will nearly always be wrong ones.

Keep calm. Get a grip on life. Realize that mid-life crisis is a phase you are going through. God is using this time of your life to deal with issues inside your heart. He is bringing unresolved things to the surface so you can deal with them in his way, put them behind you, and get on with your life. If you will keep your cool and follow God's instructions, you will come out better on the other side.

Second	**Accept the fact that mid-life is a part of God's plan for you.**

> There is an appointed time for everything. And there is a time for every event under heaven. He has made everything appropriate in its time. (Eccl. 3:1, 11)

There is an appointed time for everything and that includes mid-life. Life is not over; God still has plans for you. You are exactly where you are supposed to be according to his calendar.

This world may tell you life has passed you by. That's why it's so important that you view life from God's perspective rather than through this world's eyes. He has prepared you to fulfill his will at this time of life.

Third	**Realize the benefits in every stage of life.**

God has made everything beautiful in its time. Every stage in life has its advantages and disadvantages. Proverbs 20:29 says when a man is young, his strength is his advantage. But the disadvantage of his age is he lacks wisdom and experience. On the other hand, the older man has wisdom and experience but lacks strength.

The mid-life person has a little of both. He has some strength and some wisdom. He has gained enough wisdom through his years of experience to avoid the mistakes many younger people make. His health is usually good enough to still enjoy doing things that elderly people can't. The secret to happiness in life is understanding the benefits of your age, whatever they may be. Otherwise, you will be like the man who spent his youth trying to gain a fortune then spent a fortune trying to gain youth.

God wants you to enjoy your life at every age. Focus on the benefits of what you have right now. If you don't make the most of the present, you will one day regret the past.

Fourth	**Find meaning in life through serving God.**

Real meaning and purpose in life does not come through impressing people in this world. It comes from serving and obeying God. We can only be fulfilled in life when we live for Him.

> Remember also your Creator in the days of your youth, before the evil days come and the years draw near when you will say, "I have no delight in them." (Eccl. 12:1)

Only a fool lives for the applause of this world. After a person dies, he will be forgotten by everyone except for a few loved ones. "For there is no lasting remembrance of the wise man as with the fool, inasmuch as in the coming days all will be forgotten" (Eccl. 2:16). Many people make the mistake of trying to find purpose in life by living either to impress others or to glorify themselves. Life only becomes meaningful when it embraces God's eternal purposes.

	Look to the future with hope.
Fifth	

"For I know the plans that I have for you," declares the Lord, "plans for welfare and not for calamity to give you a future and a hope." (Jer. 29:11)

If you are in mid-life, God is not finished with you yet. The back nine still needs to be played. The game is not over at halftime. You can't turn back the hands of the clock and replay the first half. But you can play the second half. The rest of your life can be the best because God still has good plans for you.

After a pastor preached his sermon one Sunday, a man commented, "Reverend, what you said today was exactly what I needed to hear. Thank you very much. It was so helpful to me. It revolutionized my life. Thank you!"

The pastor replied, "I'm glad I said something that was so helpful to you, but I'm curious—what in particular was it?"

"Well, you began your sermon by saying that you wanted to talk to us about two things this morning. Then in the middle you said, 'That completes the first part of what I wanted to tell you, and now it's time I moved on to the second part.'

"At that moment I realized I had come to the end of the first part of my life and it was high time that I got on to the second part. Thank you, Reverend!"[1]

That's the message to the mid-lifer. The first half of your life is behind you and can never be recalled. But the second half, if played on God's terms, can be the most fulfilling and enjoyable stage of your life.

Playing the Second Half

- List some benefits you have now that you didn't have earlier in your life.

- "Pull the plug" on all desires to relive the past.

- Prayerfully make plans for the future years of your life and look forward to them.

CHAPTER 17

When Your Life Is Missing Something
Lepers Anonymous

As He entered a certain village, ten leprous men who stood at a distance met Him; and they raised their voices, saying, "Jesus, Master, have mercy on us!" And when He saw them, He said to them, "Go and show yourselves to the priests." And it came about that as they were going, they were cleansed. Now one of them, when he saw that he had been healed, turned back, glorifying God with a loud voice, and he fell on his face at His feet, giving thanks to Him. And he was a Samaritan. And Jesus answered and said, "Were there not ten cleansed? But the nine—where are they? Was no one found who turned back to give glory to God, except this foreigner?" And He said to him, "Rise, and go your way; your faith has made you well."

(Luke 17:12–19)

CAROL DECIDED SHE WANTED to do something nice for her neighbor Mrs. Smith, so she baked a pie and carried it next door.

When Mrs. Smith opened her door, she was surprised to see Carol holding a pie. She replied, "For me? Oh, thank you so much! You just don't know how much I appreciate it! You are so thoughtful for doing this. Thank you!"

Because Mrs. Smith liked the pie so much, Carol decided the next week to bake her another one.

When she took it over, Mrs. Smith opened the door and said, "Thank you so much. You are so kind!"

Carol took another pie over the following week. Mrs. Smith simply replied, "Thanks."

Carol took another pie over the next week, and Mrs. Smith responded, "You're a day late with that pie."

The following week, Carol baked her another pie. This time her neighbor said, "Try using a little more sugar, and don't bake it quite as long. The crust has been a little bit hard lately. And I'd like cherry instead of apple filling next time."

The next week Carol was so busy, she was unable to cook for her neighbor.

When Carol passed by her house on the way to the store, Mrs. Smith looked through the window and noticed she wasn't carrying a pie. She then stuck her head out and yelled, "Where's my pie?!"

It's so easy to get used to our blessings. After enjoying them for a while, we begin to think we deserve them. Then instead of being thankful, we complain. It's a process that occurs so slowly, we don't even realize it's happening. Our attitude has changed from being grateful to ungrateful.

Do you consider yourself to be an ungrateful person? Most people don't. Mrs. Smith probably didn't. I'm sure those nine lepers who were healed by Jesus didn't consider themselves to be ungrateful either. We are usually blind to our own ingratitude. It's not that we don't want to be grateful. We just "forget" to be.

"I really did appreciate the gift that Uncle Bob gave me for Christmas, I just got so busy with other things I forgot to write a thank you note. I'm not really ungrateful. I'm just forgetful."

Umm, yeah, right. The nine lepers forgot to write thank-you notes, too. It's easy to get upset with the lepers when we read it in the Bible. After all, it is pretty obvious they weren't thankful. It's just not as obvious when we forget to thank God.

The difference between being grateful and ungrateful is a lot more than two letters. It's the difference between pleasing God and grieving him. It's also the difference between rejoicing or complaining, being content or restless, appreciating blessings or taking them for granted.

If you were one of those ten lepers on the road that day, would you have returned to thank Jesus? Or would you be like the nine who "forgot" to return to give thanks? Read on and you decide.

Fact #1	Obedience goes the first mile, but gratefulness goes the second mile.

Because lepers were unclean according to the Law, they had to be removed from society lest they defile anyone. The Jewish Talmud instructed them to stay a hundred paces or about three hundred feet from other people. As outcasts of society, a leper's fellowship was confined to those with the same disease. Although the Jews normally hated Samaritans, an exception was made in this case. The group of ten lepers included a Samaritan. The leprosy which made them outcasts among their own people caused them to accept this foreigner whom they would normally reject.

One day Jesus was passing between Samaria and Galilee. When the ten lepers saw him, they knew this was their opportunity. They stood at their prescribed distance, and cried out with loud voices, "Jesus, Master, have mercy on us!"

When Jesus saw them, he yelled, "Go and show yourselves to the priests!" The reason he said this was because the priests were the only ones who could declare that a leper had been cleansed so he could be permitted to enter society again.

As they began their journey toward Jerusalem, God's healing power cleansed their leprosy. The lepers were filled with excitement as they watched their leprosy disappear. Joy overflowed in their hearts when they realized they could now rejoin their families and go back to work. No longer would they be outcasts of society.

The ten lepers believed what Jesus had said. Then they obeyed what he commanded them to do. When they began walking toward the priests, God healed them of their leprosy. But nine of those cleansed lepers forgot one very important thing. They failed to return and thank him for their healing.

I must confess, there have been times before a meal when I have thanked God out of ritual, not because I'm truly grateful. The prayer comes out of my head, not my heart. At other times, I have needed God to answer a prayer. When he did answer, I was excited about it, but thanking him didn't enter my mind. I had spiritual amnesia of the heart. I responded just like the nine lepers who received healing but forgot to give thanks.

Most Christians put a great emphasis upon believing and obeying but very little upon gratefulness. It is possible for us to hear God's Word, believe it, even obey it—and still miss doing God's will. "In everything give thanks; for this is God's will for you in Christ Jesus" (1 Thess. 5:18). God's will becomes complete only after we give thanks for what he has done.

Obedience and gratefulness are not the same thing. Gratefulness always goes beyond obedience. Obedience goes the first mile, but gratefulness goes the second mile. It's not enough for us just to be obedient. God also commands us to be thankful.

Fact # 2	**People who have been blessed are divided into two categories.**

Whenever we receive from God, we are separated into one of two categories: Grateful or Ungrateful. When Jesus healed the ten lepers, the two groups were immediately formed. The Grateful Group had a membership of only one leper. The Ungrateful Group had nine members, better known as Lepers Anonymous. They have gone into obscurity, never to be heard from again. Every person on earth is a member of one of those two groups. Compare your attitude to the descriptions below to see whether you are grateful or ungrateful.

Ungrateful people always see the bad in every good situation.
Grateful people always see the good in every bad situation.

Ungrateful people immediately find the negative in any given situation. In a pile of a hundred things, the ungrateful person is able to detect the one bad thing in a matter of seconds.

One family sat down to a meal, and the father asked his son to say the prayer of thanksgiving. The son said, "It won't do any good."

"Why not?"

"Because we're having broccoli!"

Some people can only see broccoli and never enjoy the rest of the meal. On the other hand, thankful people have the ability to immediately detect the good in any given situation. They are able to see the vitamins in the broccoli, even if they don't care for the taste.

Ungrateful people complain about how bad they have it.
Grateful people realize how good they have it.

Steve Farrar tells of moving into a nice house in Arkansas. One day he mowed the yard and went inside to get a glass of tea. As he sat down on the deck, he picked up a magazine and flipped through the pages. He saw where a couple in Des Moines had remodeled their kitchen. The "before" and "after" pictures impressed him. They had put in new tiles, French doors, a rotating pantry, and other luxuries. Then he turned the page and saw where a couple in Boise had remodeled their back deck, built a barbecue area, and an amphitheater in their back yard. It was incredible.

When he had finished drinking his tea, he went back inside to get some more. He stopped and looked at his kitchen. The countertops and Formica looked horrible! Then he opened the pantry. It didn't rotate like the one in the magazine. He didn't have any French doors, either. He said to himself, "How can we live in a roach trap like this?" He went outside and looked at the deck he had enjoyed all day and said to himself, "I've seen firewood in better shape than this!"

In seven minutes he had gone from the state of contentment to discontentment, simply because he thought about how bad he had it compared to others.[1] He realized he shouldn't have complained and quickly changed his attitude back to being grateful.

But the truth was clearly demonstrated: We will always complain when we think about how bad we have it compared to others. Grateful people, on the other hand, understand how good they have it compared to others.

A depressed man called his counselor to set up an appointment. His counselor said, "You have so much going for you. Why are you depressed?"

All the man could say was, "You just don't understand my problems." So an appointment was made for the next day.

When the man came into his office, the counselor said, "I'll visit with you in a few minutes, but I want you to watch a short video with me first." He turned on the VCR and they watched events taking place all over the world. They watched mass starvation in Africa where little children had bloated bellies due to malnutrition. They viewed dead bodies lying on the streets, covered with flies—nothing but skin and bones due to starvation.

The scenes switched to the overpopulated streets in India with open sewage. Then they saw people living in third world countries living in thatched huts and eating mush. They watched blood running in the streets because of upheaval as people rebelled against dictatorships.

After the video had ended, the counselor asked, "Now, what was the problem you wanted to talk about?"

The man replied, "Doc, I don't have any problems!"

A person becomes grateful when he realizes how good he has it compared to those less fortunate. No matter how bad we may have it, it could always be much worse.

Ungrateful people think they deserve more than they get.
Grateful people realize they don't deserve what they get.

One elderly lady gave some candy to a little girl.

The girl's mother said to her, "Now, what do you say?"

The girl looked at the lady and said, "You got any more?"

Ungrateful people are like that with God. Rather than thanking him, they complain they don't have enough. In contrast, thankful people realize they don't deserve anything at all. When they receive something, they know it is by God's grace they have it. God is kind to ungrateful men (Luke 6:35), but he enjoys blessing his grateful children.

| *Fact # 3* | **Grateful people take extra steps that ungrateful people don't take.** |

The grateful leper was on his way to show himself to the priests, but when he saw that he had been healed, he "turned back." He had already walked some distance and decided to turn around. His attitude of gratitude separated him from the fellowship of the ungrateful. He took extra steps to return to thank Jesus. He had to walk further than those lepers who kept walking toward the priests.

Thankfulness always requires that we take extra steps. It will also require extra time out of our schedule. Because this leper turned back to thank Jesus, his journey to Jerusalem would take him longer.

Tanya Gentz was a twelve-year-old girl who traveled with her parents 1,300 miles to thank the man who saved her life. They drove from Galveston, Texas, to Charlotte, North Carolina, through a record snowstorm in Tennessee that held them up for two days.

Tanya had one purpose in mind. She wanted to thank and hug the man who gave his bone marrow to cure her leukemia.

The man who had saved her life said, "I'm the only person who could have done this for her."[2]

It would have been unthinkable for Tanya to ignore the man who had saved her life. She and her parents proved their gratefulness by taking the extra time to travel those many miles to thank him.

> *Fact # 4* **Grateful people never have to be reminded to give thanks.**

God never forces anyone to be grateful. We will never find Jesus begging us to thank him. When this lone leper returned, he glorified God with a loud voice. No one had to wonder if he was truly thankful or just being courteous. His loud voice answered any questions about his sincerity. True thankfulness always arises from within our soul and can never be extracted by external forces.

Jesus didn't heal the lepers and then remind them to thank him. "Now, what do you s-a-a-a-y?"

No, this Samaritan leper looked at his new flesh which grew back in front of his eyes—new flesh on his fingers and toes—and he ran back to Jesus. (I know the Bible doesn't say he ran, but I can hardly imagine him walking.) He fell on his face, and with his face in the dirt at Jesus' feet, he cried out, "Thank You! Thank You! Thank You!"

By the way, when was the last time you got down on your face in prayer and truly thanked Jesus for all he has done for you? We are so quick to ask him to answer our prayers, but then we forget to thank him when he does.

One boy came home from school very excited. He said, "Dad, today I learned how to say *please* and *thank you* in French!"

His father replied, "When are you going to learn how to say it in English?"

Saying it is one thing. Meaning it is something completely different. No matter which language we say it in, it needs to come from both our mouths and our hearts.

I want to let you in on a little secret. Have you ever eaten a meal that was somewhat bland, and thought to yourself, "Something's missing"? Thankfulness is the ingredient missing in most people's lives. Giving thanks is the seasoning which makes life an enjoyable experience.

A meal always tastes better to a thankful person than to an ungrateful one. One poor lady didn't have much to eat but would always thank God before she ate.

A man ridiculed her by saying, "Why even bother to thank God for that pitiful meal?"

The lady answered, "Cause vittles always taste better when you're thankful!"

Fact # 5	**Jesus also expects the ungrateful people to thank him.**

When the one thankful leper returned, Jesus asked where the other nine lepers were. He wasn't just expecting the grateful leper to return, he was also expecting the other nine lepers as well. Even though Jesus never forces us to thank him, he still wants to be thanked.

Whenever we do something for someone, we always expect to be thanked in some way. We are usually bothered if we are ignored. God is also grieved and disappointed when he blesses us and we neglect thanking him.

Jesus had done an incredible miracle for these lepers. No one can put a price tag on new fingers and toes. Their entire lives were changed because of their healing. Not only were they made whole, but now they could go home, return to society, and fellowship with people once again.

Jesus was grieved in his heart that the other nine refused to thank him. Those members of Lepers Anonymous never knew how much their ingratitude disappointed Jesus because they weren't there to see the look on his face. Only the one with the thankful heart truly understood how Jesus felt.

The Leprosy of Ingratitude

Although we may not have leprosy, we may need to be cured of the leprosy of ingratitude. This disease can only be cured by giving thanks to God for what he has done.

What do we have to be thankful for? How about running water, indoor toilets, heating, air-conditioning, electric lights, televisions, VCRs, hospitals, medicines of all kinds, eye glasses, closets full of clothes, canned food, fresh food, refrigerators, freezers, microwaves, cars, bicycles, motorcycles, and entertainment features most of the world has yet to see—just to name a few things. A few hundred years ago, even kings and the most wealthy didn't live like the average person in America today. And don't forget about salvation. How can we ever thank God enough for Jesus dying for us so we could spend eternity with him?

Yes, we've got it good. Probably too good. Certainly much better than we deserve. And yet, with so much to fulfill us, many people remain empty inside. Something is still missing.

I'll tell you what's lacking. The biggest thing missing in a person's life today is a thankful heart.

Replacing the Missing Ingredient

- Make a list of every blessing God has given you. Pray through the list every day, thanking God for them.

- Whenever someone gives you something, find a unique way to thank that person.

- Make a concentrated effort to see the positive, even in negative situations.

CHAPTER 18

When You Carry Heavy Burdens
Check Your Baggage Here

"Come to Me, all who are weary and heavy-laden, and I will give you rest. Take My yoke upon you, and learn from Me, for I am gentle and humble in heart; and you shall find rest for your souls. For My yoke is easy, and My load is light."

(Matthew 11:28–30)

ACCORDING TO LEGEND, a Christian, weary from carrying his cross, passed through a small village. He noticed a sign in front of a store which read, "Crosses Traded Here." Thinking his load was unfair and his cross too heavy, he decided to enter the store. He was amazed to discover it filled wall-to-wall with crosses. "I'm tired of carrying this cross," he told the owner, "and I would like to trade it for a different one."

The owner replied, "Very well. You can trade your cross for any one of these carried by saints throughout the ages. Choose the easiest one."

The man approached a stack of crosses, comparing them for size and comfort. He picked one up, but it was much heavier than his. "I don't want this one," he said. He picked up the next cross, and it was even heavier than the first. He moved to the next one, then the next, but they were all much heavier than his.

After going through the entire store, he finally came to the last cross and picked it up with ease. "I'll trade my cross for this one!" the relieved man told the owner.

"But sir," the owner replied, "that is the cross you carried in here!"[1]

Sometimes we think our burdens are too heavy until we compare them with the persecutions of the saints from the past. Even though our trials are light in comparison, some of the burdens we carry can still be overwhelming. At times, they can almost seem unbearable. And if not dealt with properly, they can devastate us.

Some people try to lighten their loads through counseling. One woman was heavily burdened with problems and went to a counselor. She explained, "I've got so many problems they are giving me a migraine headache."

The counselor said, "Please sit down and tell me about it."

She unloaded her problems for three hours. When she was finished, she said, "I feel so much better now. My headache has disappeared!"

The counselor replied, "No it hasn't. I've got it now!"

We can't release our concerns without giving them to someone else. Jesus said he wants to take our burdens and give us rest. But if this is true, why do so many Christians still feel weighed down with problems? Surely, Jesus wasn't lying when he said we could find rest for our souls.

Perhaps there is another explanation. Maybe the problem lies with our inability to release our burdens.

The Luggage of Life

Burdens are the luggage bags we carry throughout life. We don't carry burdens in our hands or on our backs. We transport this unseen baggage on our souls. When we are burdened down, we can't see a physical load on top of us. Yet, we aren't just imagining this pressure that weighs us down. Even though we can't see a burden in the physical realm, we will be able to feel the weight from a real spiritual load on our souls.

We acquire these burdens when we think about problems for prolonged periods of time. Of course, no one is exempt from having problems. But if we begin to dwell upon them, those burdensome thoughts will become weights upon our souls. And we will be forced to carry those invisible weights with us everywhere we go unless we learn how to release them.

Accumulating Excess Baggage

The burdens we carry on our souls are produced by difficulties we encounter every day. They may be real or imaginary, but both will affect us in the same way. Even what we perceive to be problems can weigh down on our souls.

Although we may carry some baggage without becoming weary, burdens accumulate with time. Just like a weight lifter adds weights to his barbell, we add weights to our souls. When we experience a difficult problem, we add that baggage to our load. When another problem comes along, if we don't learn how to release it, the new problem is also added.

If we continue to stack one problem on top of another like layers of a sandwich, we will become depressed. Jesus referred to this state of the soul as being "weary and heavy-laden." The accumulation of numerous burdens always brings heavy pressure on our souls. That's why Jesus said we could find rest for our souls if we would come to him.

Some time ago, a small airplane crashed because it carried too much baggage. The extra weight kept the plane from climbing to its desired altitude after takeoff, and the plane crashed into some trees. Too much baggage loaded on our souls will hinder us from reaching our highest potential and may even cause our downfall.

In order to rid ourselves of excess baggage, we must understand how we accumulate it as we travel through life. Most of us never stop to think how we pick up these extra loads.

A little girl is teased and humiliated by other students in school. It devastates her, causing her to think no one will ever accept her. A burden was just placed on her soul that she will carry for the next fifteen years.

A young lady makes a vow to stay a virgin until she gets married. But in the backseat of a car, her boyfriend goes too far. She gave in just one time, but she picked up a burden that night. It will continue to haunt her, especially on her wedding night. Until she receives God's forgiveness, her relationship with him and her husband will be affected. A ten-year burden.

A businessman can't get all his work done at the office, so he brings it home. He has no time for his wife or children. Bills need to be paid, so work comes first. He's carrying too many burdens and doesn't even realize it until his wife asks for a divorce. A burden for the rest of his life.

Just because we may have dealt with a problem twenty years ago doesn't mean it no longer affects us. We may have packed it away in one of our suitcases we are carrying through life.

We pack our excess baggage in three distinct suitcases—the past, the present, and the future. We must all carry some luggage as we travel toward our destination in life, but we don't need to carry more bags than are necessary. If we are going to have a successful journey, we must check the baggage we are lugging and leave unnecessary bags behind.

Checking Your Baggage

Maybe you haven't identified with my baggage metaphor yet. If you're wondering what I mean, let me explain some of the baggage most of us carry.

Past Baggage: Regrets

Burdens from the past are known as *regrets*. As we travel down Bad Memory Lane, we drag all of our regrets from the past as excess luggage.

People who live in the past drive down the highway of life with their eyes fixed on their rear-view mirrors. Their conversations usually revolve around hurts or mistakes that occurred earlier in their lives. They want more than anything to go back into the past and change their circumstances. But because it is impossible, they vent their frustration by talking about how they wish things could be different.

People who cling to the past are called "if-only" people. "If only I hadn't made that mistake in the past. If only I had married Bill instead of Bob. If only I had not been molested as a child. If only I had chosen a different career." They recall things that happened ten or twenty years ago as if they happened yesterday. Those incidents from the past have been forgotten by everyone else in the world, but the "if only" person carries the past baggage on his soul every day. We cannot change our past, but our past can change us if we choose to carry the extra luggage.

Future Baggage: Worry

Burdens from the future we call *worry.* This is the luggage we pack for all the future trips we worry about for the years to come. Worry concerns itself with every bad possibility which might occur in the future. We may envision disasters that might happen to us or those we love. We may be afraid God will forget about providing our future needs, so we worry. The fear of car wrecks, disease, misfortune, and Murphy's law (if anything can go wrong, it will) are also carried as extra luggage.

People who worry are "what-if" people. "What if I get cancer? What if I lose my job? What if my house is burglarized?" The list of "what-if" questions is endless.

While faith is the assurance of things hoped for (Heb. 11:1), worry is the assurance of things *not* hoped for. Worry is actually *negative* faith because it believes bad things will come to pass. Even if no disasters actually occur, we visualize these calamities in our minds as if they have already happened. Worry is always caused by a lack of trust in God.

Present Baggage: Stress

The pressure we feel in our present situation is called *stress.* The present is the only time when we can manage our burdens. However, we can still become overloaded with present burdens by being involved in too many responsibilities. Our baggage can become too heavy to carry.

Present baggage may involve marital difficulties, overdue bills, strained relationships, or problems at work. Overcharging our credits cards and our own failure to fulfill our obligations will also bring unnecessary pressure on our souls. Many times we are overloaded with excess baggage simply because we have been negligent in our daily responsibilities.

Now imagine carrying the past, future, and present baggage on top of your soul. Can you feel the pressure? That's a lot of baggage! There comes a time when we must let go of some of the suitcases and leave them behind.

Don't Claim Your Baggage

Until we learn how to release our extra baggage, we will continue to carry it with us throughout life's journey. Just because we have brought it this far doesn't mean we have to continue carrying it. We must leave behind any excess luggage at the Baggage Claim. Sure, there are a lot of memories in those bags but carrying too many suitcases will make future travel both difficult and wearisome.

First	**Let go of your excess baggage.**

Casting all your anxiety upon Him, because He cares for you. Cast your burden upon the Lord, and He will sustain you. (1 Pet. 5:7; Ps. 55:22)

We can only let go of our excess baggage by giving all our regrets, worry, and stress to the Lord. Because he cares for us, he is concerned about every one of our problems. God does not automatically remove our excess baggage from us. By a deliberate act of our own wills, we must cast our burdens on him.

Whenever we cast something, we throw it in a certain direction. Two people are playing catch; one person lets go of the ball and hurls it into the hands of another person. When we cast our burdens to the Lord, we release them out of our hands and place them in his hands. Then we will no longer regret the past, be depressed by the present, or worry about the future. All are now in God's hands.

Casting always involves letting go of something. That's why we can't just hand them over to God, because we can still hold on to them. We can easily deceive ourselves into thinking we have let go of our cares when we really haven't. We may cast them to the Lord with a string attached and then, like a yo-yo, pull them back to ourselves. Although we make an attempt to release them, we never really do. In order to get rid of our excess baggage, we must let go of the suitcase handles permanently.

A little boy once got his hand stuck in an expensive vase. His parents tried everything to get his hand out. They tried soap and grease, but nothing worked. They thought they had no choice but to break the expensive vase.

His father got out a hammer and was ready to shatter the vase. Just before he hit it, he asked his son a question. "Jimmy, are you holding on to anything in the vase?"

Jimmy answered, "Yes, Daddy."

"What are you holding on to?"

"I'm holding on to a nickel."

"Let go of the nickel, Jimmy," his father commanded.

"But I don't want to."

"Son, you have to let go if you want to be set free."

The little boy let go of the nickel, and his hand was easily freed. Many people hold on to their excess baggage, refusing to let go. If they would simply release whatever they are holding on to, they would be set free from the things keeping them in spiritual bondage.

One lady in my church was repeatedly struck by tragedy. Her young daughter was diagnosed with diabetes, her young son was diagnosed with juvenile rheumatoid arthritis, her mother-in-law had a heart attack, her own mother died suddenly, some non-Christian relatives were persecuting her, and her house caught on fire—all within a seven-week period. Her burdens brought her to the verge of a breakdown.

She realized if she didn't find a way to let go of the excess baggage, she would collapse under the pressure. She decided to write down twenty-five burdens on a piece of paper, along with a prayer to God. Then she put them inside five balloons, filled them with helium, and released them to the Lord. She watched the balloons float free until they were out of her eyesight. She felt a tremendous release and a lifting of her spirit. The invisible weights on her soul were gone.

When we truly cast our burdens to the Lord, we will be relieved of the pressure weighing us down.

Joe was walking to the laundromat, carrying a duffel bag stuffed with dirty clothes over his shoulder. On the way he met his friend Darlene, who was having difficult problems. Joe reminded her she needed to cast her burdens to the Lord rather than carry them herself.

Darlene said, "I thought I gave them to the Lord, but I'm still burdened. How do I know when I've released them?"

Joe let go of the sack, and the laundry bag fell off his back to the ground. He asked, "How do I know I dropped the sack? I haven't looked around to see if it is off my back."

"You know because it isn't weighing you down any more."

"And that's how you'll know if you've released your burdens to the Lord. You'll feel the weight lifted off your soul."

Second	**Only carry enough baggage for today's journey.**

So don't be anxious about tomorrow. God will take care of your tomorrow too. Live one day at a time. (Matt. 6:34 TLB)

We would be foolish to pack suitcases for our next five trips in the future. Any luggage we don't need for today's trip is excess baggage. Living one day at time keeps us from adding the excess weight from the past and future onto our souls.

It is impossible to go back in time and relive the past. We can't unscramble eggs, but we can make an omelet out of them. We also cannot live in the future. The vast majority of things people worry about never occur. Although we may not know what the future holds, we know who holds the future. Trusting God to control our future will keep us from handling that extra luggage. We can *learn* from the past, and we can *look* to the future, but we can only *live* in the present.

A clock thought about how often it would have to tick during the coming year. Figuring two ticks a second, 120 a minute, 7,200 each hour, 172,800 a day, and 1,209,600 ticks every week, the clock realized it would have to tick nearly 63 million times in the next year. The more it thought about this, the worse it felt. Finally, the clock had a nervous breakdown. It went to the clock psychiatrist and said, "I can't go on. I don't know how I will ever make it through the next year."

The doctor responded, "How many ticks can you tick at a time?"

"Only one."

"Well, if you will simply tick one tick at a time and not worry about the next tick, you'll be just fine."

So the clock followed his advice and ticked through the next year, then the next, and the next . . . And, as all good stories end, it ticked happily ever after.

Just like a clock can only tick one tick at a time, we can only live one day at a time. If we learn to take each day as it comes without dragging the past or grasping for the future, life will become amazingly easy.

Once God has lifted your burdens, don't try to reclaim your excess baggage. If you will keep your hands off those suitcase handles, your journey through life will be a lot more enjoyable.

Casting Your Cares upon Him

- What excess baggage are you carrying? Identify past, present, and future baggage by writing each one down on a piece of paper.

- Cast and release every burden individually to the Lord. Symbolically place each burden into your hands, lift your cupped hands up to the Lord, and release it into his hands.

- After releasing each burden, thank God for taking it away. Tear up or burn the list of former burdens. After letting go, make sure you don't reclaim the baggage by dwelling upon the past and future.

- Read chapter 10, "When You Feel Like Quitting."

CHAPTER 19

When Opinions Differ
Is Right Ever Wrong?

One man regards one day above another, another regards every day alike. Let each man be fully convinced in his own mind.

(Romans 14:5)

THE GAS TANK WAS nearly empty when I pulled into the service station. While my wife and kids piled out of the car, I filled the tank and noticed the restaurant named "Eddie's" next door. It looked like it might be a good place for us to grab a bite.

After paying for the gas, I walked into the rest room. Someone had left a message scrawled on the wall, designed to be read by weary travelers like me: "Eat at Eddie's—50,000 flies can't be wrong!"

Well, that was one man's opinion. But that wasn't the way I liked to pick my restaurants. "Opinions," Darrell Royal once said, "are like noses. Everyone's got one." All of us have different tastes. Not everyone likes the same food, music, hairstyle, hobby, or football team. That can add up to a lot of trouble, especially if we don't learn how to handle our differing opinions.

In Romans 14, Paul was writing to a group of opinionated believers. As a matter of fact, they were so opinionated they began to withdraw fellowship from one another. At one time, their fellowship was in Jesus Christ but then it shifted to their opinions.

In Rome, the hot topics were diets and days. The Jewish Christians observed the Sabbath day, while the Gentile Christians regarded every day alike. Many Jewish believers became vegetarians (14:3) rather than run the risk of eating forbidden or unclean meat. The Gentiles, on the other hand, had no problem eating meat.

When they went out to Pizza Hut, the Gentiles ordered pepperoni pizza with pork sausage on thick crust. The Jews got the vegetarian pizza on unleavened bread. And I guarantee you, they didn't sit at the same table together. Their food became more important than their fellowship.

We get hung up on different issues today. Now we argue over music, movies, and makeup. We all have different opinions over what is right and wrong. For example, some people think that it is a sin for a woman to wear makeup. And then other people believe it is a sin for a woman to not wear makeup.

Disagreements Can Cause Division

A minister returned to visit a church he once served. He ran into Fred who had been an elder when the pastor was there but had left the church. The minister asked, "Fred, what happened? You used to be there every time the doors opened."

"Well, Pastor," said Fred, "a difference of opinion arose in the church. Some of us couldn't accept the final decision, so we left to start a church of our own."

"Is that where you worship now?" asked the pastor.

"No," answered Fred, "we found that there, too, people weren't cooperating. So a small group of us began meeting in a rented hall at night."

"Has that proven satisfactory?"

"No, I can't say that it has," Fred responded. "Satan was active even in that fellowship, so my wife and I withdrew and worship on Sunday at home by ourselves."

"Well, at least you and your wife have found inner peace."

"No, I'm afraid we haven't. Even my wife developed ideas I wasn't comfortable with, so now she worships in the living room and I worship in the bedroom."

If we can't agree to disagree, division is inevitable. In order to preserve the unity of the faith, we must give freedom to others to disagree on certain issues. Some churches have split over the 3 percent they disagree upon, rather than being unified over the 97 percent in which they agree. A pastor told me his church split over where to put a water fountain! We can easily lose perspective if we don't look at the whole picture.

How People Form Opinions

If I could design a plaque to hang in my kitchen, it would read, "Not Everyone Thinks Like You Do!" Sometimes it's good to be reminded of that fact. How do people form their opinions?

Some beliefs are formed by our backgrounds—the way we were raised. Corinth had a meat-eating problem there, too. Some of them were raised sacrificing meat to idols (1 Cor. 8:7). They became convinced that eating meat sacrificed to idols was the same thing as idol worship. Paul informed them this wasn't true, but nevertheless, they formed their beliefs based upon their past experiences.

Many people today have their minds made up. They have held their beliefs so long, they think they must be correct because, "That's the way I was raised."

But what if what we were taught when we were growing up was incorrect? We must form our beliefs based upon truth rather than our past experiences.

It would be nice if everything we were taught growing up was absolutely correct, but it is unlikely. Our initial beliefs we formed as children need to be reexamined as we mature into adults. "When I was a child, I used to...think as a child, reason as a child; when I became a man, I did away with childish things" (1 Cor. 13:11). We must sort through what we have been taught, keep the things that are true, and leave behind misconceptions. "But examine everything carefully; hold fast to that which is good" (1 Thess. 5:21). It is so easy to form our beliefs upon wrong foundations. Someone once said, "In a day of illusions and utter confusions, upon our delusions, we base our conclusions." We shouldn't form our beliefs upon illusions and delusions, but upon truth.

Convictions and opinions can also be formed by our teachers. Jesus said that a pupil, after he has been fully trained, will be like his teacher (Luke 6:40). Beliefs can be transferred from the teacher's mind to the student's. Sitting under incorrect teaching will form incorrect beliefs. This is why it is so important to choose the right teachers.

Other beliefs are determined by our stage of spiritual maturity. What we once believed as baby Christians is quite different than what we will believe after growing spiritually for twenty years.

One man was teasing a little boy about his baby brother. The man asked, "What can he do? Can he walk?"

The boy answered, "Nope."

"Can he talk?" asked the man.

"Nope."

"Can he feed himself?"

"Nope."

"Can he dress himself?"

"Nope."

"Well, what good is he?"

The little boy answered, "Good grief, Mister, just give him some time!"

Sometimes we need to be patient with other believers as we wait for them to grow and mature spiritually.

Wrong Ways to Handle Differing Opinions

> Oh, to dwell above
> With the saints we love,
> My, how that will be glory!
> But to dwell below
> With the saints we know,
> Well, that's a different story!

When we encounter a person who disagrees with us, what are we supposed to do? Listed below are a couple of things to *not* do:

Don't force your opinions on others through arguing.

When someone disagrees with us, we often try to convince the other person we are right. One man said, "If I want your opinion, I'll give it to you!" Some people believe if they argue and harp on the issue long enough, others will change their minds. That's why some wives nag their husbands and parents yell at their children. They are trying to force them to change through using pressure tactics. It doesn't work.

Have you ever seen a debate team convince another debate team that they are right? No. Because what is right is not the issue. Who wins the argument is the real issue. Trying to force other people to change their minds won't work because a man convinced against his will is of the same opinion, still. You can't change a mind that doesn't want to be changed.

Don't use guilt trips to make others change their opinions.

This technique makes people feel guilty if they have differing opinions. A cartoon depicted a girl telling her friend, "Do you know that kid who sits behind me in school? I convinced him my religion is better than his religion."

Her friend asked, "How did you do that?"

The girl replied, "I hit him with my lunch box!" If we hit people over the head enough times with the lunch box of guilt, they will feel condemned for what they believe. That's not the way Jesus changed people's minds.

I knew a lady who attended a legalistic church. Members made her feel guilty because she didn't wear dresses which had sleeves down to her wrists. They told her someone might lust after her because her arms were exposed.

She tried to explain to this was unlikely since she was almost eighty years old. They continued, however, to make her feel condemned for wearing short sleeves.

Finally, she bowed to their pressure and bought a pretty dress covered with strawberries with sleeves down to her wrists. She was excited to go to church, thinking the guilt trips would be over. She asked the pastor's wife, "Well, how do you like my dress?"

She answered, "Those strawberries are much too red. The dress is worldly. You are just trying to attract attention to yourself!"

Legalism uses guilt to make other people change their beliefs.

How to Handle Differing Opinions

Now that you've seen examples of wrong ways to handle differing opinions, here are some hints on right ways to handle them.

First

Don't make a big deal over minor issues.

"You blind guides, who strain out a gnat and swallow a camel!" (Matt. 23:24)

People have argued about trivial matters for centuries. Some great theological debates occurred over the following issues:

- What was the shape of the angel Gabriel's wings?

- How many angels can sit on the head of a pin?

- Did Pilate use soap when he washed his hands?

- How much wine did they drink at the wedding in Cana?

- Could Christ have changed himself into a pumpkin?

- Are there any angels with baritone voices?

The Christians in Rome were also arguing over trivial matters. These believers were in agreement on the major issues, such as the deity of Christ and salvation by grace, but were dividing over their minor differences. They were minoring on the majors and majoring on the minors. As they watched for tornadoes which might destroy the house, they forgot to inspect for termites. Just like the Pharisees, the Romans strained out gnats and swallowed camels.

The Pharisees had perfected the art of gnat-straining. They would strain their wine through a cloth to make sure a gnat did not accidentally get into it. Gnats were unclean, and the Pharisees shuddered at the thought of swallowing one. The camel, on the other hand, was the largest unclean animal. Jesus said they "strain out a gnat and swallow a camel" to illustrate their error. Christians can fall into the same trap by making too much of minor issues. We must never lose sight of the big picture.

Second

Accept one who differs, because God has accepted him.

Now accept the one who is weak in faith, . . . for God has accepted him. (Rom. 14:1, 3)

Someone defined the "weaker brother" as anyone who disagrees with me! Paul said to accept the brother who disagrees because God has accepted him. If God can accept him, then I can too. We can be brothers without being twin brothers. If God calls someone his child, then I should call him my brother.

Acceptance is more important to God than agreement on trivial matters. What if he only accepted people who were correct on every theological position? No one would be accepted.

	Be right in your heart, not just in your head.
Third	

The Jews considered the Sabbath to be a higher day than other days, but the Gentiles viewed every day the same. These were two completely different theological positions. Rather than telling them who was right, Paul said:

> One man regards one day above another, another regards every day alike. Let each man be fully convinced in his own mind. He who observes the day, observes it for the Lord, and he who eats, does so for the Lord, for he gives thanks to God; and he who eats not, for the Lord he does not eat, and gives thanks to God. (Rom. 14:5–6)

In other words, it doesn't matter who is right on these issues if your convictions are attempting to glorify God. However, an additional factor needs to be considered. If your theological position is used to destroy someone, then you are wrong.

> For if because of food your brother is hurt, you are no longer walking according to love. Do not destroy with your food him for whom Christ died. (Rom. 14:15)

An amazing truth is presented here that many people overlook: You can be right in your head in what you believe, but if you are wrong in your attitude toward your brother, you will be wrong. You can also be wrong in your head in what you believe, but if you are right in your attitude, then you will be right. You can be right but be wrong, and you can be wrong but be right! Right is wrong when correct opinions are used to destroy someone. Wrong can be right when incorrect opinions are intended for the glory of God.

| Fourth | **Don't violate your own conscience or your brother's conscience.** |

But rather determine this—not to put an obstacle or stumbling block in a brother's way. I know and am convinced in the Lord Jesus that nothing is unclean in itself; but to him who thinks anything to be unclean to him it is unclean. (Romans 14:13–14)

Now we who are strong ought to bear the weaknesses of those without strength and not just please ourselves. (Romans 15:1)

Paul said there were two kinds of believers in the church: the strong and the weak. We usually consider ourselves strong and right and the other person weak and wrong. The strong brother is the one who understands his liberty in Christ. The weak brother only understands rules and regulations. He may not agree with what you say, but he will punch you in the mouth if you say it!

Do you consider yourself to be a stronger one? Fine. Here's what to do. The "strong ought to bear the weaknesses of those without strength." Paul puts the responsibility on the stronger brother to put up with the wrong convictions of the weaker brother. The weaker brother needs to grow in his knowledge because his beliefs are wrong. The stronger brother needs to grow in his love because he must learn to tolerate the wrong opinions of the weak. The stronger brother must put his right to be right on the altar. You don't have to convince everyone else you are right in what you believe.

H. L. Menchken, a magazine editor in the first half of the century, received a lot of criticism from people with differing opinions. When people wanted to argue with him concerning an issue, he would simply respond, "You know, you may be right!" He didn't say they were right. He simply gave the opinion that they might be. The mere suggestion that they might be right caused them to back off from their attacks.

Of course, we cannot deny some beliefs. We cannot deny the Trinity, the deity of Christ, the finished work of Jesus on the cross, his resurrection, and salvation by grace. But many of our differences are nothing but minnows in the wide ocean of faith. Our theological position on the second coming of Jesus, our preference of worship style, the clothes we wear to church, and where to put the water fountain are nothing but minnows.

What minnow are you allowing to torture you? We are being minnowed to death when we fight over insignificant matters.

Augustine, concerning differences of beliefs, put it this way:

> In essentials, there must be unity.
> In non-essentials, there must be liberty.
> In all things, there must be charity.

And with that, I agree!

Adjusting to Differing Opinions

- Write down some ways you have strained out gnats and swallowed camels.

- List the beliefs that you hold because of the way you were raised. As you reexamine your beliefs in light of Scripture, hold on to the correct beliefs and release all incorrect ones.

- In what ways can you bear the weaknesses of the weak?

CHAPTER 20

When You Are Angry
The Danger of Anger

And He entered again into a synagogue; and a man was there with a withered hand. And they were watching Him to see if He would heal him on the Sabbath, in order that they might accuse Him. And He said to the man with the withered hand, "Rise and come forward!" And He said to them, "Is it lawful on the Sabbath to do good or to do harm, to save a life or to kill?" But they kept silent. And after looking around at them with anger, grieved at their hardness of heart, He said to the man, "Stretch out your hand." And he stretched it out and his hand was restored.

(Mark 3:1–5)

 ESUS LOOKED at the Pharisees with anger. His hot button was also pushed when he drove money changers out of the temple. The same Jesus who kissed babies threw the rascals out.

It may surprise you that anger in itself is not sinful. Otherwise, Jesus would have sinned when he became angry. Because he never sinned, his anger was holy. I wish I could say the same thing for every time we become angry.

We experience anger when things aren't going the way we would like them to. We can tell we are angry when the temperature in the room goes up fifteen degrees and no one has touched the thermostat. Although anger is not necessarily sinful, it can quickly turn into sin if we don't take control of it.

When does anger become sinful? That's a good question. God's Word gives us several guidelines to show us how anger turns into sin.

| Guideline # 1 | **Anger becomes sin when it is rises quickly.** |

But let every one be quick to hear, slow to speak and slow to anger; for the anger of man does not achieve the righteousness of God. (James 1:19–20)

In seven different books in the Old Testament, it specifically says that God is slow to anger. On the other hand, Galatians 5:20 describes one of the works of the flesh as "outbursts of anger." This describes a person who explodes quickly when something doesn't go his way.

What does it take to set you off? Someone once said you can measure a man by the size of whatever it takes to make him mad. Are you slow—or quick to anger?

A man from Philadelphia killed a driver who cut in front of him on the expressway. The traffic on the freeway had slowed down and was being funneled into a single lane. The man had waited fifteen minutes until he could enter the flow of traffic. But just as he was about to do so, another car passed him on the shoulder of the highway and cut in front of his car. Then the other driver laughed and made an obscene gesture at him.

It was too much for the man. When the traffic stopped, he took a gun out of his glove compartment, got out of the car, walked up to the side of the car of the man who taunted him and shot him to death.[1]

E. Stanley Jones, the great missionary to India, once observed, "Action has killed its thousands but reaction its ten thousands." Anger is a reaction to people and circumstances that are displeasing to us. We can "kill" people, spiritually speaking, through venting our anger in an unrighteous way. Whenever we react quickly and explode in an outburst of anger, it becomes sinful.

| Guideline # 2 | **Anger becomes sin when it is directed at sinners instead of sin.** |

Jesus looked around at the Pharisees with anger because he was grieved at their hardness of heart (Mark 3:5). It was the sin in their hearts that made him angry.

We have often heard the expression, "Hate the sin, love the sinner." We have quoted it so much we have forgotten how to practice it. It really is true. We must learn to direct our anger against the sin, not the sinner. When a doctor is operating on a patient to remove a cancerous tumor, he hates the tumor but loves the patient. In the same way, we should channel anger against sin and not against the person who is sinning.

| Guideline # 3 | **Anger becomes sin when it is out of control.** |

He who is slow to anger is better than the mighty, and
he who rules his spirit, than he who captures a city. (Prov. 16:32)

A person with self-control has control over his spirit. This verse tells us ruling our own spirits is more important than ruling over an entire city. Some people have power and authority over millions of people but have no power or authority over their own spirits. I won't mention any politicians by name.

Alexander the Great, the commander of the Greek Empire, conquered the world. After he had accomplished this feat, he went into his tent weeping and cried out, "There are no more worlds to conquer!"

On one occasion, Cletus, a dear friend of Alexander's and a general in his army, became intoxicated and ridiculed the emperor in front of his men.

Alexander, seized with anger, snatched a spear from the hand of a soldier and hurled it at Cletus. He intended to only scare him, but the spear hit him and took the life of his childhood friend.

Alexander was quickly filled with remorse, realizing what he had done. Overcome with guilt, he attempted to take his own life with the same spear but was stopped by his men. For days he lay sick, calling for his friend Cletus whom he had murdered. Alexander the Great had conquered many cities and countries, but he had failed to conquer his own spirit.

| Guideline # 4 | **Anger becomes sin when it is not accompanied with grief.** |

Although Jesus looked at the Pharisees with anger, he was also grieved. Anger needs to be mixed with grief to keep it balanced. An element of sorrow was involved in his anger. If grief had not accompanied Jesus' anger, he would have been like Clint Eastwood holding the gun on the criminal saying, "Go ahead, punk. Make my day!"

Jesus took no pleasure in his anger. Since it was mixed with grief, it was as if he were saying, "Why don't you open your eyes and soften your hearts?" He wanted them to change so he wouldn't have to be angry with them.

| Guideline # 5 | **Anger becomes sin when it is not resolved quickly.** |

Be angry, and yet do not sin; do not let the sun go down on your anger. (Eph. 4:26)

To not let the sun go down on our anger means we must resolve it before the day is over. Phyllis Diller once said, "Don't go to bed angry. Stay up and fight!" But this verse doesn't mean to get in as many punches as possible before the sun goes down. It means that if our anger is two days old, it has turned into sin.

Something happens to our anger after holding it for more than one day. It becomes repressed and pushed down into the soil of our hearts. This two-day-old anger then turns into the seed of unforgiveness. After we nurture the seed of unforgiveness in the soil of our hearts, it sprouts into the root of bitterness.

See to it that no one comes short of the grace of God; that no root of bitterness springing up causes trouble, and by it many be defiled. (Heb. 12:15)

John Powell has said, "When I repress my emotions, my stomach keeps score." We will feel turmoil inside our stomachs if we do not properly deal with our anger.

What if a doctor came to you with a ball of torment that was churning, twisting and looking terrible. He says, "I will pay you $1,000 per day if I can operate on you, cut you open, and implant this ball of turmoil inside. You will lose your peace and joy, and the only thing you will be able to think about all day and night is this torment inside of you. Well, how about it?"

You would say, "It's not worth $1,000 per day to carry that ball of torment inside. As a matter of fact, I wouldn't carry it for all the money in the world!" But whenever we repress anger which eventually turns into bitterness, we are saying, "I'll carry that ball of turmoil inside of me free of charge!"

How to Handle Your Anger

Sometimes anger seems stronger than you. But there are ways you can handle it.

| *First* | **Admit you have an anger problem.**

Until you admit you have an anger problem, you cannot deal with it. People often manifest their anger in a couple of ways. One way is through simmering anger. Just like a pan sits on the burner and slowly burns, some people simmer with anger. This anger is turned inward, buried, and is usually manifested through resentment and a critical spirit.

Another way anger is manifested is through explosive anger. A rattlesnake in a cage doesn't rattle if it is left alone. But if you poke the snake with a stick, it will rattle and coil as it gets ready to strike back. It has been provoked to anger. Explosive anger is usually dormant until something triggers it, then an eruption like Mount Vesuvius occurs. The anger is turned outward as the person releases the hostility.

As long as we excuse our anger through blaming others, our problem will remain. We must admit that anger is controlling us, rather than us controlling it. Regardless of which way your anger is manifested, the first step is to admit you have an anger problem that must be dealt with.

	Identify the cause of your anger.
Second	

Anger is always caused by something, whether you realize it or not. Suppose you are at your job one day. You look out the window into the parking lot, and see someone with a hammer pounding on your new car. He smashes your windshield and dents your hood and roof. Your face turns red as your blood pressure quickly rises. You are outraged as you watch him demolish your car.

Why are you angry? Because he is destroying your car. The hammer hitting the car causes your anger. The damage your car sustains (the wound) makes you angry with the person doing the harm to your property.

Many people's anger is rooted in something that happened in their past which has never been resolved. If your car was damaged a half an hour ago, you have been angry for thirty minutes. You can pinpoint where your anger originated by tracing it back to where it first began. Detecting its origin will help you discover the issue that must be resolved.

In the movie *Forrest Gump,* Jenny, Forrest's love since childhood, returned to her old home after her father died. The old farmhouse was dilapidated and abandoned. As she reflected on the sexual abuse she endured as a child, she was overcome with rage and threw rocks at the house. Jenny went out of control as she repeatedly picked up rocks and angrily threw them at the house. Finally she fell to the ground in exhaustion.

Forrest commented on the incident by saying, "Sometimes there just aren't enough rocks."

Jenny identified the cause of her anger, but she didn't know how to remove it.

When I was a boy living in New Orleans, the snow-cone truck would to come to our neighborhood. When the truck rang its bell, all the kids would be attracted to it like flies to a piece of watermelon. One day, a group of boys was gathered around the truck.

One of them asked me, "Can I borrow fifteen cents? I promise I'll pay you back. Scout's honor." Back then, everyone used scout's honor, even if they weren't Boy Scouts.

I was reluctant to lend it to him because I didn't have much money or know him very well. Nevertheless, I lent him the money. The next day, he was nowhere to be found. I never saw him again.

Funny, that was over thirty years ago, and I still remember it. I can't remember what he looked like, but I can remember losing the fifteen cents. That wouldn't bother me today. But for a little boy, it was like losing your life savings.

I can still feel how I felt back then. It made me angry that he tricked me. I'm sure he had no intention of paying the money back. I forgave him years ago, but the memory is still there. And here I am, writing about fifteen cents because it was so deeply embedded in my memory.

This event of my childhood remains in my memory, not because I am angry now, but because I was angry then. If I felt this way about something as insignificant as fifteen cents, can you imagine the painful memories of those who were physically abused or sexually molested? We may think our past hurts don't affect us today, but they do. In order to resolve how we felt back then, we cannot keep denying our past. We must get to the root of our anger. Some people never realize the anger they hold today was birthed during events that occurred during their childhoods.

| Third | **Accept the things you can't change.** |

Many times we become angry over things completely out of our control. Years ago, I remember becoming angry watching the national news every night. I gritted my teeth at the stupid decisions the government made. When the media put their own slant on reporting the news, it made me boil. Watching television often irritated me because ministers were usually stereotyped as greedy, self-promoting idiots. I know many people in the ministry, and believe me, nearly every one is hardworking, self-denying, and under-appreciated.

Then it occurred to me I was angry about things I couldn't change. I thought my anger against these evil things was the righteousness of God in me. Then one day I read James 1:20, "For the anger of man does not achieve the righteousness of God."

I decided right then I wouldn't stay angry over things I couldn't change. I had been foolish for allowing anger to steal my joy for all those years. If I couldn't change my circumstances, I decided, then I would accept them.

By acceptance, I am not talking about agreeing with the situation. Many things that happen are neither good nor right, and we certainly would prevent them from occurring if it were possible. Events in our past can't be altered, no matter how much we may wish we could change them. Some people, whom we once knew, we will never see again. We may never have an opportunity with them to clear up unresolved differences. There are things that happen on a national and international level that we can do nothing about, except to watch them take place.

In these cases, we must accept the fact this is the way it is and we can do nothing to change the outcome. If we do not accept the things we cannot change, we will continue to use our anger in an attempt to alter the things that won't budge. This will only lead to more frustration and increased anger.

| *Fourth* | **Remove your anger.** |

Let all bitterness and wrath and anger and clamor and slander be put away from you, along with all malice. And be kind to one another, tenderhearted, forgiving each other, just as God in Christ also has forgiven you. (Eph. 4:31–32)

The solution to the problem is to put away all bitterness, wrath, and anger. God never commands us to do something we aren't capable of doing. The real issue, then, is our willingness to obey his commands.

To "put away" means "to remove." If we remove garbage from our house, we decide to carry it out to the trash receptacle and dump it. In order to put away anger, the first thing we must do is decide to remove it from our lives.

A surgeon named Dr. Kane searched for a candidate to undergo surgery so he could prove that appendectomies could be done under local anesthetic. At last, a patient was found. He was prepared for surgery and wheeled into the operating room. A local anesthetic was applied, leaving the patient able to talk and respond as the surgery progressed.

As he had done hundreds of times, Dr. Kane located the appendix, skillfully removed it, and finished the surgery. During the operation, the patient complained only of minor discomfort. The volunteer was taken to a hospital room, recovered quickly, and was dismissed two days later. Dr. Kane had demonstrated that local anesthesia was a viable and sometimes preferable alternative—thanks to the willingness of a brave volunteer.

What I didn't tell you was that the courageous volunteer for surgery by Dr. Kane—was Dr. Kane. He had performed surgery upon himself. He had removed his own appendix![2]

Sometimes the surgery you need can only be performed by yourself, on yourself. You can't wait for someone else to remove your anger and bitterness for you. You must remove and release it yourself.

There was a time when I remember slowly building up anger against my wife. I found things wrong with what she did, even when she didn't do anything wrong. One morning while I was praying, God spoke to my heart, "You are angry with Cindy."

Immediately, a blanket of conviction wrapped itself around me. I was so ashamed of my unholy attitude, I wept before the Lord for about an hour. I repented of my sin, removed my anger, and asked Cindy to forgive me. I don't have any doubt I was delivered from a spirit of anger that day.

In order to remove our anger, we must forgive those who have hurt us. We also need to ask their forgiveness. Anger and bitterness usually come as a result of a past hurt. The bitterness is not the wound itself, but comes as the result of a wound. An unhealed wound causes us to become angry, and unresolved anger leads to unforgiveness and bitterness.

When we forgive those who have hurt us, we reverse the process. Forgiving frees us to remove our feelings of anger, and removing the anger allows God to heal our wounds from the past.

But it is not enough just to remove the anger. It must also be replaced with kindness and a tender heart (Eph. 4:32), which is only possible through submitting to the control of the Holy Spirit. The fruit of the Spirit is self-control (Gal. 5:23), which means anger can't control us when we walk in the Spirit.

Angry people usually take life too seriously, so relax. Loosen up. Look at the big picture. Let go of your anger. In light of eternity, it's not worth spending your short time on earth being angry.

Cooling Down Your Anger

- Identify the things that make you angry. Accept the fact you can't change some things.

- Take whatever steps are necessary to correctly remove the anger from your life. (You will probably need to go to some people in person and ask forgiveness.)

- Make a decision to resolve your anger before you go to sleep each night.

- Read chapter 5, "When You Can't Forgive Someone."

CHAPTER 21

When Bad Things Happen

The Rest of the Story

And we know that God causes all things to work together for good to
those who love God, to those who are called according to His purpose.

(Romans 8:28)

PAUL HARVEY HAS BECOME famous for his books and radio
broadcasts in which he tells interesting stories about people
going from rags to riches, tragedy to triumph, and failure to
success. He keeps the character's identity a secret until the end, then
reveals the well-known person's name and declares, "And now you
know—the rest of the story!"

Romans 8:28 is the Christian's "rest of the story" because it tells
us how the story of the believer's life is going to end. This verse is a
mystery because we don't know why certain things happen to us or
how God makes those things work together for good. We mistaken-
ly believe we must understand this promise before we can trust that
God really is in control. But his promise doesn't depend upon our
understanding it. As a matter of fact, many people need to unlearn
some things they believe about this verse. Let's look at what Romans
8:28 doesn't say before we can understand what it does say. Allow
me to present five facts about this scripture.

Fact # 1 We don't hope God is in control, we know it.

Most people quote this verse as, "God works all things
together for good." But they leave off three very important words,
"And we know." The problem is most Christians don't know it; they
only hope it's true.

194

The apostle Paul, in spite of his trials, said he knew it was true. He didn't write to the Romans, "I've been persecuted, beaten, and stoned, and to tell you the truth, I don't see how any of this can possibly turn out for good." Nor did he say, "I know I am writing this letter to many different people, and I can't say for sure how your situations will turn out. I hope things work out for you. Good luck!"

Even though Paul didn't know what the readers in Rome were going through or what we would be going through today, he made a universal statement of truth under the inspiration of the Holy Spirit informing us we can know God works all things together for good to those who love him.

Life is like a jigsaw puzzle. God sees the completed picture, but we see only one piece at a time. Some pieces have us puzzled while we wait for them to fit together. But after the pieces come together, we can look at the completed picture and say, "Now I see. Now I understand!" The key is trusting that God will fit the pieces together before we see it. We don't have to understand before we can believe what God says is true.

When Jesus gave a man his sight in the ninth chapter of John, the blind man didn't understand how the eyeball functioned to make sight possible. When Jesus healed the paralyzed man (Mark 2:1–12), he didn't first require him to understand how his spinal injury would be corrected. When Jesus raised Lazarus from the dead, Lazarus wasn't capable of understanding how he was going to be resurrected. He was dead!

Neither do we need to understand in order to trust. A college student once commented to the great theologian Charles Spurgeon, "I'm having a hard time understanding why bad things happen to people. It doesn't seem fair."

Spurgeon replied, "Young man, give God credit for knowing some things that you don't!"

Fact # 2	**God doesn't cause all things to happen, but causes all things to work together.**

Some people wrongly believe that God causes everything to happen, even evil and tragedy. That is why tornadoes or hurricanes are called "acts of God." While he does not cause all things, he is in control of all things. "Cause" means "to initiate." "Control" means "to have a hand upon."

For example, God does not tempt anyone (James 1:13). He does, however, allow temptation to take place. First Corinthians 10:13 says God will not allow us to be tempted beyond what we are able to handle but will provide the way of escape. God allows the way into the temptation, but he makes the way out.

Satan may tempt someone to sin against God. Even though the devil causes the temptation, the Lord controls the parameters by allowing it to only go so far. Then he intervenes to make a way out of the temptation. This shows God does not cause temptation, but he is definitely in control of it. He also doesn't cause all things to happen to us, but he is able to take those things and work them together for our good.

 Fact # 3 | **Not all things are good, but God works all things together for good.**

Not everything that happens to us is good. Nor is everything that happens God's will, but he will work all things into his will.

> Also we have obtained an inheritance, having been predestined according to His purpose who works all things after the counsel of His will. (Eph. 1:11)

Many people have no problem believing Satan can take something good and turn it to evil. But those same people have a hard time believing God can take evil and turn it to good.

Satan in the Garden of Eden took something good and turned it to evil. Did it ever occur to you that the forbidden fruit was good? It wasn't evil. "God saw all that He had made, and behold, it was very good" (Gen. 1:31). The forbidden tree was one of those things he had made, and it was good.

Some things may be good, but we can't have them because they are forbidden. Our neighbor's refrigerator may be filled with good food, but we don't have the right to walk into their home and help ourselves. The food is good, but it is forbidden.

In the Garden of Eden, the forbidden fruit was good. Satan deceived Eve into believing that because the fruit was good, it wasn't forbidden. "When the woman saw that the tree was good for food, . . . she took from its fruit and ate" (Gen. 3:6). Satan tempted her to take something good and turn it to evil. If he can turn good to evil, can't God, who is much more powerful, turn evil to good? Of course, he can! We have numerous examples throughout Scripture proving it.

Look at *Joseph*. Because of his brothers' great hatred for him, they threw him into a pit in the wilderness. That wasn't good. Then some Midianite traders sold him into slavery. He was taken to Egypt where he was falsely accused by Potiphar's wife, and was thrown in prison for doing the right thing. While there, he helped a man get out by interpreting a dream, but the man forgot to help get Joseph released. He spent two more years in prison. Those weren't good things. He had spent thirteen years of his life in slavery and in prison.

Now if you had been reading this and closed the book at this point, you would have thought God had abandoned him. And you would have missed the rest of the story.

As it turned out, Joseph was released from prison, became second in command over Egypt, and was reunited with his brothers. He saved them and an entire nation during a time of famine. And now you know—the rest of the story!

Look at *Esther*. The Jews were in captivity in a foreign country, where Esther was part of a harem. An evil man named Haman hated the Jewish people and sought to have them destroyed. He then built a gallows to hang a righteous man named Mordecai. Those things weren't good. And if you had closed the book at this point, you would have missed the rest of the story.

As it turned out, Esther was promoted from slave girl to queen. Haman was hanged from the gallows rather than Mordecai, and Esther saved the entire Jewish nation. And now you know—the rest of the story!

Look at *David and Bathsheba*. David committed adultery with Bathsheba, then he lied trying to cover it up. Finally, he murdered Bathsheba's husband, Uriah the Hittite. Those weren't good things. Now if you had closed the book at this point, you would have missed the rest of the story.

As it turned out, David repented, and God forgave him. David and Bathsheba had a son named Solomon, who became the king of Israel. Solomon built the temple in Jerusalem where Israel offered their sacrifices. He became the wisest man on earth and wrote the books of Proverbs, Ecclesiastes, and The Song of Solomon. In Matthew 1:6, David, Bathsheba, and Solomon are listed in the genealogy of Jesus. And now you know—the rest of the story.

Look at *Jesus*. God became a man and lived on earth. The religious leaders refused to listen to him. He was betrayed by one of his own disciples. Then he was falsely accused, scourged, and crucified. The disciples who had followed him for three years even forsook him. Those weren't good things. If you had closed the book at this point, you would have missed the rest of the story.

As it turned out, he rose from the dead, ascended into heaven, is seated at the right hand of the Father, and he will reign forever and ever. And now you know—the rest of the story!

How does God make all things work together for good? He does it by blending blessings and tragedies together. If you ate a raw egg, you would say it wasn't good. The same would hold true if you ate butter, sugar, shortening, flour, flavorings, and spices separately. But if you beat them together in a mixing bowl and bake them, those ingredients blend together to become a delicious cake.

God takes the ingredients in our lives, both bad and good, and works them together for our good. He is the Chef who can make something good out of things that, by themselves, are not good.

In the early 1970s, one of the big college football games of the year was Notre Dame versus the University of Southern California. Notre Dame dominated the first half of the game and built a 28–0 lead just before halftime. Thousands of USC fans left the stadium, thinking there was no possible way their team could win.

In the second half, USC tailback Anthony Davis ran the kickoff back for a touchdown. Southern California refused to give up and scored again—and again—and again. Final score? Notre Dame 28— USC 55! The people who left at halftime missed the greatest comeback in the history of college football.

Don't make the mistake of thinking evil will triumph because it appears to be winning at halftime. You will miss out on the rest of the story.

> **Fact # 4** — **God doesn't do this for everyone, but for those who love him.**

The Bible tells us God works all things together for good because he knows ahead of time who will choose to love him.

> For whom He foreknew, He also predestined to become conformed to the image of His Son, that He might be the first-born among many brethren; and whom He predestined, these He also called; and whom He called, these He also justified; and whom He justified, these He also glorified.(Rom. 8:29–30)

This verse is a picture from eternity past to eternity future. We are currently sitting in the present, looking at our situation. But God sees things from a different perspective. Because he sees all of time, he can intervene and make things turn out for his glory.

Eternity Past	Present	Eternity Future
Foreknew Predestined	*Called Justified*	*Glorified*

Just because God knows everything ahead of time doesn't mean he foreknows everyone. The word *know* can mean different things. "Know" can mean "to have knowledge of" (Gen. 3:7), or it can mean "to know intimately" (Gen. 4:1 KJV). That's why Jesus, who knows all things, will say to many people, "I never knew you" (Matt. 7:23). He has knowledge of them, but he doesn't know them intimately. Just like Jesus can have knowledge of someone without knowing him, he can have foreknowledge of someone without foreknowing him.

God knows everything before it happens, which is foreknowledge. That means he knows ahead of time who will call on him to be saved and who won't. Because he has foreknowledge of those who desire to be saved, he foreknows those same people.

Even though God does the choosing, we are given the opportunity to ask him to choose us. It's like the army general who asked his soldiers, "Whoever would like to volunteer to go on a dangerous mission with me, please step forward." About one-third of the soldiers stepped forward of their own free wills, separating themselves from the other soldiers. The general then went up to each soldier who stepped forward and said, "I choose you and you and you." He chose everyone who stepped forward, but he didn't choose anyone who didn't volunteer. He gave them their free wills, but he did the choosing. In the same way, God allows us to have free wills, but he chooses everyone who wants to love him.

But doesn't the fact that he knows ahead of time what we will decide mean it is now impossible to have free wills? Doesn't it also mean he has already predestined whomever he wishes? No, because his predestination is based upon his foreknowledge of what we will choose to do. "For whom He foreknew, He also predestined" (Rom. 8:29). First Peter 1:1–2 says, "Peter, an apostle of Jesus Christ, to those who reside as aliens, . . . who are chosen according to the foreknowledge of God the Father."

Think about it this way. You record a basketball game on your VCR because you are busy while the game is being played. That night you rewind the tape and watch the game exactly as it was played. Did the basketball players have free wills in playing the game? Yes. But the results are already fixed on the video tape. You watch the game not knowing the outcome, but you know the results are already determined and recorded on the tape. You are watching the players exercise their free wills, even though the outcome is already decided. Foreknowledge is just like that video tape, except instead of playing the tape after the game, God sees the tape before the game.

Now, let's add to the illustration to help us understand predestination. You and God are basketball players on the same team. When you shoot and miss, he gets the rebound and dunks it. Throughout the game, you keep making mistakes, but God gets the ball and overrules your mistakes. Your team wins because he is on your side. He stepped in and compensated for your failures and mistakes.

Because of his foreknowledge, God knows your mistakes ahead of time. Through his predestination, he chooses to intervene and turn your mistakes around for good. He did it in Joseph's life, he did it in Esther's life, and he will do it in your life, too.

God's purpose is not to just make us happy, but to make us like Jesus.

The promise is for those who are "called according to His purpose." We tend to think the Bible was written only to this generation of Americans in order to make us happy. The moment we experience one ounce of pain, we are thrown into a tailspin of doubts and questions. "God, where are you? Why is this happening to me?"

Did you notice what we are predestined to? Not heaven. Not hell. We are "predestined to become conformed to the image of His Son" (Rom. 8:29). Although God works all things together for good, he is also using our trials and difficulties to chisel off our rough places. He is in the process of making us like Jesus, so he's more interested in developing our character than in making us comfortable.

God truly does work all things together for good for those who love him. A Christian named Bernard Gilpin was falsely accused of heresy by Bishop Bonner and was on his way to London for trial. His favorite saying was, "All things work out for the best." On his way, Gilpin broke his leg, which delayed his arrival.

Someone mocked him saying, "Is your broken leg for the best now?"

Gilpin replied, "I believe so." Although he couldn't understand how a broken leg could possibly be in God's plan, he continued to trust. It was for the best, as it turned out. During the time he was delayed, Queen Mary died, the charges were dropped, and rather than being burned at the stake, he returned home in triumph.[1]

Yes, Romans 8:28 really is true. And now you know the rest of the story!

Rethinking Romans 8:28

- Ask God to forgive you for blaming him for tragedies that may have happened to you.

- Even though what happened to you may have been terrible, quit trying to find an explanation as to why it occurred.

- Place your situation in God's hands, and trust him to work it together for good.

CHAPTER 22

When You Have Drifted from God
Heartbreak Highway

The backslider in heart will have his fill of his own ways, but a good man will be satisfied with his.

(Proverbs 14:14)

A SON IN A LARGE FAMILY resented his youngest brother. When he thought the "baby" received special privileges, he tormented his brother.

He whacked him, then as soon as the younger brother cried, the older would become remorseful. "I'm sorry," he'd say. "I didn't mean to hurt you. Don't tell Mom and Dad." This episode was repeated month after month.

One day the older brother hit the child and with apparent sincerity said, "This time I really am sorry. I mean it. Don't cry. I'm sorry."

The younger one, fed up with his hypocrisy, replied, "I know you're sorry. What I want to know is, when will you be sorry enough to quit?"

Many people are sorry for what they do but not sorry enough to quit. There is a difference between being remorseful and repentant. Remorsefulness is sorry for the past but doesn't want to change the future. Repentance is also sorry for the past but makes a change in heart so the future will be different. It changes future behavior so the past mistakes won't be repeated.

When a child of God rebels against his heavenly Father, God has set up a process by which he can bring that child back to himself. The parable of the prodigal son reveals an amazing ten-step pattern of repentance that occurs when a person backslides. When God removes his hand of blessing, the conditions in a backslider's life become so miserable, he will want to come back home. Here's what happens when someone travels down Heartbreak Highway.

| Step # 1 | **Rebellion against the Father.** |

"A certain man had two sons; and the younger of them said to his father, 'Father, give me the share of the estate that falls to me.' And he divided his wealth between them." (Luke 15:11–12)

In this passage, the father represents the heavenly Father. Rebellion is an inward separation in heart from him. We always rebel on the inside before it shows on the outside. This son wanted his inheritance even though his father was still living. He didn't want to wait until his father died. That could be years of waiting. So he demanded to receive it right then.

Even though he didn't want to live with his father, he wanted to live off his father's money. He wanted the father's presents, but he didn't want his presence.

| Step # 2 | **Rejection of the Father's presence.** |

"And not many days later, the younger son gathered everything together and went on a journey into a distant country, and there he squandered his estate with loose living." (Luke 15:13)

An inward separation in the heart is always followed by an outward separation in action. "Not many days later," the son packed his bags to leave home. It doesn't take long for the outward separation of the rebellious heart to manifest itself.

You can picture the scene in the house that day. The father's heart broke as he watched his son gather his belongings. Although it is not recorded in Scripture, this unwritten verse is just a thought: "And the father wept." He knew the son was about to make a painful journey down Heartbreak Highway, the road that leads to the distant land. Even though the son didn't realize the suffering he would experience in the foreign land, his father knew.

As much as the father loved his son, he didn't chase him down the road, begging him to return. No, he let him go. Sometimes the hardest thing to do when you love someone is to let him go, especially when you know what that person is about to experience.

This a painful road to travel. It is so easy to backslide down Heartbreak Highway. It leads to the distant land, where famines occur and hearts break. The only way back to the Father's house is to return with a changed heart.

I've watched a lot of people travel down this road. I've seen husbands leave their families and go down this path. Many rebellious teenagers and bitter people have also traveled down this highway.

Some people return in a few days with their clothes torn and scratches on their bodies. They have seen enough to know it is not the right way, and will humbly return to the Father's house. Others are gone much longer. And the further down the road they go away from the Father, the worse it gets. The son was a long way down the road. He was in the distant land.

| Step
#3 | **Removal of the Father's provision.** |

"Now when he had spent everything, a severe famine occurred in that country, and he began to be in need." (Luke 15:14)

When we are in fellowship with God the Father, he blesses us because he is the source of all blessings. But when we run from the Father, the blessings run out. He refuses to bless rebellion.

When Muhammad Ali was boxing as the heavyweight champion of the world, his opponents would stay away from him in the ring. Ali used to shout, "You can run, but you can't hide!" The prodigal son was trying to run from God, but he couldn't hide from him.

After the son spent everything, a severe famine hit the land. It always does. God will allow a famine to hit our lives when we are away from him. It's part of the process in repentance. God will not send milk and honey to the foreign land. Milk and honey are reserved for the promised land.

The son became destitute. He went from luxury in the father's house to poverty in the foreign land. Part of the process God uses to bring a person to repentance is to strip him of everything so he can see his true condition. People often have to hit bottom before they will look up to God. Sometimes things have to get worse before they get better. The removal of God's provision is a very important part in bringing a person to repentance.

Realignment with the wrong fellowship.

"And he went and attached himself to one of the citizens of that country, and he sent him into his fields to feed swine." (Luke 15:15)

The son no longer wanted to be with his father, which left a void in his life. So he attached himself to a foreigner. It won't be long after we leave God's fellowship that we will attach ourselves to the wrong fellowship.

God has put within us a need for fellowship. We need to be with people. If we do not fellowship with the right people, we will associate with the wrong people. Have you ever noticed how bitter people always choose to be with other bitter people? Why do rebellious teenagers always hang out with other rebellious teenagers? The reason is because like hearts attract each other.

The foreigner sent the prodigal son out to feed his pigs. What a horrible thought! Pigs were unclean animals according to the Mosaic Law and greatly detested by the Jews. This was not what he had in mind when he left his father's house. The companionship he once had with his father was now replaced by the disgusting company of pigs.

"And he was longing to fill his stomach with the pods that the swine were eating, and no one was giving anything to him." (Luke 15:16)

No one was giving him anything to eat. His father hadn't sent any "care packages" to help meet his needs. Sometimes refusing to help a rebellious person in need is the most loving thing we can do.

This is why 2 Thessalonians 3:10 says, "For even when we were with you, we used to give you this order: if anyone will not work, neither let him eat." Hunger pains can motivate a person to change!

When a person needs to suffer the consequences of a wrong decision he has made, it is important to not bail him out. The pain experienced through harmful consequences can teach him to not make the same wrong decisions again.

 Step # 5 **Realization of his true condition.**

> "But when he came to his senses, he said, 'How many of my father's hired men have more than enough bread, but I am dying here with hunger!'" (Luke 15:17)

He saw the pigs and heard them oinking. He smelled the mire, tasted the pods, and felt the mud that filled the pig pen. His five senses brought him to his senses. The light bulb clicked on inside his head.

His miserable conditions in the pigpen caused him to recall fond memories of living in his father's house. He remembered the delicious food at the dinner table, the comfortable bed, and the closet full of clothes. He had to lose everything he had in order to see the contrast between life with his father as opposed to life away from his father. Sometimes we don't realize what we have until it is taken away.

He finally realized his father's kindness by remembering the way he treated his hired men. The son was now himself a hired man, but not like the men hired by his father. His father's hired men always had more than enough to eat, but he was about to starve to death. It only made sense to leave the foreign land, go back home, and try to get a job working for his father.

Step # 6 **Repentance in his heart.**

> "'I will get up and go to my father, and will say to him, "Father, I have sinned against heaven, and in your sight; I am no longer worthy to be called your son; make me as one of your hired men."'" (Luke 15:18–19)

We know the son repented because he was willing to take the blame for his disastrous life. Repentant people don't point fingers, except back at themselves. "Father, I have sinned." He realized he had sinned against heaven and his father.

Repentance always produces a change of heart. His broken heart became humble and submissive rather than arrogant and rebellious. He realized he was no longer worthy to be called his father's son because he had squandered his inheritance. He was willing to return, not as a son submitting to his father, but as a servant submitting to his master.

A worker in an orange grove in Florida was known as "The Snake Man." His real name was Walt, but for a long time no one knew it. His friends called him Snake Man because he caught snakes and scared everyone with them.

One day he picked up a ground rattler and waved it at some workers. The snake twisted in his hand and bit him on the thumb. Snake Man's arm swelled horribly, and he was rushed to the hospital where it looked as if he might die.

Several weeks later, he returned to work looking pale and weak. One of the men called out to him, "Snake Man! It's good to see you back!"

Snake Man looked at the group and announced, "I'm not Snake Man anymore. My name is Walt."[1]

The Snake Man had repented of his snake handling because he learned he couldn't continue to play with snakes without getting bit. The prodigal son repented of his ways because he learned a painful lesson after traveling down Heartbreak Highway. He had been deceived by the lure of the foreign land, thinking it was something it wasn't. Now he was ready to return home.

Step # 7

Returning to his father.

"And he got up and came to his father." (Luke 15:20)

Dr. J. Vernon McGee once asked, "Do you know the difference between the son in the pigpen and the pig? The difference is that no pig has ever said to himself, 'I will arise and go to my father.'" The son's inward heart change toward his father was manifested outwardly by his actions. A truly repentant person will always get up out of the mud, leave the foreign country, and return to the Father.

The son rose up out of the pigpen, scraped the mud off his sandals, and took the first of many steps in a long journey. The road to his father's house had a luring power, drawing him back home. As he walked, he rehearsed his speech he would give the moment he met his father, "Father, I have sinned . . . I'm no longer worthy to be called your son . . . Father, I have sinned . . ." In his mind he was nervous and afraid, expecting his father to reject him because of the terrible things he had done.

| *Step # 8* | **Reconciliation with the father.** |

"But while he was still a long way off, his father saw him, and felt compassion for him, and ran and embraced him, and kissed him." (Luke 15:20)

The father hoped his son would return. Every day he stood on the porch watching for him. Then one day he saw someone limping toward his house, apparently from blisters received from having walked a long way. At first he thought it was a stranger. Then he realized, "It's my son! My son has come home!"

The father jumped off the porch and ran down the road to welcome him. He threw his arms around his son and held him, never wanting to let go. As he kissed him, he wept uncontrollably. His father, who had shed tears of sorrow when he left, was now crying tears of joy.

The son was stunned. Instead of being rejected by his father, he was warmly received and accepted. At that moment, it dawned on him that his father had always felt this way about him, but his rebellion had blinded him to his father's goodness.

God has a divine order. Reconciliation occurs after repentance, not before. The father did not run after the son when the boy left because the son's heart pointed away from him. No amount of chasing the son down the road would ever convince him to return home.

But now because his son's heart was turned back toward his father, he could run to receive his son. James 4:8 tells us, "Draw near to God and He will draw near to you." Once the son had decided to draw near to his father, then his father was free to run to him.

Restoration of the son's privileges.

"And the son said to him, 'Father, I have sinned against heaven and in your sight; I am no longer worthy to be called your son.' But the father said to his slaves, 'Quickly bring out the best robe and put it on him, and put a ring on his hand and sandals on his feet.'" (Luke 15:21–22)

The son began his rehearsed speech, "Father, I have sinned. . . . I'm no longer worthy to be called your son," when the father interrupted and gave orders to his slaves. "Bring the best robe and ring." The best robe and ring were symbols of the privileges of sonship. Rather than the son becoming a slave and waiting on the father, the father had the slaves waiting on his son. The privileges of his sonship had been restored.

Rejoicing in the father's house.

"And bring the fattened calf, kill it, and let us eat and be merry; for this son of mine was dead, and has come to life again; he was lost, and has been found.' And they began to be merry." (Luke 15:23–24)

Because the son had returned home, the father threw a party. Joy had once again returned to the father's house. Rejoicing can only come after repentance and reconciliation have taken place. If you have lost your joy, it may be because you have been away from the Father. When you return home, the joy of your salvation will be restored to its fullest (Ps. 51:12).

Robert Robinson was converted under the preaching of George Whitefield. He became a pastor and wrote the hymn, "Come, Thou

Fount." Later in his ministry, he neglected his fellowship with God and drifted away from the Lord.

In an attempt to find peace, he traveled. During one of his journeys, he met a young woman on a stagecoach who sang the hymn "Come, Thou Fount." The third verse contained the phrase, "Prone to wander, Lord, I feel it, prone to leave the God I love." The woman asked Robinson what he thought of the hymn.

He was overcome with emotion and said, "Madam, I am the poor, unhappy man who wrote that hymn years ago, and I would give a thousand worlds if I had them to enjoy the feelings I had then."

The young lady reminded him that the "streams of mercy" mentioned in his song were still flowing.

Robinson, convinced this was a divine appointment, turned his wandering heart back to the Father and was restored to fellowship.[2]

Maybe you have wandered from the Father. You have traveled to the distant land and have lived in the pig pen. You want to come back home, but you are afraid the Heavenly Father will reject you because of the terrible things you have done.

I've got good news for you. He is still waiting on the porch, watching and hoping you will come home!

Returning Home

- In what ways have you rebelled against God?

- Make a definite turn in your heart from the "foreign land" to the "promised land."

- Take the steps necessary to leave your backslidden condition and return home.

- Pray the following prayer:

"Heavenly Father, forgive me for rebelling against you. I will get up out of my pigpen and return to fellowship with you. Thank you for loving me in spite of the things I have done. By your grace, I won't do them again."

CHAPTER 23

When You Are Afraid of Dying

Scared to Death of Death

You do not know what your life will be like tomorrow. You are just
a vapor that appears for a little while and then vanishes away.

(James 4:14)

ANTHONY FERNANDO, a twenty-one-year-old man living in
Colombo, Sri Lanka, went fishing one day off the coast of
the island. He had no idea he would never make it back
alive. If you would venture to guess how this man lost his life, what
would you say? That he died from a heart attack? Perhaps he fell out
of the boat and drowned? Or how about a shark attack?

It was none of these things. A forktail gar fish jumped out of the
water and cut him on the neck with its tail. He bled to death before a
fellow fisherman could get him to a hospital.[1] If you had told him before
he left to go fishing this would happen, he wouldn't have believed it.

Lance Foster, a twenty-three-year-old student at the University of
Kansas was studying at his desk one night. Little did he know he
would be dead a few minutes later.

How did he die? Was he shot by a roommate? Or did lightning
come through his window and strike him? It was neither. He was
killed by a soda machine.

Foster became thirsty and walked down the hallway to get something to drink. He put his money in the machine, but the drink did-
n't come out. When he rocked the vending machine back and forth
to get the can of soda, the machine fell on top of him. He died from
internal injuries shortly thereafter.[2] If you had told him he would die
when he got a drink, he wouldn't have believed it.

If you would have told Ali-Asghar Ahani he would be shot to
death by a snake, he wouldn't have believed it. But it happened.

Although he could have shot the snake, this man from Iran was trying to capture it alive. He pressed the butt of his shotgun behind its head, and the snake coiled itself around the gun. With its tail thrashing, the snake pulled the trigger, fired one of the barrels, and shot Ahani in the head.[3] This man also died an unexpected and unusual death.

After winning $3.6 million in the lottery, William Curry must have thought he was the luckiest person in the world. But he wasn't lucky for very long. Two weeks after hitting the jackpot, Curry, at the age of thirty-seven, died of a heart attack. His sister-in-law said the stress of winning the lottery killed him.[4]

None of these people knew or even imagined that death was just moments away. Death can come unexpectedly to anyone.

Have you ever thought about how you will die? Will you be cut by a fishtail? Crushed by a soda machine? Shot by a snake? Maybe your heart will just stop beating. You probably won't be able to predict how or when your death will occur. Nevertheless, you have an appointment with death. You have a one-way ticket to the grave, and the fact you are getting older is a reminder that the train has not stopped.

Everyone is biodegradable. Statistics show one out of every one person is going to die. It is coming, whether you like it or not. When your turn comes, you need to be prepared. No, you can do better than that. You can actually look forward to it.

Why People Fear Death

The truth is, many people are scared to death of death. King Louis XV of France was so afraid of death he ordered that the word "death" was never to be spoken in his presence. He believed if no one mentioned death, it wouldn't happen to him. It didn't work. He still died.

People are afraid of dying because they don't know what lies beyond the grave. Actually, it's the fear of God's judgment that makes most people afraid to die. Judgment can be a terrifying thing for people who don't know the Lord.

When W.C. Fields was on his deathbed, a visitor found him reading the Bible. The visitor asked why he was reading it, and Fields replied, "Looking for loopholes, my friend. Looking for loopholes." He didn't find any, but at least he found the right resource to answer his questions. When people face death, they instinctively know where to go to find the answers.

Not everyone is afraid of death. Sinicia, the pagan philosopher, realized Christians view death differently than non-Christians. He once stated, "Only Christians and idiots are not afraid to die." Those who have trusted Jesus to save them have been delivered from the fear of death.

> Since then the children share in flesh and blood, He Himself like-wise also partook of the same, that through death He might render powerless him who had the power of death, that is, the devil; and might deliver those who through fear of death were subject to slavery all their lives. (Heb. 2:14–15)

When Jesus Christ is Lord of your life, he will give you grace to face death. W. E. Sangster (1900–1960), one of England's outstanding Methodist preachers, was on his deathbed. He wrote to his young friend Billy Graham this note of hope: "All my life I have preached that Jesus Christ is adequate for every crisis. I have but a few days to live, and oh, Billy, Christ is indeed adequate in the hour of death. Tell everyone it is true."[5] God places a supernatural peace and confidence within each believer that calms the fear of death.

Throughout history we find numerous examples of Christians who were not afraid to die. In the early fourth century, a believer named Phocas lived outside the city of Sinope. He often welcomed travelers to his house to share his faith with them. During the reign of the Emperor Diocletian, an order was issued that all Christians were to be put to death. The name of Phocas of Sinope was high on the list given by the magistrates.

The officers of the magistrates, hot and weary from a long day's journey, arrived at Sinope.

Phocas, as he had done with so many travelers, welcomed them into his home. As the soldiers refreshed themselves, Phocas asked them their business in the area.

The commanding officer told him, "We have orders from Rome to execute a local Christian named Phocas. Do you know him and where he lives?"

"I know him well," Phocas replied. "Why don't you and your men rest for the night, and I will direct you to him in the morning."

When the men from Rome retired, Phocas went into his garden and began to dig. By sunrise, the hole he dug was large enough to bury a human body. He then woke the Roman soldiers, informing them, "I am Phocas, the man you are looking for."

The soldiers were astonished and insisted they couldn't put to death a man who had been so kind to them.

"Oh, please do," said Phocas. "I am a Christian and am not afraid to die. If you do not fulfill your orders, you will get into trouble. You must do your duty. It will not alter my love and affection for you."

Phocas was executed and lowered into the grave which he had dug in his own garden.[6] He was not afraid to die because he knew where his spirit would go after they killed his body.

Once you are assured that your spirit will be received by Jesus into heaven, the fear of death will leave.

What Happens When You Die

God did not create you to live forever in your natural body on this planet. He made you to last for eternity, but you must first live on earth for a while in a natural body. Your body is like a space suit which an astronaut wore when he walked on the moon. The suit enabled him to exist while he was away from earth. When he returned from his mission, he didn't need the space suit any longer.

When you go to someone's funeral, you are looking at the space suit that is not inhabited anymore. Nobody is in that body. It is a vacant shell—an empty house. The real person has left the body.

One young minister was doing his first funeral. He explained to the congregation how the spirit departs from the body when a person dies. Then he pointed to the corpse in the open casket and said, "Folks, what you see here is just a shell. The nut has already departed!"

Perhaps those weren't the best choice of words, but the point is clearly illustrated: When a person dies, the spirit departs from the body. James 2:26 tells us the body without the spirit is dead. The spirit lives on after death and enters into eternity while the body is left behind. Death does not stop your existence. It is simply the door through which you must go to exit this world and enter the next world.

At death your spirit immediately goes to stand before God for judgment to determine where you will spend eternity. Hebrews 9:27 says, "It is appointed for men to die once and after this comes judgment."

God desires for everyone to be saved (1 Tim. 2:4). That includes you. He doesn't want anyone to go to hell but for everyone to repent (2 Pet. 3:9). God wants you to go to heaven, but he can't save you if you reject his provision through Jesus Christ's death. He is the only way to heaven (John 14:6). He paid for your sins when he died on the cross (1 John 2:2), but if you refuse to accept him as your Savior, you must pay the sin debt yourself. Hell is a place where people pay for their sins throughout eternity because the debt will never be paid off.

However, if you accept Christ into your life, the sin debt is paid by Jesus on your behalf. You don't have to pay for your own sins, so you escape the judgment and pass from death into life (John 5:24). Instead of going to hell to pay for your sins, you are saved and will spend eternity with God in heaven (2 Cor. 5:8). (See the next chapter, "When You're Not Sure You're Saved," concerning how to be saved.)

What Death Is Like for the Christian

The thought of passing through the death door bothers most people. What will it be like? Jesus said death for the Christian is like sleep. It doesn't hurt when you go to sleep. Neither does it hurt when a believer dies because when Jesus rose from the dead, he took the sting out of death. "O death, where is your victory? O death, where is your sting?" (1 Cor. 15:55). Just like a bee loses its stinger when it stings, death lost its sting when it stung Jesus.

One little boy asked his mother what death was like.

"Do you remember when you fell asleep in the living room?" she asked. "Your father picked you up in his big, strong arms and took you to your bedroom. When you woke up, you found yourself in another room. Death for the Christian is like that. You go to sleep in one room and wake up in another."

Better on the Other Side

Paul said he had "the desire to depart and be with Christ, for that is very much better" (Phil. 1:23). Heaven will be far better than life on earth could ever hope to be. It is filled with eternal joy, without pain or suffering. It is a place where we will reside in God's kingdom forever and ever.

Whenever a believer dies, you miss the person on this side. But never forget that your loved one is greeted by Jesus on the other side.

Picture yourself standing on a seashore. A ship at the dock spreads its white sails to the morning breeze and slowly sails away. You watch it get smaller and smaller until it seems to disappear. Then someone at your side says, "There, she is gone."

But gone where? Gone from your sight, that is all. The ship is not gone; it is only gone from your view.

But on a distant shore, other eyes are watching as the ship grows larger and larger. Someone welcomes the ship with a great shout, "Here she comes!"[7] Although you can't see the person from this shore anymore, never forget Jesus is on the other shore greeting the person into his kingdom.

Understanding the joy of heaven will shatter your fear of death. Heaven is a place of unimaginable joy. People in heaven don't experience one iota of mental, emotional, or physical pain. And if you think heaven will be boring, you are wrong. It will be a place of eternal ecstasy. God has exciting jobs in heaven for those who have faithfully served him during their lives on earth. But these jobs will be fun and without stress, much like hobbies. This is why Paul said he preferred to be in heaven with Christ than to remain on earth.

If you are a Christian, you need not fear death. The sting of death is gone. A place has been reserved for you in heaven. And Jesus is on the other side, ready to welcome you into your eternal home!

Conquering the Fear of Death

- Ask Jesus to come into your life and forgive all your sins.

- Read Revelation 21 and 22 concerning your future eternity in heaven.

- Read chapter 13, "When You Are Afraid."

CHAPTER 24

When You're Not Sure You're Saved
Heaven's Entrance Exam

These things I have written to you who believe in the name of the Son of God, in order that you may know that you have eternal life.

(1 John 5:13)

A COLLEGE FOOTBALL COACH recruited an outstanding football player to play for his school. The football player, however, did not score well enough on his entrance exam to get into college. The coach went to the dean of admissions and said, "We have to get this player into our school. Do whatever you can to get him in."

The dean, who was a big football fan said, "I'll give him an easy entrance exam, and if he passes it, we'll let him in."

The coach called the player in and said, "We're going to give you another entrance exam. There are only three questions on the test, but you have to get all of them correct in order to pass."

The dean asked him the first question, "How many days of the week begin with the letter T?"

The football player thought for a minute and said, "Two!" As the dean and the coach breathed a sigh of relief, the player added, "Today and tomorrow!"

The coach looked at the dean and said, "Well, we did ask how many, and he answered correctly."

The dean said, "Very well. He got the first answer. The second question is, how many seconds are in a year?"

The football player got out a piece of paper and pencil and began figuring. He wrote, then erased, then wrote again. Then he answered, "Twelve. January 2nd, February 2nd, March 2nd..."

The coach said to the dean, "We didn't clarify what kind of seconds we were talking about. We've got to give him that one."

"I agree," said the dean. He then asked, "How many *d*'s are there in 'Rudolph the Red Nosed Reindeer'?"

Again the football player scribbled on the paper.

The coach and dean grew nervous because he was doing too much writing for such a simple answer.

Finally, the football player said, "One hundred and ten!"

"How did you arrive at that number?" the coach asked.

The athlete answered, singing to the tune of "Rudolph the Red Nosed Reindeer," "Dee-dee-dee-dee-dee-dee-dee…"

God also has an entrance exam to get into heaven with three questions on it. These deal with your perception of Jesus, how you view the cross, and what is required to enter heaven. Unless you answer all of them correctly, you won't get in.

| *Question # 1* | **Who is Jesus?** |

In Matthew 16:15, Jesus asked the disciples, "Who do you say that I am?" He is asking you that same question. You must answer it correctly, or you will not be admitted into heaven.

Some say Jesus was just a man. One cult teaches Jesus was an angel. Some say he was a prophet. Still others refuse to believe he even existed.

Peter answered, "Thou art the Christ, the Son of the living God" (v. 16).

That's the correct answer, but what does "Son of God" mean? The term "Son" refers to his humanity and the term "God" refers to his deity. Although he was born as a human in Bethlehem, he also existed in eternity past as God (Micah 5:2). Jesus existed as God in heaven, then put on flesh and lived among us (John 1:1, 14).

Imagine a sponge represents the deity of Christ and a glass jar represents his humanity. Jesus existed as the eternal Word in eternity past (the sponge). The Word becoming flesh can be illustrated by putting the sponge into the glass jar. He is both God (the sponge) and man (the jar). Jesus was only begotten, meaning he had a one-of-a-kind birth. He was all God, yet he was also all man.

| Question # 2 | **What did Jesus do on the cross?** |

We all know that Jesus died on the cross. But something occurred on the cross in the spiritual realm which was not visible to the human eye. He Himself bore our sins in His body on the cross" (1 Pet. 2:24).

He bore your sins on the cross. The people watching Jesus die could not see what was happening in the spiritual realm. Because people can't see sins with their physical eyes, those watching the crucifixion couldn't see him bearing their sins.

Jesus died for the sins of the whole world (1 John 2:2). That includes my sins and your sins. Somehow when Jesus died on the cross, he reached into the future and gathered up all of my sins and your sins and placed them upon himself. On that day, the price for your salvation was paid by Jesus.

But not everyone views the cross in the same way. The cross is foolishness to those who are perishing, but to us who are saved, it is the power of God (1 Cor. 1:18). What do you say happened on the cross?

The Archbishop of Paris was once preaching to a large congregation in Notre Dame Cathedral. He told the story of three carefree, worldly, godless men who wandered into the cathedral one day. Two of the men made a bet with the third man that he could not make a bogus confession to the priest. He accepted the bet. During the confession, he made up a story about a sin he committed.

The priest realized what was happening. When the third man finished, the priest said, "Go to the crucifix, kneel down before it, and repeat three times, 'All this you did for me, and I don't care.'"

The young man did what the priest asked. After kneeling down, he said, "All this you did for me, and I…" Immediately, his heart was torn in two with repentance, and tears rolled down his cheeks. His life was changed, and he became a new creation in Christ Jesus.

After completing the story, the archbishop announced to the congregation, "I was that young man!"[1]

What does the cross mean to you? Once you realize what Jesus did for you, you won't be the same. People who look at the cross and walk away unchanged do not see what happened there. Do you see what really happened at the cross?

Question # 3	**What must I do to be saved?**

A Philippian jailer once asked Paul and Silas, "What must I do to be saved?"

They answered, "Believe in the Lord Jesus, and you shall be saved" (Acts 16:30–31). You can get the first question right, and you can get the second question right, but if you miss the answer to this third question, you have failed the entrance exam.

The first thing we need to understand is we cannot save ourselves. Imagine being on a ship in the middle of the Atlantic Ocean and falling overboard. Because no one saw you fall in, the ship continues toward its destination, leaving you hopelessly lost. After treading water for several hours, you find yourself surrounded by sharks. You face certain death at any moment. Exhausted from trying to stay afloat, you slip underwater and begin to drown. Somehow, you force your way to the surface for one more gasp of air.

As you are about to go under for the last time, a helicopter appears miraculously out of nowhere. The rescue squad throws out a rope and lassoes your hand, pulling you out of the water just seconds before the sharks move in for the kill. The helicopter flies you back to shore, where you receive treatment in the hospital.

After you recover, you brag about how you saved yourself. "I'm really proud of my hand. This hand saved me. Let me tell you how I found the helicopter in the middle of the ocean…"

Just like we can't save ourselves if we were stranded in the Atlantic, we are also helpless to save ourselves from hell. God doesn't want our help, either. Because Jesus does all of the saving, we have no right to brag about anything we have done. "For by grace you have been saved through faith; and that not of yourselves, it is the gift of God; not as a result of works, that no one should boast" (Eph. 2:8–9). The Father sent the Son to be the Savior of the world (1 John 4:14). The Savior of the world is not the Son plus (fill in your name). Jesus is the only Savior.

The only thing we can do to be saved is to trust Jesus to save us. We cannot work long enough or hard enough to merit salvation. Some people once asked Jesus, "'What shall we do, that we may work the works of God?' Jesus answered and said to them, 'This is the work of God, that you believe in Him whom He has sent'" (John 6:28–29).

Because salvation is a free gift, it cannot be earned as a wage. Jason wanted to do something nice for his friend Darrin, so he bought him two 50-yard-line tickets for a Green Bay Packers football game. He drove to Darrin's house and rang the doorbell. When Darrin opened the door, Jason said, "These tickets are a gift to you from me."

Darrin was excited about the tickets, but instead of receiving them, he jumped in his car and drove away. Jason was puzzled by his friend's strange behavior.

Later, when Jason returned home, he discovered Darrin mowing his yard.

Huffing and puffing, with sweat dripping off his brow, Darrin said, "Jason, I'll take those tickets now!"

"Why didn't you take them when I first offered them to you?" Jason asked.

"I didn't feel worthy enough to take them as a free gift," Darrin replied, "so I decided I would earn them by mowing your yard."

Darrin tried to earn the tickets as a wage rather than receive them as a free gift. In the same way, many people attempt to earn their salvation as a paycheck from God by attending church, confessing sins, being baptized, taking communion, and giving money. All these things are good but will never be good enough to purchase the ticket. "Now to the one who works, his wage is not reckoned as a favor, but as what is due. But to the one who does not work, but believes in Him who justifies the ungodly, his faith is reckoned as righteousness" (Rom. 4:4–5).

The only thing you can add to the cross that Jesus died on is your sins, not your works.

One lady argued with her pastor because she believed her religious works would help get her into heaven. "I think getting to heaven is like rowing a boat," she said. "One oar is faith and the other oar is works. If you use both, you get there. If you use only one, you go around in circles."

"There is only one thing wrong with your illustration," replied the pastor. "Nobody is going to heaven in a rowboat!"[2]

Too many people are trying to paddle their way to heaven rather than simply trusting in the finished work done by Jesus on the cross.

He paid the price for the ticket to heaven. You don't have to mow any yards to earn it either. You simply need to receive it.

If you don't know if you are a child of God, you can receive Jesus right now by praying this prayer and meaning it with your heart:

> "Heavenly Father, I know that I have done a lot of bad things. I have sinned against you, and I need to be forgiven.
>
> "Jesus, I thank you that you died on the cross for me. Thank you for paying for every one of my sins. I open the door of my heart and invite you to come in. I receive you and your forgiveness into my life right now.
>
> "Fill me with the Holy Spirit and empower me to live for you.
>
> "Thank you for saving me! Amen."

Now I want to ask you, did he come into your life? Yes, he did! He promised that he would (Rev. 3:20), and he wants to live through you. You now need to grow as a Christian. Tell someone that you have received Jesus into your life. Read at least one chapter of the Bible every day. Find a church that preaches God's Word, then get involved there.

I'll see you in heaven!

Passing Heaven's Entrance Exam

- Have you prayed the above prayer?

- If you received Jesus into your heart, write down the date on this page or in your Bible.

- Tell others how to be saved, and pray the above prayer with them.

SOURCE NOTES AND STUDY GUIDE

Chapter One
When You Need God to Provide

1. *Faith & Renewal,* March/April, 1993, 29.
2. *The Best of In Other Words.* Raymond McHenry, 1996, 32-22.
3. Graham, Franklin. "When the Lights Went On."In *Snowflakes in September.* (Nashville: Dimensions for Living, 1992), 38.

Chapter Three
When You Are Discontented

1. Hyles, Jack. *Revival Fires!* April 1995, 6.
2. *Garden City Telegram,* September 30, 1996, B-10.

Chapter Four
When You Are Tempted

1. Tan, Paul Lee. *Encyclopedia of 7700 Illustrations.* Rockville, MD: Assurance Publishers, 1979, 1534.
2. Anderson, Neil. *Victory Over Darkness.* Ventura, CA: Regal Books, 1990, 162-163

Chapter Five
When You Can't Forgive Someone

1. Windsor, Carl. *On This Day.* Nashville: Thomas Nelson Publishers, 1989, 93.

Chapter Six
When You Can't Forgive Yourself

1. *Reader's Digest,* September 1991, 32.
2. *Our Daily Bread,* RBC Ministries, Grand Rapids, MI.
3. *Leadership,* Fall 1983, 86.

Chapter Seven
When You Are Disappointed

1. Taylor, Ken. My Life: A Guided Tour. Wheaton: Tyndale House, 1991, 75.

Chapter Eight
When You Need to Make A Change

1. McCullough, Don. "Reasons to Fear Easter." In *Preaching Today,* Tape 116.
2. Knight, Walter. *Knight's Master Book of New Illustrations.* Grand Rapids, MI: Eerdmans Publishing Co., 1956, 510.

Chapter Nine
When You Are Depressed

1. Duncan, King. *2,000 Quips, Quotes, and Anecdotes.* Knoxville, TN: Seven Worlds Corporation, 1994, 5-6.
2. *Our Daily Bread,* RBC Ministries, Grand Rapids, MI.
3. *The Saturday Evening Post,* September/October 1992, 61.
4. Leman, Kevin. *Parenthood Without Hassles.* Eugene, OR: Harvest House, 1979, 136.
5. Thorn, W. E. *Watching The World Go By.* 1987, 125.

Chapter Eleven
When You Are Being Criticized

1. Powell, Paul. A Pastoral Letter, July 1993. As cited in *The Best of In Other Words,* Raymond McHenry, 1996, 146-147.
2. Source unknown.
3. Tan, 296.
4. Hay, Peter. *The Book of Business Anecdotes.* New York, New York: Facts On File Publications, 1988.

Chapter Thirteen
When You Are Afraid

1. Larson, Bruce. *The Presence.* HarperCollins Publishers, 1988, 10-11.
2. *USA Today,* October 23, 1989.
3. *Quote,* August 1992, 248.

Chapter Fourteen
When You Have to Make a Decision

1. *A Treasury of Bible Illustrations,* Chattanooga, TN: AMG Publishers, 1995, 113.
2. Carroll, Lewis. *Alice in Wonderland.* New York, New York: The MacMillan Company, 1943, 89.

Chapter Fifteen
When You Feel Like Complaining

1. Harbour, Brian. *Brian's Lines,* May 1991.

Chapter Sixteen
When You Are Middle-Aged

1. Peck, M. Scott. *Further Along the Road Less Traveled.* Simon & Schuster, 1993, 155-156.

Chapter Seventeen
When Your Life Is Missing Something

1. Farrar, Steve. *Pastor to Pastor.* Tape interview, Focus on the Family, Vol. 13, 1994.
2. Stackel, Robert. "Four Pictures of God's Grace." *The Clergy Journal,* November/December 1993, 13.

Chapter Eighteen
When You Carry Heavy Burdens

1. Bess, C.W. *Nothing Can Separate Us.* Nashville, TN: Broadman Press, 1986, 25-26.

Chapter Twenty
When You Are Angry

1. Campolo, Anthony. *Seven Deadly Sins.* Wheaton:IL: Victor Books, 1987.
2. The Voice of the Village, July/August 1996.

Chapter Twenty-One
When Bad Things Happen

1. Tan, 1509.

Chapter Twenty-Two
When You Have Drifted from God

1. McPhee, John. Oranges, New York: Noonday Press, 1966, 53.
2. McHenry, 27.

Chapter Twenty-Three
When You Are Afraid of Dying

1. Associated Press article, March 8, 1988.
2. Associated Press article, May 8, 1989.
3. Associated Press article, April 24, 1990.
4. *USA Today,* September 26, 1990.
5. Carlson, Paul. *Before I Wake.* Elgin, IL; David C. Cook, 1975, 143.
6. Barclay, Jan. *Living and Enjoying the Fruit of the Spirit.* Chicago, IL: Moody Press, 1976, 14-15.
7. Boettner, Loraine. *Immortality.* Philadelphia, PA: The Presbyterian and Reformed Publishing Co., 1956, 29-30.

Chapter Twenty-Four
When You're Not Sure You're Saved

1. Harbour, Brian. *Brian's Lines,* February, 1992.
2. Wiersbe, Warren. *Be Joyful,* Wheaton, Illinois: Victor Books, 1974, 84.

Lesson 1 / Chapter 1
When You Need God to Provide

Using the example of the fish with the coin in its mouth, discuss from God's perspective how he performed the miracle.

According to Jeremiah 32:17, 27, what problem is too difficult for God?

Fact #1: God knows our needs before we ask.

Read Matthew 17:24–27 and make a list of the things Jesus knew before they happened.

Read Psalm 139:1–4. What are seven things mentioned in this passage that God knows about you?

Is God is fully aware of your present situation?

If God knows our needs before we ask, why should we pray?

Fact #2: God controls events that we can't control.

Discuss the reasons why Jesus told Peter to use a hook rather than a net.

The fish with the coin in its mouth bit on Peter's hook. How does this demonstrate that God controls circumstances beyond our control?

How does this apply to the problems we face every day?

Fact #3: God's timing is perfect.

A "divine appointment" occurs when God causes two paths to cross at a predetermined time. Discuss what can be learned from the following divine appointments:

• Jonah was caught by the whale (Jonah 1:15–17).

What would have happened if the whale was late for the appointment?

Discuss God's purpose for the whale.

• The ram was caught in the thicket (Genesis 22:10–14).

Do you think Abraham was expecting God to provide a ram? (Hebrews 11:17–19)

What is the correlation between obedience and provision?

What does this teach us about God's ability to provide at the last moment?

Fact #4: God supplies needs to those who obey him.

God didn't cause the fish to jump into the boat. Sometimes we must throw out some lines in order to see God's provision. What are some modern day examples of "throwing out lines"?

Have you ever thrown out a line? Discuss.

What are some modern day examples of "fishing in the Dead Sea"? Have you ever done this? Discuss.

If Peter had thrown out of net instead of a hook, what would have been some possible consequences of his disobedience?

In this example of the fish with the coin in its mouth, what have you learned about God's provision?

In what ways can you exercise this new faith in God to provide?

Lesson 2 / Chapter 2
When Your Faith is Weak

Read James 1:5–8. Doubt wavers between faith and unbelief, unable to make up its mind what it wants to be. Why is the one who doubts like the surf of the sea driven and tossed by the wind?

How can doubt affect the decisions we make? (James 1:8)

How can every wind of doctrine toss us to and fro? (Ephesians 4:14)

How to Deal with Doubts

Read Matthew 14:28–31. When Peter was walking on the water, what caused him to doubt? (v. 30–31)

What role do circumstances play in causing us to waver in our faith?

First, Question your doubts, not your faith.

What does it mean to question your doubts, rather than your faith? Give an example.

John the Baptist was confused because he expected Jesus to correct all injustice, which he will do at his second coming to earth. How did John's misunderstanding of Scripture cause him to doubt?

How can misunderstanding the Scriptures can us to doubt?

Second, Concentrate on what you know, not on what you don't know.

Read John 9:1, 6–8, 18–21, 25. When the blind man was healed, the Pharisees wanted to know how Jesus performed the miracle. Rather than trying to explain something he didn't understand, what was his response? (v. 25)

We don't have to understand everything completely before we can believe. What lesson can we learn from this former blind man?

Read Philippians 4:8. How can letting our minds dwell on the right things keep us from doubting?

Third, Trust in the Lord with your heart, not your head.

Read Proverbs 3:5. What does it mean to lean on your own understanding?

What does it mean to trust the Lord with all your heart?

How can depending upon our logic keep us from trusting God?

Lesson 3 / Chapter 3
When You Are Discontented

Contentment-Deficit Disorder isn't a real disorder, but simply a scapegoat on which to blame our restlessness. Name several ways discontentment is manifested.

First, Accept the fact that God has given you an assigned seat.

Read Philippians 4:11–12. Paul said he *learned* how to be content in every circumstance. How did he learn this valuable lesson and how can we also learn it?

Paul said he learned the *secret* of being content. Name some facts about secrets.

Paul believed God assigned him a seat in prison. What does this say about God's control of our circumstances?

How does our view of circumstances influence our contentment?

Second, Learn to coexist with the crab.

Why does the grizzly bear choose to coexist with the skunk? What can we learn from this example?

How can fighting your crab make your situation worse?

Discuss some ways God is using the crab in your life.

What attitude should we have toward the crab? (Luke 6:32)

Third, Realize changing seats does not solve the problem.

Myth #1: "If I could be with someone else, then I would be happy."

Single people want to change seats and get married, while married people want to change seats and be single again. Discuss how people have illusions about life "on the other side of the fence."

Discuss the statement, "Discontentment is an internal problem, not an external one."

Myth #2: "If I could just go somewhere else, then I would be happy."

Why does the grass always look greener somewhere else?

Myth #3: "If I could just get something else, then I would be happy."

Read 1 Timothy 6:17. If God has given us all things to enjoy, what keeps people from enjoying them?

Why must we first be happy with what we already have before we can enjoy the new things we receive?

Fourth, Don't allow the crab to ruin your trip.

What does it mean to "enjoy the trip"?

How can a crab keep us from enjoying the trip through life?

What can we do to keep the crab from ruining the trip?

Lesson 4 / Chapter 4
When You Are Tempted

Lesson #1: **We can reduce temptations by avoiding the places of temptation.**

How are some ways we can avoid places of temptation?

What did Jesus mean when he said, "Lead us not into temptation"?

Lesson #2: **We open ourselves to temptation when we decide to provide for the flesh.**

Read Romans 13:14. What does it mean to provide for the flesh?

How is your *decision* the pivotal point in the temptation process?

Lesson #3: **When we move into the place of temptation, Satan will be waiting there to tempt us.**

How did Satan know to wait for Adam and Eve at the forbidden tree?

What does it mean to make no place for the devil? (Ephesians 4:27)

Lesson #4: **After we have entered into temptation, we become blinded to the consequences.**

How do we view temptation's consequences when we are outside the temptation versus after we have entered into it?

Why do we become blinded after we have entered into temptation?

Lesson #5: **The pull of temptation increases the closer we get to the forbidden fruit.**

How does the statement "It is hard to pick fruit if you are a hundred yards away, but it is easy at arm's length" apply to us today?

Why does willpower grow weaker as we get nearer to the temptation?

Lesson #6: **We must run away from temptation rather than try to resist it.**

Why is it impossible to successfully overcome temptation by trying to resist it? (Matthew 26:41)

How is the best way to get out of temptation? (1 Corinthians 6:18; 2 Timothy 2:22)

When we flee, what are we running *out of?*

Lesson #7: **Forbidden fruit is never as sweet as you have been told it will be.**

Discuss what Adam and Eve must have thought immediately after they ate the forbidden fruit.

From observing others who have eaten forbidden fruit, does it look like they are enjoying it? Compare their immediate satisfaction with long-term consequences.

What can we learn from this?

Lesson #8: **When we are full of God's fruit, we won't be hungry for forbidden fruit.**

Discuss how eating the legitimate fruit would have prevented Adam and Eve from eating forbidden fruit. How does this apply to us today?

What is God's remedy for victory over temptation? (Galatians 5:16)

Lesson 5 / Chapter 5
When You Can't Forgive Someone

Read Matthew 18:23–30. Why do you think the first slave forgot how much he was forgiven ($50 million)?

First, **We base our forgiveness on what God has done for us, rather than on what the person has done to us.**

What do most people base their forgiveness of others upon?

Explain how Christ's death on the cross changed our perspective on how we view others and what they may have done to us.

Discuss the difference between the $15 debt and the $50 million debt.

Second, **We must let God heal our past wounds.**

Discuss the story about the boy sitting on a bumble bee. How does this apply when we have been hurt by someone?

Third, **We need to feel compassion for the person who hurt us.**

The king felt compassion of the slave. How can feeling compassion toward others motivate us to forgive?

How can we increase compassion for those who have hurt us?

Fourth, **We choose to pay off the debt the person owes us.**

When the king forgave the slave, he paid off the debt himself. What does it mean to "pay off the debt" when we forgive someone?

What is proof we have done this?

Fifth, **We stop replaying the hurt on the screen of our minds.**

What does it mean to hit the "play" button on the VCR in our minds?

How does replaying the hurt cause the pain to be multiplied worse than the original wounding?

How can we "erase the tape" in our minds?

Sixth, **We must release the person from our prison.**

The king forgave *and released* the slave from the debt. Forgiveness is not complete until you release the person from the dungeon of your soul. Why does it take an act of your will to release someone out of your prison?

How does releasing people from your dungeon set *you* free?

Lesson 6 / Chapter 6
When You Can't Forgive Yourself

Read Matthew 27:20–25. Why do you think Pilate washed his hands?

Method #1: Blame It On Someone Else

How did Pilate use this method?

How did Adam and Eve use this method?

In what ways do you use this method?

Method #2: Run and Hide

What happened to Peter after he denied Jesus? (Matthew 26:75)

How do people today use this method when it comes to Christian fellowship?

If you know someone who has dropped out of church or fellowship, what might be an underlying reason?

Method #3: Cover It Up

Explain how Judas used this method at the Last Supper in the upper room.

How is this method related to hypocrisy?

Method #4: Get Some Professional Help

Why does this method fail so many times?

How do many counselors deal with the guilt problem?

The Only Cure for the Guilt Problem

Read Matthew 27:25. How did the crowd give the answer to the guilt problem without realizing it?

First, **Admit what you have done.**

Why is confession the first step in canceling guilt trips? (Psalm 32:5)

From a guilty person's perspective, how can confession benefit?

Second, **Receive the cleansing.**

Because Jesus has already died for our sins on the cross, what is the only thing left?

How does a person receive a gift?

How can a person receive something he or she can't see?

Explain how the duck story relates to the lies of Satan.

Lesson 7 / Chapter 7

When You Are Disappointed

Leftovers: Second-Choice Casserole

Read Genesis 13:5–9. Although Abram had the right to choose first, he gave Lot the first choice of land. What does this show concerning Abram's belief in God's sovereignty (God's ability to control outcomes)?

What attitude did Abram have while making this land deal?

How can we apply his example to our lives today?

Why did God wait until after Lot made his choice to tell Abram his land was the promised land?

Lot's land, which appeared best at first, became a nightmare. Abram's land, which appeared to be leftovers, turned out to be the promised land. What can we learn from this?

Leftovers: Canaanite Crumb Cake

Read Matthew 15:21–28. Why did Jesus ignore the Canaanite woman's requests?

How did the seemingly cold response by Jesus develop her faith?

What can we learn from this concerning God's will and persistence?

What did this Gentile woman possess that the Jews didn't have?

Leftovers: Andrew's Fish and Chips

Read John 6:5–13. After Jesus performed the miracle of feeding the multitude with five loaves and two fish, twelve baskets were left over. Why didn't he make the food come out even?

Why did Jesus tell his disciples to gather up the leftovers?

What can we learn from this?

Have the group discuss some examples when they received leftovers. Are there any testimonies where leftovers turned into blessings? Pray for those who are still waiting for God to do a miracle.

Lesson 8 / Chapter 8
When You Need to Make a Change

Read Matthew 14:25–31. What is a comfort zone?

What is the greatest danger of a comfort zone?

Comfort Zone Principles

Principle #1: We break through comfort zones when we do something that makes us feel uncomfortable.

Why is it important for us to break through our comfort zones?

How does the boat represent a comfort zone?

Why do we feel uncomfortable whenever we break through a comfort zone?

Principle #2: We break through comfort zones by refusing to listen to our fears.

Why We Stay in the Boat:

How can fear of criticism keep us in the boat?

How does the fear of failure keep us in the boat?

How can failure help make us successful?

Give some examples of imaginary dragons that keep people in the boat.

Principle #3: We break through comfort zones by taking a step of faith.

Why did Peter ask Jesus to command him to come?

What commitment did Peter make when he stepped out of the boat?

Using the analogy of feet and the boat, explain the difference between unbelief, doubt, and faith.

Explain how taking a step of faith can shatter the stronghold of fear.

Principle #4: We break through comfort zones in order to fulfill God's will.

What is the primary motivation for breaking out of a comfort zone?

Why did Peter need to hear Jesus say "come" before he got out of the boat?

Before we can make a change, what do we need to understand?

Principle #5: We break through comfort zones to experience freedom on the other side.

Why did Peter sink after taking a few steps on the water?

Why is freedom found outside of every comfort zone?

What are some comfort zones you need to break through? What steps do you need to take?

Lesson 9 / Chapter 9

When You Are Depressed

Read 1 Kings 19:1–4. The Elijah Complex is when we lose all sense of God's presence, protection, and provision.

Thought #1: Your problem appears to be bigger than God.

When we get depressed, why do our problems appear so large?

Read Romans 12:1–2. How can renewing our minds day by day bring back the correct perspective?

Thought #2: You see yourself as the only one with problems.

Elijah thought he was the only one left who served God (1 Kings 19:10). Why does depression make us think we are alone in dealing with our problems?

Read 1 Peter 5:9. How can knowing that other Christians are experiencing the same problems encourage us?

Why did God tell Elijah that 7,000 in Israel had not bowed to Baal?

Thought #3: You lose hope for the future.

Read 1 Kings 19:4. How do we know Elijah was depressed?

Read the "Thought-Analyzer Test." Discuss how our thoughts can affect our emotions.

What is the cause for most depression?

Read Proverbs 17:22. How can a joyful heart be good medicine?

Explain why the two sons of the alcoholic father were completely different when they became adults.

How can we apply this lesson to our own lives?

What to do when you are depressed:

First, Put your hope in God.

In Psalm 42:5, David commanded his soul to hope in God. When we are depressed, why is it important to regain our hope?

How can we put our hope in God? (Hebrews 4:16)

Second, Sing in the dark.

David said, "And His song will be with me in the night" (Psalm 42:8). Why is singing praise and worship to God important during times when we are depressed?

Read Acts 16:25–26. Discuss the correlation between Paul and Silas' singing to God and the miracle of being set free from prison.

What parallels do you see in the spiritual realm?

Third, Rejoice it the Lord.

According to Philippians 4:4, how often should we rejoice?

Give two reasons when we should rejoice, even when we don't feel like it.

Fourth, Reach out and help other people.

According to Dr. Viktor Frankl, those in the prison camps who focused on helping others were mentally and physically stronger. Explain why.

Why is it necessary for a depressed person to turn their eyes from inward to outward?

Fifth, Change the way you view your problem.

When Moses sent the twelve spies into the promised land, ten returned with a bad report and two had a good report. Even though they all had seen the same set of circumstances, why did they have differing reports?

How does this apply to our outlook on life?

What was the key factor in Barbara being set free from her depression?

Lesson 10 / Chapter 10

When You Feel Like Quitting

Read Galatians 6:9. Burnout is a modern-day term for "growing weary." What is the primary cause for burnout?

Stage #1: We become disillusioned.

What causes us to become disillusioned?

Give some examples (marriage, job, etc.) how someone can get disillusioned.

Stage #2: We become discouraged.

What does it mean to "lose heart"?

Why is it important to not lose heart?

Fill in the blanks and briefly what the consequences will be if we quit.

Don't lose heart in _____ (Luke 18:1) _____

Don't lose heart in _____ (2 Corinthians 4:1) _____

Don't lose heart in _____ (Galatians 6:9) _____

Don't lose heart in _____ (Colossians 3:21) _____

Don't lose heart in _____ (Hebrews 12:3) _____

Stage #3: We become discontented.

What are some signs that we have become discontented?

Why does discontent...ent disrespect God's will?

How does discontentment distort our view of life?

Stage #4: We become disassociated.

Once we decide to quit, we forfeit the reward of the harvest. What is the great tragedy of quitting?

How to Prevent Burn-Out

First, Rest from your labor.

Read Exodus 20:9–10. Why did God command us to rest one day a week from our labors?

Second, Reduce your workload.

What is the first thing we must do to reduce our workloads?

Third, Regulate your schedule.

What does it mean to live one day at a time?

What happens to us if we become pre-occupied with the burdens of tomorrow?

Fourth, Refuel your spirit.

According to Ephesians 5:18–19, what will happen to our hearts after we are filled with the Holy Spirit?

According to Ephesians 5:20, what else will we do?

Have the group share testimonies of being filled with the Holy Spirit gave them new power. If someone wants to be filled, pray with them to receive it by faith.

Fifth, Renew your vision.

Proverbs 29:18 says, "Where there is no vision, the people perish." Give a definition of "vision."

Why is having vision important?

How can we regain vision?

Lesson 11 / Chapter 11
When You Are Criticized

Six Reasons Why People Criticize:

Reason #1: Some people criticize because they have critical spirits.

Using the story about the dirty windshield, discuss how the dirt on a person's heart can affect how they view others.

Reason #2: Some people criticize because they don't know the whole story.

How can having partial information cause a person to make an incorrect judgment? Give some examples.

Reason #3: Some people criticize because it makes them feel better about themselves.

Why did the women's song make Saul angry?

How did Saul's self-image influence his treatment of David?

How does this explain why some people criticize today?

Reason #4: Some people criticize because it's easier to complain about problems than to solve them.

In what ways can people become critical when problems arise in their marriages or jobs?

Reason #5: Some people criticize because the person is godly.

Read 2 Timothy 3:12 and John 15:18–19. Why is it normal for a Christian who is living godly to be criticized?

Reason #6: Some criticize because a real fault needs correcting.

Read Proverbs 17:10. How is the one who has understanding different than the fool?

How does this apply when a critic discovers a real fault in you?

How to Respond to Criticism

First, View you critics as being sent by God.

Explain why David and Abishai had different perspectives concerning Shimei's cursing.

We can view our critics in one of two ways. What did Jesus say we must do when we are hated for His name? (Luke 6:22–23). Why?

What does this teach us about viewing our critics from heaven's perspective?

Second, Find the grain of truth in the criticism.

What was the grain of truth in Shimei's criticism?

How did Gen. Dwight Eisenhower use his critics to his advantage?

How can we apply this principle to our lives?

Third, Don't counter-criticize your critics.

Why didn't Jesus defend Himself against His accusers?

What happens to us if we counter-criticize our critics?

Fourth, Don't allow the critics to discourage you.

If you are laboring for the Lord, why does Satan raise up critics?

Why should we remember the Judgment Day when we are being criticized?

Lesson 12 / Chapter 12

When You Are Tired of Waiting

Symptom #1: Trying to help God

After waiting ten years to have a child, why did Sarai tell Abram to have a child through Hagar? (Genesis 16:1–3)

Read Genesis 17:18–19. What does this reveal about Abram's and Sarai's decision to use Hagar?

Discuss the story about Henry and Mr. Smith. What are some things we can learn from this about trying to help God?

Symptom #2: Overstepping the boundaries

What was Saul's excuse for not waiting for Samuel to offer the burnt offering? (1 Samuel 10:8; 13:8–12)

In what ways do we overstep our boundaries and do what is forbidden?

Because Saul overstepped his boundaries, what was his penalty? (1 Samuel 13:13–14)

What does this teach us about the consequences of not waiting for God's timing?

Symptom #3: Becoming restless and irritable

What does restlessness and irritability reveal about our spiritual condition?

Why Should We Wait on the Lord?

Reason #1: We may not be ready for what God has for us.

What would have been the consequences if Hannah started driving when she wanted?

What should a single person do while he or she is waiting to get married?

Reason #2: What God has planned for us may not be ready.

What does it mean, "There is an appointed time for everything?" (Ecclesiastes 3:1)

To find God's timing, why must we "watch the conductor" instead of the other musicians?

Reason #3: God is using the waiting period to develop patience within us.

Using the illustration of lifting weights, explain how patience can make life easier for us.

Reason #4: God wants to do a greater miracle for us.

What did Jesus do when he heard that Lazarus was sick? (John 11:6)

When Jesus arrived in Bethany, why was Martha upset at Jesus? (John 11:21)

How do you normally react when God doesn't perform according to your schedule?

Although Mary and Martha were not aware of the reason, why did Jesus delay his coming to Bethany? (John 11:4–6, 11–15)

Compare Martha and Mary's thoughts with Jesus' thoughts.

What can we learn from this?

How Do We Wait on the Lord?

Using Psalm 37:3–7 as a prescription for waiting, write a brief description of the four things we must do while waiting.

- **Trust in the Lord**
- **Delight yourself in the Lord**
- **Commit your way to the Lord**
- **Rest in the Lord**

Lesson 13 / Chapter 13
When You Are Afraid

Fear Isn't Logical

Using the illustration of the boxer, explain why fear isn't logical.

Have the group identify their fears by choosing the two things they fear the most from the list on page 119. (Allow them to share fears that are not on the list.)

How Fear Affects You

Share how fear can affect us:

Genesis 3:7–10 _____

Acts 9:19–21, 26 _____

Matthew 25:14–19, 24–25 _____

1 John 4:18 _____

Other ways: _____

_____

What can we learn from the French defeating the Austrian soldiers about how Satan controls people?

How to Deal with Fear

First, Seek the presence of the Lord and trust him.

Read Psalm 23:4. How can being aware of God's presence help us deal with fear?

Read Matthew 8:23–26. Discuss the relationship between fear and faith.

The disciples had to awaken Jesus to tell him the boat was sinking. What does this tell us about what Jesus believed?

What is the lesson we should learn when storms come our way?

Second, Face up to your problem.

Discuss how the lady who was afraid to fly on a plane overcame her fear.

How does this apply to every kind of fear?

Third, Stand on God's promises.

Read Psalm 91:5–10. What must we believe about God to not be afraid of the "terror by night" or the "arrow that flies by day"?

In order to overcome fear, what must we do? (Psalm 91:1–2).

How did the overnight camp-out resemble the situation of the disciples in the boat when the storm came?

What brought peace into the tent during the electrical storm?

Lesson 14 / Chapter 14, part 1

When You Need to Make a Decision

Guideline #1: Consult God's Word

Read Psalm 119:89. How long is God's Word "settled"? Why does this make God's Word the clearest revelation for us?

Read Psalm 119:105. Discuss the differences between the "lamp" and the "light"?

What is the relationship between the "feet" and the "path"?

How does this apply to guidance from God's Word?

Guideline #2: Pray for God's wisdom.

Read James 1:5–8. What does it mean to lack wisdom?

What does God tell us to do when we don't know what to do? (v. 5)
Why?

If God generously gives wisdom to all men, why aren't all men wise?

How can doubt keep us from receiving God's wisdom? (vv. 6–8)

Guideline #3: Gain insight through wise counselors.

• Choose godly counselors (Psalm 1:1)

Why is it important to not choose ungodly counselors?

What advantage is a godly counselor over an ungodly counselor?

• Choose wise and knowledgeable counselors (Proverbs 24:6)

If you are about to enter a war, what kind of counselor would you choose to advise you?

How does this apply to other decisions we need to make?

• Choose caring counselors (Proverbs 27:6)

What does it mean when it says the "wounds of a friend" are faithful?

Why is it important to choose a counselor who cares about us if we follow his or her advice?

• Choose a multitude of counselors (Proverbs 24:6).

Why is choosing several counselors the last factor to be considered?

Guideline #4: God will speak to your heart.

First, He will put desires in your heart (Psalm 37:4–5)

What does "desire" mean?

What does it mean to delight yourself in the Lord?

What does it mean that God will give you the desires of your heart?

Second, He will put peace in your heart (Colossians 3:15)

How can the peace of God act as an umpire when we are making a decision?

Read Philippians 4:6–7. What two things will the peace of God guard?

What does this mean?

Lesson 15 / Chapter 14, part 2
When You Need to Make a Decision

Guideline #5: God may speak through a sign.

What does a "sign from God" mean?

What are the two categories of signs?

God answered Gideon's two requests for signs (Judges 6:36–40). If God confirms our signs, what is this usually followed by?

Guideline #6: Look for open and closed doors.

An "open door" means a "door of opportunity." Does God want us to go through every open door? Why or why not?

Does every closed door mean it is not God's will? (Matthew 7:7–8)

Guideline #7: Gather all the facts about the decision.

Before we make a major decision, why is it important to "sit down"? (Luke 14:28)

What does "counting the cost" mean?

If you are thinking about moving, what are some factors to consider when "counting the cost"?

Guideline #8: Be sensitive to God's timing.

What does it mean that God has made everything appropriate in its time? (Ecclesiastes 3:11)

Read Psalm 32:8–9. Discuss some ways that God will lead us in the way we should go.

What does it mean when God says He will counsel us "with My eye upon you"?

How did Felix miss God's timing? (Acts 24:24–27)

What can we learn from his mistake?

Lesson 16 / Chapter 14, part 3
When You Need to Make a Decision

Guideline #9: Begin to make plans in the direction you are being led.

According to Proverbs 16:9, what is our responsibility?

What does it mean to plan your way?

What is God's responsibility?

How do plans give us direction?

How do plans keep us from getting diverted?

Guideline #10: Walk in the light you have.

What does it mean to "walk in the light you have"?

Read Psalm 119:105. Picture yourself walking at night, but your lamp only shines light on the path three feet in front of you. How does this illustrate "walking in the light you have"?

Guideline #11: God may lead without you knowing it.

When Abraham was called by God to leave his home and travel to another land, did he know where he was going? (Hebrews 11:8)

As he was traveling toward his unknown destination, what do you think was going through his mind?

How did Abraham know he had arrived at the correct place? (Genesis 12:7)

What can we learn from this about how God might lead us?

Guideline #12: Make your decision, and don't look back.

Why are we to remember Lot's wife? (Luke 17:32)

Why did she look back?

If what ways can we safeguard ourselves from looking back on the decisions we make?

Why will looking back cause problems for us, even if we have made the correct decision? (James 1:8)

Lesson 17 / Chapter 15

When You Feel Like Complaining

The pessimist says: "We wasted the day because we didn't catch anything."

The optimist says: "God had a reason why we didn't catch anything."

Discuss how viewpoint can determine whether a person becomes an optimist or a pessimist.

From God's perspective, what was the primary reason Charles Francis Adams needed to take his son fishing?

Discuss why we need to look beyond our human viewpoint in order to keep our attitudes right.

The pessimist says: "The fish aren't out there. It won't do any good."

The optimist says: "I will trust and obey, though I don't understand."

Discuss several reasons why it was God's will for them to fish all night and not catch anything.

Why do you think Peter decided to let down the nets again after they had worked all night and caught nothing?

Why does God sometimes allow us to exhaust our resources before he performs a miracle?

The pessimist says: "Look at the nets!"

The optimist says: "Look at the fish!"

How can the object of our attention determine whether we complain or rejoice?

How can focusing upon our blessings (fish) reduce the burden of our problems (broken nets)?

The pessimist says: "God is sinking our boats!"

The optimist says: "God is blessing our boats!"

Why did God allow them to catch so many fish that it filled the boat and began to sink?

What are "good" problems?

The pessimist says: "I'm not a bad person!"

The optimist says: "I'm a sinful man!"

Why does a pessimist think he's not a bad person?

Why did Peter call Jesus "Master" in verse 5, but called him "Lord" in verse 8?

The pessimist says: "I am losing my fishing business!"

The optimist says: "I am gaining eternal life!"

Why would they leave everything behind after they caught the tremendous haul of fish?

Why weren't they worried about the loss of income if they followed Jesus?

List some things we can do to change our attitudes from pessimistic to optimistic?

Lesson 18 / Chapter 16
When You Are Middle-Aged

Factor #1 The Aging Factor: The realization you are getting old.

What are some things that make people realize they are getting old?

How can this affect the way they view the future?

Factor #2 The Time Factor: Time seems to pass more quickly.

According to James 4:14, why is life compared to a vapor?

Read Psalm 90:12. What does it mean to number our days?

Factor #3 The Boredom Factor: Life becomes monotonous.

What makes people get bored with life?

Factor #4 The Failure Factor: Goals you haven't reached.

What does Proverbs 24:16 tell us about failure?

Factor #5 The Reflection Factor: Regrets over past decisions.

Why is it dangerous to try to start life over again?

How does Romans 8:28 give us a different view on our past decisions?

Calming Mid-Life Crisis:

First, **Don't panic!**

What can happen to us if we panic?

What is God's remedy for panicking? (Philippians 4:6–7)

What does it mean that the peace of God will surpass all comprehension?

Second, **Accept the fact that mid-life is a part of God's plan for you.**

"He has made everything appropriate in its time" (Ecclesiastes 3:11). How does this verse apply to mid-life?

Third, **Realize the benefits in every stage of life.**

Read Proverbs 20:29. What are the benefits of youth, mid-life, and old age?

Fourth, **Find meaning in life through serving God.**

Why is it foolish to live for the applause of this world?
(Ecclesiastes 2:16)

Why is it important to find meaning through serving God?

Fifth, **Look to the future with hope.**

According to Jeremiah 29:11, who has the plans for the future?

Why can we look to the future with hope instead of panic?

Lesson 19 / Chapter 17
When Your Life is Missing Something

Using the story of Carol making pies, how did Mrs. Smith's attitude change from grateful to ungrateful?

Describe some differences between being grateful and ungrateful.

Fact #1: Obedience goes the first mile, but gratefulness goes the second mile.

How did the nine lepers prove they weren't grateful?

How does this apply to us today?

Why do we place a great emphasis upon believing and obeying, but so little upon gratefulness?

What must we recognize about God in order for us to be truly thankful? (James 1:17)

What is the missing ingredient in fulfilling God's will?
(1 Thessalonians 5:18)

Fact #2: People who have been blessed are divided into two categories.

Discuss how the way we view life determines our level of gratitude.

Why is it important to realize we don't deserve what we receive?

Fact #3: Grateful people take extra steps that ungrateful people don't take.

How did the grateful leper take extra steps the ungrateful lepers didn't take?

In what ways can we take "extra steps" to show our gratitude?

Fact #4: Grateful people never have to be reminded to give thanks.

Why doesn't a grateful person have to be reminded to give thanks?

How does an attitude of gratitude make life's experiences different?

Fact #5: Jesus also expects the ungrateful people to thank him.

Why did Jesus ask where the other nine lepers were?

What does this tell us about what God desires from us?

The Leprosy of Ingratitude

What kind of leprosy do we need to be cured from today?

What are some things for which you are grateful?

In what ways will you thank God for these things?

Lesson 20 / Chapter 18
When You Carry Heavy Burdens

The Luggage of Life

Discuss some reasons why burdens can be compared to luggage.

Accumulating Excess Baggage

How do we accumulate burdens on our souls and how does it affect us?

What did Jesus call this state of the soul?

How can Jesus solve the problem?

Checking Your Baggage

Past Baggage: Regrets

How can you tell if a person is living in the past?

How can the past keep us from enjoying the present?

What does God command us to do with the past and how can we do it? (Philippians 3:13)

Future Baggage: Worry

Why is worry always concerned about the future?

How does worrying rob the present of its joy?

How is worry "negative faith"?

Present Baggage: Stress

Give some examples of things that can produce stress.

Don't Claim Your Baggage

First, **Let go of your excess baggage.**

Read Psalm 55:22. Using the analogy of two people playing catch, how do we know when we have released our burdens?

When Joe released the duffel bag of dirty clothes, how did he know dropped the sack when he couldn't see it? How does this relate to our souls?

Give an example of how you were burdened down, but finally released your burdens to the Lord.

Second, **Only carry enough baggage for today's journey.**

What does it mean to "live one day at a time"?

How is our thought-life involved in the process of living one day at a time?

How can we plan for the future without being preoccupied with the future?

What are some lessons you learned from the story of the clock that had a nervous breakdown?

Lesson 21 / Chapter 19
When Opinions Differ

Disagreement Can Cause Division

What was the real reason why Fred couldn't get along with others?

What can this teach us concerning how to preserve unity?

How People Form Opinions

How did the way the Corinthians were raised affect their convictions after they became Christians? (1 Corinthians 8:7)

Although it would be nice if everything we were taught growing up was correct, it is unlikely. After we mature, how should we sort through what we have been taught? (1 Thessalonians 5:21)

What are some things we were taught as children that we need to leave behind?

Wrong Ways to Handle Differing Opinions

Why can't people sincerely change their minds through being pressured?

What does legalism (man-made rules) do to make someone change his or her mind?

How to Handle Differing Opinions

First, **Don't make a big deal over minor issues.**

Explain what Jesus meant when he said the Pharisees "strain out a gnat and swallow a camel." (Matthew 23:24)

How do we strain gnats and swallow camels today?

Second, **Accept one who differs, because God has accepted him.**

What does it mean to "accept" the one who is weak in faith?

Why would God accept someone who is weak in faith?

Third, **Be right in your heart, not just in your head.**

Why does Paul say in Romans 14:5–6 for each to be "fully convinced in his own mind"?

Fourth, **Don't violate your own conscience or your brother's conscience.**

What does it mean to violate someone's conscience?

What responsibility does Paul put on the stronger brother? (Romans 15:1)

What does the stronger and weaker brothers each need to grow in?

Lesson 22 / Chapter 20

When You Are Angry

Guideline #1: Anger becomes sin when it rises quickly.

Read James 1:19–20. How can being quick to hear help us become slow to anger?

How can being slow to speak help us become slow to anger?

Guideline #2: Anger becomes sin when it is directed at sinners instead of sin.

Using the illustration of the doctor operating on the patient, explain why it is important to make a distinction between the sin and the sinner.

Guideline #3: Anger becomes sin when it is out of control.

Read Proverbs 16:32. Explain how this passage was demonstrated through the life of Alexander the Great.

How might we do the same thing today?

Guideline #4: Anger becomes sin when it is not accompanied with grief.

Although Jesus was angry with the Pharisees, He was also grieved in His heart. Explain why it is necessary to balance anger with grief.

Guideline #5: Anger becomes sin when it is not resolved quickly.

Read Ephesians 4:26. Why is it important to resolve our anger before the day is over?

How to Handle Your Anger

First, **Admit you have an anger problem.**

If we don't admit to having a problem with anger, what will we do?

Why is admitting we have a problem the first step to curing it?

Second, **Identify the cause of your anger.**

What do we need to do to identify the cause of our anger?

Third, **Accept the things you can't change.**

What does it mean to "accept" the things you can't change?

Fourth, **Remove your anger.**

Read Ephesians 4:31–32. How can removing anger be compared to taking garbage to the trash receptacle?

What is the primary lesson from Dr. Kane's surgery?

How is forgiveness an important part in removing our anger?

Lesson 23 / Chapter 21

When Bad Things Happen

Fact #1: We don't hope God is in control, we know it.

How is life like a jigsaw puzzle?

Why is it important to know God is in control when we go through difficult times?

Fact #2: God doesn't cause all things to happen, but causes all things to work together.

Read James 1:13. How does this prove God does not cause all things to happen?

Read 1 Corinthians 10:13. Discuss how God doesn't "cause" temptation but is still in control when we are being tempted.

Fact #3: Not all things are good, but God works all things together for good.

Why do you think some people have no problem believing Satan can turn good to evil, but have a difficult time believing God can turn evil to good?

How did God demonstrate his power to work all things together for good in Joseph's life?

How did God demonstrate his power to work all things together for good in Esther's life?

Using the illustration of the cake, how does God work all things together for good?

Fact #4: God doesn't do this for everyone, but for those who love him.

Using the illustration of the army general and soldiers, explain how God can choose us and still give us a free will.

How does God's foreknowledge and predestination play a part in working all things together for good to those who love Him?

Fact #5: God's purpose is not to just make us happy, but to make us like Jesus.

Romans 8:28 says we are "called according to His purpose." What is His purpose?

Why is God more interested in our character or our comfort? (Romans 8:29)

Lesson 24 / Chapter 22

When You Have Drifted From God

Step #1: Rebellion against the Father. (Luke 15:11–12)

What was the proof that the son was in rebellion against his father?

How does this indicate he would soon be leaving the house?

Discuss the statement: "We always rebel on the inside before it shows on the outside."

Step #2: Rejection of the Father's presence. (Luke 15:13)

When the son left home, why didn't the father chase him down the road, begging him to return?

Why is it important to "let go" of a rebellious person?

Step #3: Removal of the Father's provision. (Luke 15:14)

Why is the removal of God's provision an important step in bringing a person to repentance?

Step #4: Realignment with the wrong fellowship. (Luke 15:15)

If people don't have the right fellowship, why do they seek after wrong fellowship?

Step #5: Realization of his true condition. (Luke 15:17)

Why was it necessary for the prodigal son to experience the pigpen for him to come to his senses?

Step #6: Repentance in his heart. (Luke 15:18–19)

How do we know the son truly repented?

Step #7: Returning to his father. (Luke 15:20)

Describe what the son probably thought as he traveled back home.

Step #8: Reconciliation with the father. (Luke 15:20)

Why did the father run to greet his son when he returned, but didn't run after him when he left?

Step #9: Restoration of the son's privileges. (Luke 15:21–22)

What was the significance of the father giving him the ring and robe?

Step #10: Rejoicing in the father's house. (Luke 15:23–24)

Why can rejoicing only take place after repentance and reconciliation?

Lesson 25 / Chapter 23

When You Are Afraid of Dying

Read the four stories about the unusual deaths. What was common in all four cases?

List some reasons why people refuse to think about dying.

Why People Fear Death

Why do people fear death?

Read Hebrews 2:14–15. According to this passage, what two things did Jesus accomplish through his death on the cross?

What does God grant to his children to calm the fear of death? (Romans 5:1)

What Happens When You Die

How can our bodies be compared to spacesuits like the astronauts wore when they walked on the moon?

According to James 2:26, what happens at death?

Where does the spirit go? (Ecclesiastes 12:7; Hebrews 9:27)

How can a person escape judgment for his or her sins? (John 5:22–24; 1 John 3:5)

What Death is Like for the Christian

What did the resurrection of Jesus do to death? (1 Corinthians 15:55)

Why is death for the Christian compared to going to sleep? (1 Corinthians 15:51)

Better on the Other Side

Why did Paul say it was better to depart this life? (Philippians 1:23)

Do you think God has things planned for us to do in heaven? (1 Corinthians 3:9)

How does a person's understanding of heaven influence his or her view of death?

Lesson 26 / Chapter 24
When You're Not Sure You're Saved

Many people aren't sure whether they are going to heaven. Can people have assurance they have eternal life? (1 John 5:13)

List some reasons why people aren't sure that they are going to heaven.

Question #1: Who is Jesus?

Read Matthew 16:13–16. Why did Jesus ask his disciples, "Who do people say that the Son of Man is?

Why did Jesus follow up with the question, "But who do you say that I am?"

How is the only way we can truly know who Jesus is? (v. 17)

Question #2: What did Jesus do on the cross?

What did Jesus do to your sins on the cross? (1 Peter 2:24)

How could Jesus pay for your sins when you hadn't committed any yet? (Hebrews 10:12)

How many of your sins were in the future when Jesus died on the cross?

How does this apply to the sins you will commit tomorrow? (Hebrews 10:14)

Why do people view the cross from different perspectives? (1 Corinthians 1:18)

Question #3: What must I do to be saved?

Read Ephesians 2:8–9. Are we saved by grace or by faith?

What does "grace" mean?

What role does faith play in salvation?

Using the Atlantic Ocean example on page 221, explain what "not as a result of works, that no one should boast" means (v. 9).

Jason bought the football tickets for Darrin (p. 222). What was the only thing Darrin needed to do?

Why did Darrin mow Jason's yard in order to get the football tickets?

How does this apply to people receiving salvation?

Read Romans 4:4–5. How can our works nullify the free gift? (v. 4)

How does the person who "does not work" become justified before God? (v. 5)

If you haven't trusted Christ to save you, pray the prayer on page 223. Then thank Him for saving you.

This Study Guide is available on the author's website:
www.kentcrockett.com